THE
SOCIAL MEDIA
MANAGEMENT
HANDBOOK

THE
SOCIAL MEDIA
MANAGEMENT
HANDBOOK

EVERYTHING YOU NEED TO KNOW
TO GET SOCIAL MEDIA WORKING
IN YOUR BUSINESS

NICK SMITH AND ROBERT WOLLAN

WITH

CATHERINE ZHOU

WILEY

John Wiley & Sons, Inc.

Published by John Wiley & Sons, Inc., Hoboken, New Jersey.
Published simultaneously in Canada.

For general information on our other products and services or for technical support, please contact our Customer Care Department within the United States at (800) 762-2974, outside the United States at (317) 572-3993 or fax (317) 572-4002.

Wiley also publishes its books in a variety of electronic formats. Some content that appears in print may not be available in electronic books. For more information about Wiley products, visit our web site at www.wiley.com.

Library of Congress Cataloging-in-Publication Data:

Smith, Nick, 1962–
    The social media management handbook: everything you need to know to get social media working in your business/Nick Smith and Robert Wollan; with Catherine Zhou.
        p. cm.
    Includes index.
    ISBN 978-0-470-65124-7 (hardback); ISBN 978-1-118-00350-3 (ebk);
ISBN 978-1-118-00351-0 (ebk); ISBN 978-1-118-00352-7 (ebk)
    1. Internet marketing. 2. Social media—Marketing.   I. Wollan, Robert, 1957–
II. Zhou, Catherine.   III. Title.
    HF5415.1265.S6147 2011
    658.8′72—dc22

                                                                                    2010037011

Printed in the United States of America

10 9 8 7 6 5 4 3 2 1

Contents

Introduction

Getting involved in social media is a bit like getting a free puppy. It doesn't cost anything to start, and it looks like nothing but fun—until it chews up the carpet, eats the neighbor's plants, and costs thousands of dollars at the veterinarian. Welcome to the world of social media.

It's not an understatement to say that social media has equally captured the attention of companies large and small with great promise. Every month, more and more people—young and old, around the world—take to their computers or mobile devices to connect with friends, post their opinions, and engage in conversations. This rare combination of such massive numbers of customers engaging in such new ways with companies and each other is making businesses take notice.

In fact, this strong undercurrent of social media activity and the impact it is having on businesses everywhere are significant—whether companies know how much it is happening with their customers or not. Given the massive rise and acceleration of social media adoption around the world, it is clear that customers are using this medium, although few can pinpoint precisely how many and what is being done. It would be a mistake to assume that social media is not a major (and growing) part of customers' lives and choose not to act. Thus, it's absolutely vital for business leaders to understand this phenomenon and determine what they need to do to prepare their organizations to thrive at a time when customers wield more power and influence over businesses than ever before.

The Audience and What to Expect from This Book

The *Social Media Management Handbook* has been written to help you with everything you need to know to get social media working in your business.

We all engage in social media in one way or another, especially in our personal lives through friends and family. But to date many of us have not practiced extensively or thought through precisely what it means to our business. Social media is undoubtedly out there and evidently important to a rapidly, exponentially expanding number of people. Our customers, our coworkers, and, therefore, our business must be connected. We can't ignore it Canutelike, hoping the changing world of digital conversations will somehow pass us by unaffected. But what do we need to do about it? How can we build our strategies and organize our customer-facing activities to continue to meet the important challenge of remaining relevant, competitive and attractive to our consumer?

If you are engaged in commerce and have a fair understanding of your customers and the growing importance of this new type of conversation we call social media but aren't entirely clear how best to respond to the challenge, this book is for you.

If you have experimented with using social media to engage directly with your customers—to establish a dialogue, manage customer complaints, shore up your reputation, sell more, prevent your customers from defecting, and understand customers' sentiments toward your business in the social media environment (or "blogosphere"), this book is for you.

If you have sought to collaborate with coworkers to improve customer service, solve problems of delivery, or create systems or products that are more relevant to your customers and more competitive; if you have sought to engage your colleagues in seeking new ways to present the business or get input into the development of advertising or communications but have done so in only a piecemeal or ad hoc way, this book is for you.

Social media is not a passing phenomenon; this new form of communication is changing behavior and expectations of consumers and employees. The consumer is no longer king, he is emperor, with the power to make or break brands. If business hasn't already woken up to the opportunity (and challenges), it had better do so soon because social media is not just here to stay; in time it will fundamentally change the way we do business.

During the course of this simple "how-to" guide, we cover the strategy, culture, metrics, policies, roles, and responsibilities related to making social media work for your business. The question we get asked most is not "How can we start?" Instead, managers and executives want to know how they can bring structure and commercial return to this new and vibrant global conversation and how they can divert funds and effort sensibly into something that is neither fully accountable nor "controllable."

The thing is, to win it, you've got to be in it. This guide should help make your welcome to the world of social media a little more thoughtful, comprehensive, and confident knowing you're aware of practical lessons learned from others in the marketplace . . . and *their* social media customers that just might be *your* social media customers.

This Book Is Just the Start . . . Access the Social Media Resource Portal

Social media and new ideas are emerging in the market all the time. To help you keep up with some of the best and latest examples of social media, Accenture has developed a social media portal. This site will give you access to updated content, other relevant documents, and project templates to download and put to use in your business. Get connected to a whole new network of social media professionals—access the site at www.socialmedia managementhandbook.accenture.com.

What Is Social Media?

Before going any further, we should confirm what we mean by "social media" in the context of this handbook.

Strictly speaking, social media is not a new phenomenon; people have been providing recommendations and opinions to friends and contacts for millennia via channels through which a two-way conversation can take place. In modern history, such channels have included face-to-face discussions, letters, the telephone, and, more recently, e-mail. So what *is* new?

We see a number of characteristics that distinguish today's "digital social media" interaction from other types of social conversations.

- It enables one-to-many or many-to-many conversations. (We use the phrase "peer-to-peer" to describe these dialogues.)
- It features content created and posted by consumers of that content.
- It is easy to use.

- It is highly accessible (everyone), highly scalable (everyone + everywhere), and operates in real time (everyone + everywhere + every time).
- It is entirely public and transparent.

In short, social media enables the swift and easy development, creation, dissemination, and consumption of information and entertainment by both organizations and individuals.

A Growing Force

The advent of social media interactions is creating a whole new ball game for the world of commerce and connection. They are materially impactful, unavoidable, and so ubiquitous that no business can afford simply to ignore them. In fact, social media already has a massive presence and just keeps growing and evolving.

Consider the growth of the most popular social networking sites. Facebook, the behemoth of the group, topped 500 million users worldwide in 2010 and is currently growing at a rate of 500,000 new users daily.[1] Twitter claims 105 million users (adding 300,000 users per day) and is projected to process 6.7 billion tweets per month by January 2011 (see Figure I.1)[2] while LinkedIn and MySpace have 60 million and 57 million users, respectively.[3] Yelp, just an idea six years ago, now serves more than 30 million visitors a month.[4] Flickr now hosts more than 4 billion images, while Wikipedia currently has in excess of 14 million articles.[5]

And unlike several years ago, when such sites were the purview of young people, older adults now are driving much of this growth. For example, a recent AARP study found that use of social networks by those over 50 has tripled in the past 18 months, and once boomers join a social networking site, one-third of them visit at least once a day.[6] A survey by Accenture found that baby boomers are connecting on social networking sites at a rate nearly 20 times faster than younger generations, with 28 percent of boomers indicating they use such sites.[7] (See Figure I.2.)

While the popularity of social media is growing, so is the frequency and duration of use. According to one study, 56 percent of social media users said they need to check Facebook at least once a day, and 12 percent check in every couple of hours just to see what's happening.[8] (Those under 25 years old are more likely than those over 25 to check in frequently.) Furthermore,

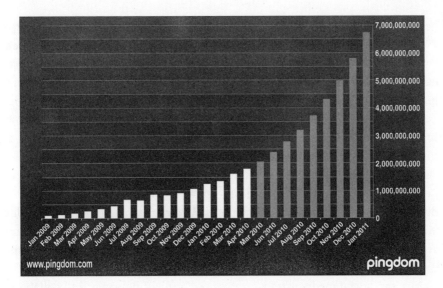

FIGURE I.1 Tweets per Month on Twitter: Predicted Growth.

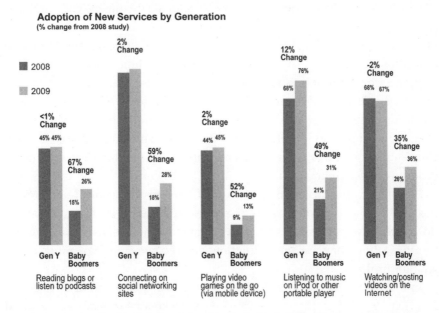

FIGURE I.2 Baby Boomers Are Adopting Social Media at a Far Greater Pace than Younger Users.

Source: Accenture 2009 Consumer Electronics Products and Services Usage Report.

between 2003 and 2009, time spent on social networking sites has surged 73 percent. The time spent on video sites has skyrocketed almost 2,000 percent during the same period.[9] These figures, combined with those in the preceding paragraph, demonstrate that not only are more people using social media, their engagement with those channels is deepening.

Social media has ties into the rise of mobile commerce as well. Interestingly, the mobile phone is beginning to overtake the personal computer as the preferred platform for social networking. According to one study, 91 percent of people use the mobile Web to socialize, compared with 79 percent of people who use the desktop to do the same.[10] This same study found that during the 2.7 hours per day people in the United States spend on the mobile Web, 45 percent are posting comments on social networking sites, 43 percent are connecting with friends on social networking sites, 40 percent are sharing content with others, and 38 percent are sharing photos.

In short, social media is transforming one-way monologues into collaborative interactions, typically conducted via the Internet. It's democratizing information and knowledge as peer-to-peer interaction becomes more dominant. It involves everyone, everywhere, in all-the-time conversations—including an organization's employees and the consumers and broader observers of its products. It's not hype, it's reality, and organizations ignore it at their peril.

In the remainder of this book, we explore the most critical aspects companies must consider and master to fully benefit from social media.

In Part I, we cover the up-front concerns—understanding why social media is so important, developing an effective social media strategy, creating and using the new metrics required to gauge success, and rallying the organization around social media.

Parts II and III focus on more functional concerns—specifically, how social media affects a company's marketing, sales, and customer service organizations and the ways in which companies can use social media to fundamentally transform how they use these functions to create and strengthen customer relationships.

In Part IV, we review what comes after the pilot phase and discuss the infrastructure changes companies must make to be able to incorporate social media into their operations effectively and do so quickly and at scale.

We wrap up with Part V, in which we cover the cultural and organizational changes an organization faces when dealing with social media, and the impact of social media on a company's employees and talent management capabilities.

Throughout these sections, we draw on our extensive research, as well as work with leading organizations around the world, to help executives and managers alike make more sense out of social media and its role in today's company. We relate practical and proven practices that companies of all kinds can begin using today to make social media an integral part of their growth strategies and day-to-day operations.

THE
SOCIAL MEDIA
MANAGEMENT
HANDBOOK

Social Media Strategy for Organizations

1

The Power and Business Risks of Social Media

Nick Smith and Robert Wollan

CHAPTER HIGHLIGHTS

Executives at companies large and small have reached the point of needing to understand exactly what is different about social media and why now is the critical time to consider *how*, not *if*, they will engage their customers.

Social media gives companies the power to create fans, not just customers; to rally the organization to become more customer-centric; and to create new revenue streams in three dimensions.

Social media use also comes with two significant risks: Those who ignore the growing demand will be caught off guard and miss out on the next wave of customer relationship building; and those who do not understand what it takes organizationally to fully embrace and leverage social media will fail to realize its promise.

In the early days of social media, companies could quickly dismiss it—for a number of common reasons:

- "We're not like Amazon or eBay. We don't need it."
- "Our customers aren't using it and likely won't."
- "We don't see how this would ever fit into our business model."

However, fast-forward five years, and it's easy to see that social media has matured and is now mainstream. In fact, social media now is dramatically influencing traditional business-to-consumer models and is well on its way to changing business-to-business models.

Why? The customer franchise is rapidly embracing social media, with three groups leading the way. The massive influence of the large millennial generation, the initial adopters of social media, has been well documented. However, as mentioned in the Introduction, baby boomers increasingly are using social media—just one example of how this group is redefining what people think of as "senior citizens." Finally, millions of first-time consumers are entering the landscape in emerging markets, and many of them see social media as a way to connect instantly with the rest of the world.

But the fact that many of their customers and prospects are using social media is only part of the reason why it should matter to companies. The more prominent factor is that social media is not simply a new channel, as some have characterized it; rather, it is fundamentally changing the business model and role of the company.

The last time companies faced such an issue was the rise of ecommerce. However, that development primarily involved adding a new channel. Yet, on a superficial level, the debate we hear among business executives today about social media bears a striking resemblance to those confusing days when the Web was being touted as the end to business as we know it. "Is it just hype?" "Do I really need to embrace it?" "How do I make best use of it?" "How do I prove the business case?" "What are the benefits?"

What Makes Social Media Difficult to Address?

Beyond the innovators and early adopters, many companies still are struggling to determine how to address the social media conundrum. And, indeed, it is a significant challenge. As noted, social media still is a new phenomenon, and, thus, there are few rules or proven best practices in place for how to manage it. It also has yet to affect the entire customer or prospect base of most companies, so companies are understandably unsure of how and where to invest in social media capabilities. Perhaps even more problematic is the fact that social media forces companies to take action based on imprecise information, which is counter to an organization's instincts.

In summing up the challenge, we've identified six factors that make social media so difficult to address because, combined, they illustrate how the conventional wisdom of customer communications and brand engagement no longer applies:

"You Give Up Control":
- There's no viable regulation of the media, so the content doesn't have to be true.
- The impact of social media cannot be stopped or undone, even in court.

"It Is Everywhere":
- Social media transcends traditional geographic, demographic, and economic boundaries.
- Social media content is amplified via the "viral effect."

"It Is Emotional, as well as Functional":
- User-generated content often is triggered by an emotional reaction.
- Social media forces companies to shift from dealing with long, predictable cycle times to having to make decisions much more quickly and with less precise information.

Each of these factors requires an organization to be extremely agile simply to keep pace. Unfortunately, such agility is not commonplace in most organizations, which is what makes dealing with social media such a challenge.

As we consider the characteristics of social media and their impact, it's clear that companies now must consider the fact there are new rules for customers, business functions, and growth strategies.

Social Media Ignites a Seismic "Shift of Power" Toward Customers and Consumers

For years we have observed a steady increase in the power consumers believe they should hold in their dealings with providers. Consumers no longer accept that they are at the end of the "conveyor belt," simply accepting marketing messages companies push out into the marketplace and passively waiting at the company's mercy when giving feedback or lodging a complaint.

Now consumers not only want to be engaged earlier in that process, but they also want to be more engaged at various points throughout the relationship (on their terms, of course)—whether that involves providing advice and feedback on the company's products and services, having access to specialized content, or getting an immediate response to their questions.

Social media provides a highly public and powerful venue for consumers to speak their minds about companies and their brands, thus enabling consumers to "call out" companies when they're not performing up to customers' expectations (and spark a real change in behavior). And it serves as a vehicle through which consumers can force conversations with a company that they can manage more actively, a departure from the one-way transaction-based communications (in which the company talks to, not with, customers) that used to characterize the customer-company relationship. Thus, social media in many ways makes consumers co-owners of a company's brand and places them essentially on equal footing with a company.

This is something that U.S. consumer electronics retailer Best Buy has recognized, and it's a fundamental driver of the company's social media efforts. "For us today, [social media] is really about deepening our customer relationships," said Tracy Benson, senior director, interactive marketing and emerging media for Best Buy. "[That means letting customers] know they can go to you for questions . . . [and] can participate in the dialogue." Benson equates the situation to a friendship. "If [my friend] only talks to me and never allows me to talk, and if they just tell me what to do all the time, it's not a great friendship, right? It's a push. Social media gives us the opportunity to push, pull, and enable, and the return is a stronger, deeper relationship. And studies have shown that when your relationships are stronger, your customers will look to you first, look to you more often and intentionally think about you when they have a product they need to purchase." Ultimately, the net result, noted Benson, is greater sales.

Social Media Has a Profound Effect on Traditional Business Functions

The scope and scale of social media leaves few areas of a company untouched. However, while all functions in a business are impacted by social media, some are more extensively and directly affected than others.

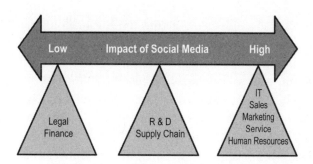

FIGURE 1.1 Social Media Affects Business Functions Differently.

One way to think about impact is to consider a spectrum of influence, such as that in Figure 1.1.

At the far left of the spectrum are functions farthest from the customer—such as legal and finance. These functions are likely to be least affected by social media (although they will, in fact, be impacted and have activities alongside other functions).

In the middle are functions that experience moderate impact. They include research and development (R&D) and the supply chain, which, while not directly connected to customers, play an instrumental role in fulfilling customer demand and will require new levels of agility to accommodate the always-on, fast-paced nature of social media.

At the far right of the spectrum are functions that are highly affected by social media. Not surprisingly, these include the three front-office functions of marketing, sales and service, as well as information technology (IT) and human resources (HR).

The most significant impact on the front office is that social media will prove to be the final nail in the coffin of the one-size-fits-all customer experience model. Companies have spent the past 20 years perfecting the one experience they aspire to, which they think will appropriately capture the essence of their brands. However, with the help of social media, the customer base continues to fragment into ever-more granular segments, each with highly specialized interests and needs. Thus, a company that continues to deliver an experience geared toward the masses can alienate as many customers as those it pleases. In the new era of social media, companies will have to become extremely adept at determining the experiences specific customer segments desire and then at delivering those experiences consistently and flawlessly.

Social media also is further blurring the lines among marketing, sales, and service. For instance, the concept of marketing as a stand-alone, "research and origination" channel rapidly is giving way to a model in which marketing and sales effectively become a single "engagement channel," where customers learn about an offer, research it, consult with friends about it, and make their purchase in a highly compressed time frame. In this environment, the traditional functional boundaries between marketing and sales disappear. Similarly, the line between sales and service is blurring, as the service process becomes increasingly responsible for bringing to life the promise made by sales. In other words, customers no longer see sales and service as two distinct transactions. Rather, they view them both as inextricably linked to the overall experience they have with the company. If service falls short, it squanders the goodwill the customer felt at the time of purchase and erodes the company's credibility. Customers are blurring the lines as well. Social Media has turned customers into marketers as they leverage social media to bring their favorite products to their own networks—via enabling web sites like Lemonade.com.

From an HR perspective, the impact of social media is twofold. Because social media can effectively make every employee a spokesperson for the company, HR must determine how to manage the ways in which employees engage in social media conversations about the company and how they represent the organization in these conversations. This is substantially different from years past, when public relations (PR) and HR only had to concern itself with the limited number of "official" spokespeople who were authorized to interact with the media, had the appropriate training, and conducted their interviews in controlled environments. Today, while employees aren't holding press conferences, they do have the ability to do good or cause harm online. Thus, they must be much more aware of the nuances of their communications and have clear boundaries regarding what they say and how they say it.

Just as important from an HR perspective is the talent question. As companies increasingly use social media in multiple business functions, HR must ensure that employees possess the appropriate social media skills and capabilities. Doing so requires considering such skills, where relevant, not only in the recruiting process but also in the training and development of existing employees. Furthermore, social media is playing an increasingly prominent role in how organizations attract employees. Prospective candidates are using social media to get a composite picture of an organization to determine whether it is a good fit for them (which means companies need to make sure the employee value proposition they present via social media is appropriate and compelling). Companies can use social media to find and vet candidates (which requires people in the HR function who are adept at incorporating social media searches into their overall recruiting process).

The IT function, by virtue of the technology-driven nature of social media, also is in the "high-impact" zone. We see three main areas in which chief information officers (CIOs) are affected. The first area relates to the propagation of data. CIOs need to determine how they will capture, organize, analyze, and leverage the vast amounts of data social media generates. The second area involves what we call "disposable technologies." Social media introduces all sorts of technologies that aren't necessarily going to be around for 15 years, so they're not infrastructure per se. But still, the organization needs to have a plan for how to acquire and retire them as well as how they fit within the overall IT portfolio. The third area relates to the overall planning and execution process for technology in the business. One of the impacts here could include shifting from annual to quarterly planning for technology to accommodate rapidly evolving social media tools and large shifts in customer bases. Another could be staffing related, as CIOs need to anticipate the kinds of skills their IT organizations require in a social media–driven world. We discuss these and other impacts in greater detail in Chapter 15.

Social Media Creates Significant New Opportunities for Strategic Growth but also Carries Substantial Risk

With any new development, both opportunities and risks abound. Social media is no different in that regard.

Managed correctly, social media enables companies to significantly accelerate their ability to launch new brands, incrementally strengthen customer relationships and drive revenues from existing customers, new customers and new local/global markets.

Social Media is being used to grow new revenues from the current customer base—finding opportunities among existing customers to provide new products or services or to augment those already offered. By identifying unmet needs among current customers and developing value-based products and services to meet those needs, companies can differentiate themselves from their competition as well as generate incremental sales and margin. Some great examples of how social media can deliver on this are Dell Swarm (which enables customers to get discounts on Dell products by banding together on social networks to make volume purchases) and MyStarbucksIdea (which enables customers to post and rate ideas for new Starbucks products and practices).

Social Media is also being used to appeal to broad ranges of new customers in new ways—recognizing opportunities in new segments 'hidden' inside and outside of the existing customer base. Growth possibilities abound for companies that devise innovative ways to identify, engage, and acquire prospective new buyers. IKEA's photo-tagging campaign on Facebook illustrates how social media can be used to spread the word to potential new customers much faster, more effectively, and less expensively than traditional campaigns. The Swedish home furnishings company wanted to promote the opening of a new store in Malmo, Sweden. It created a profile page for the store manager on Facebook and posted on that profile page photos of various IKEA products. To generate excitement about the store and IKEA products, the company put the word out that the first person to tag his or her name to a product in the pictures on the profile won the product. In short order, thousands of people tagged themselves in photos of products ranging from beds, to vases, to sofas in an attempt to win. Not surprisingly, the campaign quickly spread across the site, generating a massive increase in awareness of the company and the new store.

Social Media is even being used to engage and grow new markets, whether that's capitalizing on opportunities in new geographies or enhancing local market execution. There's no doubt that emerging markets—which, for many companies, are still largely untapped—offer the greatest opportunities for growth in the coming years. Yet there is still plenty of untapped potential in companies' existing local markets. Companies can use social media to enter new global markets more successfully by developing market-specific insights and approaches to tailor products and offers to customer segments as well as expand more effectively in existing local markets by gaining a more granular picture of existing and prospective customers and how those customers differ from market to market. Nokia Beta Labs demonstrates how, through social media, companies can transcend physical boundaries and distances to interact with customers. Nokia Beta Labs is a web site through which Nokia makes its beta applications available for public download anywhere in the world.

Users submit feedback on the applications, which is passed on to the product development team for consideration. Such feedback is invaluable to Nokia's ability to understand the unique needs and preferences of customers in particular regions or markets and build relationships with them without the need for a physical retail presence.

Social media also provides an opportunity for a company to engage and energize its employee base in the promotion of its brand. With employees already participating credibly in online conversations as part of the consumer population, it's a natural extension for a company to encourage employees to use that position to serve as fans and facilitators.

What's at risk if companies don't engage? Ignoring social media will not make it go away or lessen its impact. Social media is here and it's happening, regardless of which companies participate. If a company chooses not to act, it will find competitors rapidly filling the gap—and, potentially, could see its brand and reputation damaged by critical comments that gain a life of their own and "go viral."

The preceding opportunities and risks are embodied in what we call "consumer activism." When a company uses social media in the right way to engage customers, it will find customers are more than willing to become an extension of its sales force and customer service organization, to help spread the good word and attract other customers. As one example, Virgin America has more than 20,000 followers on Twitter, which gives the airline incredible access to an engaged and loyal community of customers. But beyond simply enabling Virgin to reach customers quickly and inexpensively, the airline's Twitter account actually does the selling for the company when newcomers ask if they should fly Virgin.[1]

Conversely, when a company ignores social media or fails to use it correctly, it risks falling victim to a customer scorned who can turn an isolated incident into an international brand nightmare. Not many people had heard of Dave Carroll or his band (except for his loyal fans) before the spring of 2008. However, after watching United Airlines baggage handlers mistreat his $3,500 guitar on the tarmac before a flight, Carroll recorded three YouTube videos ("United Breaks Guitars") about his experience.[2] In four days, the videos attracted more than 7 million viewers, and he—and United's mistake—became known by people all around the world. One journalist asserted that the video was the biggest reason the airline's stock price fell 10 percent (cutting its market cap by $180 million).

A Change in Mind-Set Is Needed: The "Fifth P"

To begin adapting a company's operations and strategy to capitalize on social media, leaders must take the first critical step of changing their mind-sets and revising some long-held beliefs about building and managing customer relationships.

In particular, they need to acknowledge that social media has fundamentally changed the traditional "four Ps of marketing": promotion, product, place, and price. When the four Ps were created, customers gathered information about their purchases mostly through their direct contact with sales channel providers, such as retailers, and information provided directly by the maker, like product labels or advertising. So it made sense for marketers to base their sales-growth efforts on manipulating those four attributes of their offerings to find the right combinations that would entice customers to buy.

Although the initial four Ps still apply, social media requires the addition of a fifth P: people. The distinction here is that the original four Ps relate to proactive things a company does *to* its customers; adding the "people" element recognizes the new collaborative nature of the customer-company relationship made possible by social media. In other words, prior to social media, people were on the receiving end of a company's actions while, today, they have joined the conversation and play a more significant role in shaping what is "done to them."

Within this context, we can view the additional fifth P, people, as having five key elements—the "five Rs": reputation, responsibility, relationship, reward, and rigor. The five Rs are the guideposts for how companies reengage with their audiences in today's collaborative world.

Reputation refers to the fact that in today's highly transparent world, brands no longer can be inconsistent in their actions versus their promise to customers—and get away with it. A company and its brand simply must deliver what they promise, because if they don't, their reputations have a significantly greater chance today of being damaged, and damaged deeply and quickly. But *reputation* also refers to how a company must respond to potentially damaging comments and criticisms. An organization must be able to use social media to engage in a dialogue with critics and unhappy customers to correct inaccuracies and address concerns head on and in a very public way.

Responsibility is a twofold issue. On one hand is the concern about privacy and the steps a company must take to be responsible with customers' information—especially given the public nature of social media and the myriad opportunities for exposure of details that are not for widespread consumption. On the other hand is the extent to which a company is socially responsible. Consumers are evaluating their providers with the social responsibility yardstick today more than ever. Companies that don't measure up in consumers' eyes risk being taken to task and exposed for all the world to see.

Relationship involves the proposition and posture a company must develop to effectively engage an individual via social media. In doing so, it must recognize the balanced nature of a true conversation as opposed to the one-way characteristic of a broadcast. For instance, marketing historically used to be about conveying a functional benefit at the right price point—such as Procter & Gamble's "Tide's in, dirt's out" slogan to convey the virtues of getting clothes cleaner with Tide laundry detergent. Function eventually evolved into emotion, where the message transcended "solving a problem" to making people feel better about themselves; witness the "Dirt is good" campaign for Unilever's OMO detergent, which is underpinned by the philosophy that playing outdoors is an essential part of a child's learning and development and that OMO can help parents by being there to clean up after their kids effectively.[3] The collaborative and conversational nature of social media creates an opportunity for companies and brands to take that emotional connection—and the resulting relationships with customers—to an entirely new level, provided customers want to "talk with them." The challenge will be for companies with inherently low-interest brands or offerings, which will have to work much harder to engage customers in meaningful dialogues.

Reward relates to the value organizations can both add to and derive from their conversations with individuals via social media. Until recently, companies typically relied heavily on transactional data—especially, purchase history—to paint pictures of their customers that could help them match their offerings with customers' needs more effectively. With the advent of social media, companies have access to a whole new world of external data they can use to augment the data in their customer databases—and, thus, create even more highly personalized (and, thus, far more rewarding) products and services for customers. Doing so, in turn, will result in more value for the organization, as it benefits from greater advocacy and share of wallet among customers.

Finally, *rigor* involves the consistency and reliability of a company's operations and how those operations deliver the right customer experience via social media. Inconsistency through poor rigor is instantly visible to consumers and demonstrates at best incompetence and at worst insincerity. The interesting point here is that unlike with traditional channels, in which companies can use a "test and learn" approach to experiment with a select, small group of customers, social media offers no such option. Each and every engagement must be personal to the individual, a segment of one. How a company acts and what it says via social media is instantly experienced and scrutinized by potentially millions of people around the world. Thus, an organization must balance carefully thinking through its actions with being able to hold a conversation in real time.

As with the classic four Ps, when organizations are operationalizing the five Rs, they must ensure they strike the right balance. Too much or too little of any one of the dimensions covered by the five Rs will very quickly and very publicly expose the organization's lack of authenticity. Ultimately it will undermine not just the social media opportunity but also the brand.

Moving Forward: Practical Lessons for Getting Started

There is no question that social media is one of the most important consumer-related developments of the past 50 years. There is also no question that it is here to stay and will continue to create significant opportunities as well as risks for companies.

Companies that have already joined the conversation and made social media a priority understand how fundamentally it affects myriad areas of their business. These organizations are well ahead of the curve and have made substantial changes in their strategies, business processes, technology infrastructures and applications, and organization and talent bases that enable them to capitalize on the opportunities provided by social media while mitigating the risks. Other companies can learn much from their experiences.

In the remainder of the book, we explore the practices and approaches that leading organizations have adopted as well as share practical insights we have gained in our social media work with influential companies around the world. We begin in the next chapter by discussing the critical first step: how to develop an effective and appropriate social media strategy.

2

How to Develop a Social Media Strategy

Chris Boudreaux

CHAPTER HIGHLIGHTS

Getting started in social media can be an inexpensive proposition—at least at the outset. But companies that have been successful in using social media have learned quickly that it requires a substantial commitment in time, people, and money.

To avoid at best stumbling and at worst being completely consumed by social media, a company must develop at comprehensive strategy. A social media management framework can help organizations create or improve a social media strategy by delivering a prioritized road map for instituting the process, technological, organizational, and cultural changes required to achieve the strategy.

Many companies, lured by the novelty and inherent interest in social media, are tempted to jump right into the fray without fully thinking through what they're doing and why they're doing it. In other words, the "fire, ready, aim" approach to social media is not uncommon. At best, that approach can result in a company's failing to fully capitalize on the benefits of social media. At worst, it can be a public relations and customer relationship nightmare. That's why developing a comprehensive social media strategy early is critical.

Typically, social media initially is adopted by marketing and public relations (PR) teams because the early-use cases for social media focused on advertising and PR. For example, many organizations launch a blog or Twitter account as alternative channels for their press releases or to publish information on the company and its products. Then they may start announcing sales promotions or links to coupons. Soon thereafter, two things typically happen that significantly increase the complexity of managing social media in the organization.

1. **Employees interacting with customers via social media realize they need more participation from other teams in the organization.** For example, they need to decide who handles a customer complaint received through Twitter. They have to coordinate announcements about sales promotions with supply chain and customer service leaders. They have to determine who will respond if a group of consumers suddenly launches an attack on the company's Facebook fan page on a Sunday morning. Or they have to figure out how they will work with human resources (HR) to ensure that the company appears well organized when people ask about job opportunities through Twitter.
2. **As more people throughout the organization understand the potential value of social media, more teams want to use social media in their department.** Figure 2.1 provides an example listing of the internal stakeholders of social media in a global financial services firm.

As a result of these two factors, the complexity of using social media in an organization gradually increases over time, impacting multiple teams and functional areas. (See Figure 2.2.)

In most organizations, the operational complexity of social media increases in four important ways—coordination, scrutiny and accountability, data management, and scalability and consistency—each of which a strong social media strategy addresses.

Coordination

Most companies can find one or more internal teams using social media today. Because many social media tools are low cost (or free) and hosted

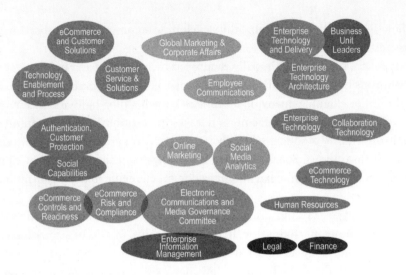

FIGURE 2.1 Internal Social Media Stakeholders at a Fortune 100 Company.

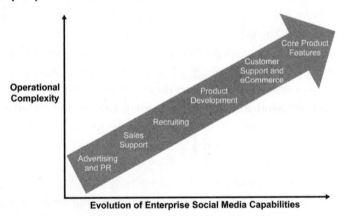

FIGURE 2.2 Increasing Operational Complexity of Social Media.

outside of the corporate firewall, it has been easy for one or a handful of people to engage in social media on a small scale. But those teams typically achieve very little impact beyond the scope of their team—for example, a few PR professionals using a listening tool, or a small team of customer support agents using Twitter to respond to customer complaints.

As more functions in an organization engage in social media, coordination grows more difficult. Different teams will have different goals, motivations, knowledge, skills, resources, and urgency. Some teams will leap forward to stay ahead of the competition while others wait and see how the market, regulations, and internal politics develop.

During that time, different teams will purchase different social media applications that may provide redundant functionality and costs to the company. As a result, they will hire and develop people with different skill sets and knowledge. For example, HR may decide to use social media listening tools to find better job candidates at lower costs. At the same time, marketing may invest in different listening technologies for brand management while customer support develops its own listening and response tools to interact with customers. At some point, someone has to coordinate these investments and capabilities for the good of the overall company. (We cover social media tools for listening in more detail in Chapter 5.)

Scrutiny and Accountability

Although many organizations began their social media experience by experimenting with free tools and the spare time of a few employees, using social media at scale requires real investment in knowledgeable and skilled employees and tools, in addition to thoughtful strategies. Those all cost money. When asked to spend money, most organizations require a business case, or at least a reasonable hypothesis about how the investment will benefit the business.

Internal champions of social media seeking to achieve real business results will have to hold themselves accountable for measurable outcomes and most likely will need to demonstrate return on investment (ROI) in a business case. (ROI and metrics are covered in more detail in Chapter 3.)

In addition to business cases and demonstrable outcomes, internal champions of social media also must solve a broad array of questions to ensure that investments in social media align to business goals and are properly controlled and managed and that the people involved are appropriately measured and rewarded. Figure 2.3 lists many questions internal champions encounter as they work to achieve material business outcomes through social media. In Chapter 4, we provide more detailed guidance for internal champions seeking organizational support for social media investments.

Example Questions Triggered by Social Media	Key Issues for Social Media Champions
• Do I get value from Social Media? • Is Social Media really helping my business? • How will we ensure an integrated view of the customer?	*How is social media aligned to the business?*
• How can I get this key initiative prioritized? • How can I ensure appropriate control over social media spend and risk? • Are we investing our time and money appropriately?	*How should social media decisions be made?*
• What should be the social media spend this year? • Who owns social media? • What skills do we need? • How will our organization need to change?	*How do we manage social media investments?*
• How do I get funding and approval for this new project? • Who is accountable for social media results? • When happens when my experiment budget runs out? • What regulations are relevant and how do we comply?	*What controls do we need in place?*
• Where do I want social media champions to focus? • What service levels should I expect from social media partners? • What areas of social media governance should I approve?	*How do we measure and reward?*

FIGURE 2.3   Key Issues for Social Media Champions.

Data Management

Online social media creates significant volumes and a more widespread set of customer behavioral data, but many organizations are limited in their ability to capture and measure the interactions. After spending years and millions of dollars to integrate their existing customer data, many organizations now find themselves frustrated by the massive volumes of valuable customer data living outside of their four walls and data centers in social media. Tools are emerging to help solve the problem. But until recently, it has been impossible with social media–generated data to achieve the level of customer insight that most organizations achieve in their traditional customer interaction channels. A social media strategy must address this need, lest the exercise result in collecting too much or too little data.

Consider a company whose call centers record phone calls and whose web sites capture every visitor click. Because it controls the phone lines and the Web servers, the company can store and analyze all relevant information—such as who the customer was, how long the interaction lasted, whether the interaction led to a new sale, and so on. In social media, however, many interactions between an organization and its audiences occur on Web servers that are outside of their data centers. For example, if a company responds via Twitter to a customer who mentions its brand, that interaction lives in Twitter's servers, not the company's; thus, until recently, the company had no way of storing and tracking that interaction. In addition, the organization probably had no idea who the real person was behind the Twitter account, so it couldn't store the interaction in that person's customer record (if he or she even was a customer).

Solutions are emerging to help integrate social media data with CRM systems, and Chapter 12 explains how to make that happen at the system level. For example, Salesforce.com and Microsoft Dynamics CRM enable a company to turn a Twitter user name into a Dynamics CRM customer record or sales lead. However, every company needs a single strategy for managing social media data across the organization to ensure maximum value from social media and to be in compliance with regulations such as privacy and disclosure.

Scalability and Consistency

Because most organizations have engaged in social media through bottom-up efforts that were not centrally funded or governed, using free tools and people's spare time, they find it very challenging to scale their initial social media efforts to achieve major paybacks. For example, in June 2009, the *New York Times* reported that Dell had generated $3 million in revenues through its Twitter account since 2007.[1] That's $3 million in two years. In its regular business, Dell generates that much revenue every 30 minutes on average.[2] The challenge for most organizations lies in determining how to scale such initial success into material outcomes for the business.

How Did We Get Here?

These challenges exist because bottom-up, fragmented approaches to social media simply do not permit large organizations to operate social media at scale, with appropriate controls and consistency across the enterprise. As a result, these approaches to social media likely won't realize their full potential. In addition, fragmented approaches to social media create significant risks, including:

- Inconsistent customer experiences across products or business units.
- Inability to ensure regulatory compliance across business units and regulatory jurisdictions.
- Redundant investments in technologies and HR.
- Fragmented or missing customer data.
- Inability to consolidate the voice of the customer across channels, products, and segments.

Although most leaders can find someone in their organization using social media with customers or employees today, the challenge lies in evolving such efforts from experimental silos into enterprise-scale capabilities.

Some organizations leap into social media with committed leadership from the top of the organization, as was the case at Zappos, where chief executive officer Tony Hsieh led the charge with his active participation and leadership by example. In other organizations, social media begins through small efforts in different parts of the company and gradually grows into something bigger.

In any case, many organizations then appoint a chief social media officer, social media "czar," or some equivalent role, who then is asked to create an inventory of all existing social media efforts and formulate a social media strategy for the organization as a whole. The problem with this approach is that development of a social media strategy is not one person's job. It requires a broad set of leaders to effectively shape and operationalize an impactful social media strategy.

In fact, we've learned that simply creating a new organizational role that owns social media accomplishes the same impact as when companies addressed quality in the 1970s and 1980s by anointing a chief quality officer. It may be very helpful to the journey, but it is a very small step. And regardless of how important this new role is in the early going, it eventually must disappear as each functional leader takes accountability for the impacts of social media in his or her domain.

Social Media Management Framework

Social media, like quality, has to become embedded in the fabric of the organization because it affects every functional area. Doing so requires a comprehensive approach to ensure consistent customer experiences, reliable content creation, compelling insights through analytics, appropriate data governance, and sufficient regulatory compliance.

To help leaders chart a path through the opportunities, threats, and risks of social media, we developed a comprehensive list of the factors critical to the success of building large-scale social media capabilities. These factors form the core of a social media management framework that can help organizations create or improve their social media strategies. It can help ensure a company gets a significantly greater positive impact from social media and delivers a prioritized road map for instituting the process, technological, organizational, and cultural changes required to effectively implement its social media strategies. As illustrated in Figure 2.4, the framework contains six elements:

1. Context
2. Culture
3. Process
4. Metrics
5. People
6. Policies

Context

Context includes external considerations such as regulations and competitive dynamics as well as the information that an organization gathers through its social media listening activities (the latter of which are described in detail in Chapter 5).

Regulations can create tremendous burdens on organizations using social media. They can restrict what the organization can say, which employees are permitted by law to interact with customers, the extent to which interactions must be recorded and archived, and more. In highly regulated industries, such as financial services, pharmaceuticals, and energy, regulatory burdens have prevented most organizations from adopting social media at the same pace as companies in less regulated industries.

Context also includes internal business objectives such as corporate priorities or major corporate initiatives. Development of a social media strategy should begin with an understanding of the business objectives that social media is expected to support. Those business objectives then may translate into functional objectives, which further can be translated into social media

CULTURE

- Habits and behaviors
- Ways of working
- Subcultures

PEOPLE

- **Training and Development:** Adequacy and accessibility of training and professional development
- **Leverage:** Extent to which best practices are identified, shared, and utilized
- **Roles:** Clarity and adequacy of roles and responsibilities

METRICS

- **Resource Management:** Level of visibility into the efficient utilization of social media assets (people and technology) and level of efficiency achieved
- **Performance Management:** Degree to which results are measured and behavior rewarded for success or failure in achieving performance targets
- **Financial Management:** Level to which costs are tracked and controlled, and the degree of ownership by the business for social media costs

PROCESS

- **Leadership:** Degree to which leadership for social media decisions is formalized and accountability for business outcomes is clear
- **Alignment:** Degree of alignment between various agendas to ensure resources and funds are appropriately allocated

POLICIES

- **Clarity:** Degree to which policies clarify boundaries for employees
- **Empowerment:** Degree to which policies empower employees to achieve business outcomes, consistent with the cultural, regulatory, and business realities
- **Differentiation:** Degree to which policies support differentiation of the organization in the market

CONTEXT

- Business environment and objectives
- Regulatory environment

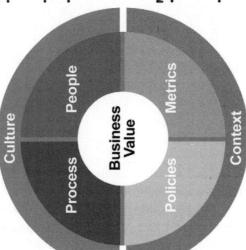

FIGURE 2.4 Social Media Management Framework.

objectives. At this point, a company then can define a social media strategy to achieve those objectives.

For example, an organization may commit to increasing revenues 20 percent in the coming year. The organization then may determine to achieve that 20 percent revenue growth by acquiring new customers and increasing revenues from existing customers. With those goals clearly understood, the organization can determine how to use social media to acquire new customers as part of its whole marketing strategy and decide how to use social media to increase revenues from existing customers, within the marketing and customer service strategies.

Clarifying the internal context is the key to establishing business cases for social media investments. For example, if business leaders set goals for increasing market share, they should evaluate proposed social media investments on such criteria as their ability to create new leads, increase lead quality, or increase customer retention. The revenue benefits from more leads, higher-quality leads or increased customer retention could form one-half of the social media business case. Of course, the other half is the investment required to generate those benefits, including the implementation and operational costs of new social media capabilities.

Culture

The culture of the organization is a critical input into successful social media strategy development. It includes habits, behaviors, ways of working, and subcultures within an organization. Chapter 15 explains ways of assessing opportunities for shaping culture to support social media strategies as well as a framework for pursuing those opportunities. In that chapter, we explain there is no single "best" culture for success in social media; however, organizations that use social media well tend to collaborate well across organizational boundaries and their information technology governance tends to possess enough flexibility to accommodate technologies and business requirements that continually evolve.

Business Processes

Developing a social media strategy requires thoughtful consideration of two types of processes: the processes a company uses to manage social media

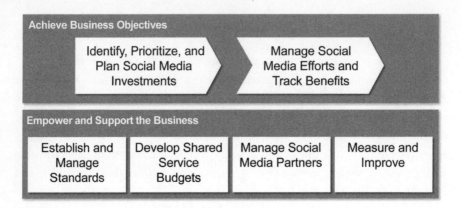

FIGURE 2.5 Social Media Management Processes.

across the organization and the business processes it intends to support or impact. We focus on the former here.

Every organization must define cross-organization processes for managing social media. For example, Figure 2.5 shows a typical framework of management processes required to ensure efficient and effective use of social media across the organization. Such common processes include those listed next.

Identify, Prioritize, and Plan Social Media Investments

- How the organization empowers employees across the organization to identify new social media investment opportunities
- How to determine opportunities for resource sharing, align the opportunities to business objectives, and prioritize the opportunities accordingly
- How to plan the execution of those investments. This process should borrow heavily from existing annual planning and information technology (IT) governance processes

Manage Social Media Efforts and Track Benefits

- How to determine ownership of social media efforts, which typically requires participation from multiple teams across the company
- How to then measure and report achievement of expected benefits during and after the investment

Establish and Manage Standards

- Who is responsible for defining standards that should apply across the organization, such as integration with customer records, data retention, disclosures, and so on?
- How will those standards evolve over time, and how will requirements be gathered throughout the organization to ensure that the standards evolve as regulations and social media technologies evolve?
- How will standards be audited and enforced or supported across the organization?

Develop Shared Service Budgets

- When opportunities are identified for resource-sharing across teams, how will the budgets be defined and managed so each team receives the support it needs?
- How are requirements gathered across teams?
- Who makes the decision when two teams disagree on requirements, tool selection, and so on?

Manage Social Media Partners

- Who owns service-level agreements with social media partners?
- How are the requirements determined for those agreements across the organization?
- How is performance tracked against the agreements and managed over time?
- Who is responsible for managing application programming interfaces (APIs) and ensuring that all dependent systems are updated when external party APIs change?

Measure and Improve

- Who owns performance measurement for social media?
- What gets measured and by whom?
- How are the metrics reported, and to whom?
- What process is used for systematically improving performance over time, including identification and sharing of lessons learned and leading practices?

Defining these processes requires participation from all of the stakeholders who participate in the processes, which typically means many functional leaders in the organization.

Metrics

Within each business process, a company must define the metrics that social media will help improve. Such metrics can include conversion rates, recruiting costs per new hire, or number of new product ideas that reach the market. Importantly, whichever metrics are chosen should align with the goals a company has for its social media initiatives—which could vary substantially from company to company and even within a company.

For instance, according to Tracy Benson at Best Buy, a company can define its return on investment in social media in many ways. She explained in the interview:

> You could look at return from an attitudinal perspective, or how customers are perceiving us based on what we do, what we're talking about and what we're enabling. You could look at it from a behavioral perspective, or how we are driving traffic, as measured by [such things as store and web site visits]. You can look at it from an organizational standpoint—what [our social media efforts are] empowering employees to do that they couldn't do before [in terms of engaging with customers]. You can also look at it from a transactional or conversion standpoint—for instance, how a customer influences somebody else or a customer's purchase of something or intent to buy something.

Benson stressed that return on investment in social media does not necessarily mean sales and, thus, the metrics a company creates to gauge its effectiveness and return should be driven accordingly. (We further explore social media metrics in Chapter 3.)

People

Once a company understands the desired business process changes that social media will enable, it then must identify the impacts of those changes on the people involved in the processes and the new roles that social media requires an organization to create. As discussed more fully in Chapter 16, this can include new training, coaching, and hiring criteria.

The next step is determining whether new tools will be used and new skills will be required. If so, a company must identify how it will develop those skills and improve them over time. For example, will the company train existing employees, or hire new employees who already have the required skills? How will it ensure that those employees maintain the relevant skills, as technologies and leading practices evolve?

Rewards and performance measurement are an important part of ensuring that a social media strategy incorporates appropriate plans for the people who will turn the strategy into reality. We discuss this topic in Chapter 15.

Policies

Policies define acceptable, unacceptable, desired, and undesired behaviors among internal and external audiences, including employees, contractors, vendors, customers, and prospects. To achieve meaningful impact from social media policies, each policy must be crafted in consideration of the six framework elements and should be unique to an organization.

Policies are uniquely important to social media strategies because of the number of people involved in achieving the strategies, the real-time nature of social media, and the need to empower employees and customers to interact with speed and at scale to a significantly greater degree than in any other business capability. Chapter 17 provides leading practices and guidance for developing social media policies.

How to Begin: Start with Business Goals

To be sure, most organizations do not have the luxury of pursuing every component of the framework at once. That is fine, because social media strategy development is an iterative process wherein the strategy should be revisited and updated periodically.

As illustrated in Figure 2.6, social media has the potential to benefit many areas of a company, most specifically product development, marketing, sales, customer service, and HR. But any company that tries to define a strategy for evaluating and then achieving all of those potential outcomes will quickly be overwhelmed for two reasons.

1. It is very difficult to coordinate such a strategy effort across an entire organization when starting from a blank sheet of paper.

Product Development	Marketing and Sales	Customer Service and Support	Hiring and Professional Development
• Increase volumes of new ideas through crowd sourcing	• Improved targeting through self-selected social media users	• New opportunities for self-serve and lower cost-to-serve channels (e.g., shift infrastructure costs to social utilities)	• Increased access to the best candidates
• Improved market research efficiency with better access to qualified test subjects	• Decreased marketing infrastructure costs through free tools (e.g., Twitter, Facebook)	• Decreased costs to maintain knowledge bases through integrated internal and external media	• Decreased costs per hire by using free or low-cost social utilities to post jobs
• Increase ability to leverage expertise and source ideas across the organization	• Increased acquisition efficiency and penetration rates through viral mechanisms	• Greater personalization through access to more customer behaviors and preferences	• Increased collaboration and access to internal experts
			• Decreased time to competence with social knowledge management applications

FIGURE 2.6 Example Business Benefits of Social Media.

2. The development of a social media strategy must begin with listening. The organization must begin by identifying and understanding the conversations that are occurring in social media with relevance to the topics that the social media strategy will support. If a company tries to listen and analyze all of the topics that are relevant across the organization, then that can get very expensive very quickly.

For example, if a company wants customers to solve each others' problems, it would analyze conversations about product issues, service issues, and so on. Then the company would identify the influencers within those conversations and the venues where those conversations occur, and the strategy would focus on those topics, conversations, venues, and influencers. If a company wants to use social media to hire new employees, the topics analyzed would be different, focusing on conversations involving jobs, career, and so on. In addition, a strategy focused on hiring likely would depend on different influencers and venues. And a strategy for increasing sales leads through social media may identify another set of topics, conversations, venues, and influencers.

This is when cost becomes a major issue. Every time a company adds a topic for analysis, its costs increase. Someone has to analyze the data and derive insights from it. Thus, adding more topics means more time for analysis, and time is money, even if a company is conducting the analysis itself. Additionally, most listening services charge by the topic in some form. Radian6 calls them "profiles," while Converseon calls them "topics." Different vendors use different terminology and slightly different definitions, but, ultimately, it all depends on the number of topics a company wants to monitor. And many listening tools base their pricing on the volume of posts or entries that a company's account aggregates and analyses—in addition to charging per topic or profile. As a company adds more topics, it adds more volume, and that increases the price it must pay.

As a result of the organizational complexity and potential costs of listening, it is generally best to begin with one business problem or one business area, such as marketing. Develop an initial strategy to address that problem or the opportunities in that area, and gradually refine and expand the strategy over time. As one business area figures out how to use social media successfully within the organization's context and culture, the strategy can expand into other areas of the business.

For example, the head of marketing may lead the first effort to define a social media strategy for the organization. Such an effort would begin by understanding the current goals of the marketing organization, then identifying how those goals could be supported by social media. This first step could look something like the illustration in Table 2.1.

Table 2.1 Defining a Social Media Strategy for the Marketing Organization

Marketing Goals for This Fiscal Year (A company probably already has these)	How Social Media Could Help (A company may need some help identifying these)
1. Increase brand awareness	• Increase conversation reach and volumes for positive-sentiment topics about the brand and products
2. Increase revenues through demand marketing	• For products where multiple people participate in the purchase decision, make it very easy for any participant to share succinct and relevant product content with other members of the purchase decision
3. Increase efficiency by decreasing average cost per converted lead	• Increase lead volumes from organic search versus paid search by increasing back-links and traffic to product-specific blogs and web properties

For this step, there are three options: (1) research it internally, (2) employ a subject matter expert, or (3) hire a consultant. In any case, it requires someone who possesses deep understanding of the business process affected and applied knowledge of the relevant social media solutions available in the industry. This effort also might include benchmarking competitors or leading social media practitioners to understand what is possible.

Case studies should be used only to generate ideas, not as evidence that any particular strategy or tactic will work for anyone other than the organization in the case study. Case studies will give companies ideas to try, but one cannot expect the same results from the same actions as those who came before. As online marketing guru Seth Godin said on his blog:

> The reason social media is so difficult for most organizations: It's a process, not an event. Dating is a process. So is losing weight . . . and building a brand.
>
> On the other hand, putting up a trade show booth is an event. So are going public and having surgery. Events are easier to manage, pay for and get excited about. Processes build results for the long haul.
>
> When you are good at social media, your audience will be somewhat unique to you: your evangelists and your fans. If you follow someone else's wake of social media success, expect your results to vary. The Early Adopters may give you tactics to try, but their results will not be yours because your process has different inputs and should take different turns.[3]

Later chapters in this book provide far more information about the kinds of goals that social media can support. The purpose here is to provide a simple example.

Once an organization articulates its goals and understands how social media might support them, it should identify the business processes involved. For example, lead generation impacts revenues, and the product ideation process impacts research and development (the costs and quantity of new products that a company brings to market each year). For champions of social media, this is the time to identify the internal stakeholders they will need to engage. With the process impacts well understood, a company then can select the metrics that will determine success, their current values, and how they need to change. For example, a team that plans to improve lead conversion rates needs to understand current conversion rates, by lead source.

To continue the example of the hypothetical head of marketing: Assume the person chooses to begin her social media strategy by focusing on increasing brand awareness through social media. She then would identify all of the people across the organization who participate in generating brand awareness. That could include anyone who blogs, tweets, or runs a Facebook fan page for the company at present as well as anyone who runs marketing campaigns on television, radio, print, or online. She also might engage the people who work with channel partners. For example, a marketing vice president at a shampoo manufacturer might engage the people at her company who work with the retailers that sell their products to consumers. IT also will need to be involved because that function will have to either build or support the eventual solutions used to implement the strategy, and it probably has people who are experienced in social media. At some point, the marketing head will need to engage someone from legal (and sooner is generally better than later) so that person can grow to appreciate the business goals and the strategy. Finally, the team will need someone from finance to help with estimates of costs and benefits. This last point is crucial, as our experience shows one never should try to build a business case without someone from the finance team at least providing feedback and guidance.

With the key players defined, the marketing head is ready to establish a clear understanding of the current situation, define the desired situation, and identify the gaps that need to be closed in order to get to the desired situation. This effort generally begins with a kickoff meeting, the purpose of which is to explain to the key players the rationale for pursuing a social media strategy and why such a strategy is important, as well as to get their commitment to participate in the initiative. After the meeting, the marketing head would conduct follow-up interviews with all the relevant stakeholders to understand their experiences with social media in their jobs, including challenges and opportunities, as well as the relevant regulations governing the selected business process(es) to appreciate the boundaries within which the team must operate. For example, financial services institutions usually have to store any product-related communications for years into the future. If an insurer plans to publish viral content that contains product information for investment products, it needs a plan for ensuring appropriate reviews and storage of the content in addition to auditability, documentation, and employee training on the process.

Following the interviews, the participants from the kickoff meeting are reconvened for a workshop in which they explore in more detail the data collected to date. Toward the end of the workshop, the group should collectively prioritize all of the possible options, based on expected costs and benefits. In the last exercise of the workshop, participants organize the options and opportunities into a timeline, thereby agreeing on the chronological order for addressing them. Throughout this exercise, it will be important to identify capabilities that should be centralized versus those that should be run within each business unit or geographic area.

Table 2.2 summarizes the most important steps in developing a social media strategy and the order in which they should be occur.

Table 2.2 Principal Steps in Developing a Social Media Strategy

1. Identify an initial business domain (e.g., marketing).
2. Understand the existing business goals for the business domain (e.g. marketing goals for the current fiscal year).
3. Identify ways that social media could support those goals, to determine which goals to focus the social media strategy
4. Identify the business processes that achieve the selected goals (e.g., lead management).
5. Engage appropriate stakeholders to help and to participate.
6. Understand the metrics used to define success of the business processes (e.g., average cost per converted lead), their current values, and target values that would demonstrate a successful social media strategy.
7. Hold a kick-off meeting.
8. Interview all stakeholders to identify the current challenges, opportunities, and options. Use the Social Media Management Framework as a checklist to understand current context, culture, processes, people, policies, and metrics.
9. Hold a workshop to review the data gathered in the interviews, discuss the themes revealed, and jointly prioritize the themes for action. Again apply the Social Media Management framework as a checklist to ensure that each element that will be required for success is considered.
10. Identify capabilities that should be centralized or shared.
11. Begin working on the themes in priority order.

Once the initial strategy is defined, it's important for a company to test and refine it over time. Social media is still a very new domain, and no one knows specifically which tactics will achieve results with audiences, who are, by definition, unique.

Conclusion

As is the case with any new development, it's easy for companies to underestimate what it takes to fully embrace and benefit from social media. Although the promise of social media can be alluring and exciting, there's so much more than meets the eye. Organizations that wade into the social media waters unprepared likely will find themselves quickly overwhelmed by the complexity and speed they encounter.

That's why it's absolutely critical for companies to have a solid, well-articulated strategy for dealing with social media before they get involved too deeply. Knowing precisely why and how they will use social media will help organizations avoid many of the pitfalls that have derailed others before them while maximizing social media's contribution to their pursuit of their business goals.

3

Social Media ROI: New Metrics for Customer Health

Kevin Quiring

CHAPTER HIGHLIGHTS

The credibility of social media is won or lost on its return on investment (ROI). The most successful companies—those that have gotten out of pilot mode—have been able to crisply define what they want to get out of social media and then identify the right metrics to help them achieve their objectives.

Organizations need a new integrated ROI measure called customer health, which provides a holistic approach to predicting the impact of social media investments to increase revenue, profitability, and long-term customer loyalty. This metric must encompass the "five Rs" discussed in Chapter 1.

Measuring the return on investments (ROIs) to attract and retain customers has never been easy. Understanding how much new business a marketing campaign generated is often the subject of debate. Was it the advertising campaign or the sales force training program that increased sales? Perhaps it was recent improvements in customer support—for example, the self-service web site that speeds the repair process. Determining precisely what a company gets from investing X dollars in a marketing, sales, or service program always has been a complex undertaking.

Now, with the advent of social media, it's become even more complex. As companies increasingly use social media to market their offerings and provide service to customers, the shortcomings of traditional processes for measuring ROI become even more pronounced.

Nonetheless, social media channels enable companies to create far better ways of measuring investments for attracting and retaining customers. But it requires a new metric, one we call "Customer Health." This metric provides a holistic approach to predicting the impact of investments to increase revenue, profitability, and long-term customer loyalty.

Challenge of Measuring Customer Investments in Social Media

Companies always have found it difficult to measure the impact of new marketing programs, service improvements, and other investments meant to attract and retain customers. Even after instituting effective measures, many organizations use them sporadically or unevenly across product lines and divisions.

Determining whether an uptick in sales is due to a sales promotion launched in stores, an ad campaign, or just a plain old improvement in the economy has given many managers fits. Far too often, they assume that a sales increase is the result of a promotion when in reality the propellant may be something else. But while making accurate correlations is extremely difficult, it's also become extremely important. The reason: Companies are making increasingly big bets in their marketing, sales, and service programs. Offering promotions or launching new advertising campaigns can erode profit margins just as easily as they can boost sales.

To understand their returns on customer-related investments, companies must be able to determine which data is relevant, gather that data, and make highly complex correlations (sales, timing, breadth, scope, quality of advertising, and many more variables). All of this is difficult. Managers often don't have all the data they need, or it's not in one place or easy to access. In other cases, marketing partners such as media buyers, ad agencies, and sales tracking companies (for example, IMS and Nielsen) have the information, but it may not be in formats that are easy to use. In still other cases, the cause-and-effect analysis is just too complex to attempt.

However, as difficult as the analysis of marketing ROI is, there is an even more daunting issue. The data a company collects in traditional ROI analysis doesn't paint a complete picture of what caused customers to take some action or what they think about that firm. In fact, the traditional things companies do to understand customer perceptions on performance can be quite ineffective at reflecting what the customer really thinks. Customer surveys are a case in point. Asking customers what they think about a firm, its products, and its service processes is often an ineffective way of capturing what they truly believe for three reasons.

1. Many people don't respond to surveys, and the ones who do may represent a highly biased sample (often the biggest complainers or biggest advocates).
2. They may answer erroneously, saying one thing ("I hate your customer service") but acting in a different manner (continuing to buy).
3. There are so many other things going on in the lives of consumers that a company can't hope to understand. The customer's bad rating of a firm in a survey may be the result of a recent family issue, problem at work, or a bad experience with another company.

Managers can only truly correlate the direct interactions their firms have with customers—a customer service or sales call, for example. Until now, attempting to correlate indirect interactions—that is, ones that are not between the customer and the company—had been trying to quantify the unquantifiable. This is the problem of "dark matter"—all of the data customers generate about a company or its direct competitors for which the company has no visibility.

The dark matter can take many forms, including conversations customers have with other people about a company—the dialogue "behind the company's back." These could be the conversations at a party or on an airplane (positive or negative) that influence other customers or potential customers. This is a form of social media, one that has gone on for centuries. Yet it is insight that has gone uncaptured. It is this dark matter that allows an organization to truly understand the feelings customers have about companies, and, to date, it has been unattainable.

Problem of Inconsistent Measures

Some companies are quite competent at gathering traditional customer information and doing the analytics to measure the impacts of marketing and customer investments. Yet they often are tripped up when they try to apply those measures across the organization and use them to continually improve the way they attract and keep customers.

What trips them up? Misaligned or split accountability is one culprit. One person may be in charge of customer satisfaction (for example, customer service). Another may be responsible for customer acquisition (for example, sales), and a third for customer awareness (for example, marketing). However, to manage the entire customer life cycle, someone has to be accountable for all these things—awareness, sales, and postsales satisfaction. But it is the rare company that has a high-ranking individual who has power over the three functions and who exercises it daily. (Theoretically, the chief operating or chief executive officer has such power. But in a large company, it's nearly impossible for such a person to find the time to monitor the life cycle of customers.)

When a company fragments its accountability to customers, functional teams can easily take conflicting actions. They can send conflicting marketing messages to the marketplace. They can institute service policies that erode sales promises. And they can choose to act or not to act on what their customer measures tell them. For example, a customer call center measured largely on efficiency—keeping call times down to a minimum—and not on overall customer satisfaction may disregard a survey commissioned by the sales force on how the company needs to improve service.

Thus, even if a company institutes effective metrics across the functions that touch customers, how it uses those measures—whether certain functions decide to ignore some and not others—ultimately determines the usefulness of its metrics.

How Social Media Complicates Measurement

Just as companies grapple with the issues of measuring the impact of their customer investments in traditional channels (advertising, direct marketing, call centers and so on), a whole new channel of customer interaction has arrived: social media. It only further complicates the ability of companies to measure customer investments and the state of customer relationships.

Social networking tools such as Facebook, MySpace, LinkedIn, and Twitter, blogs that command large audiences, video-sharing sites such as YouTube, and other Internet-based social media channels have attracted a huge audience around the world in less than a decade. For companies, the result is a whole new ecosystem of customer touch points—millions of them. These touch points are not just between a company and its customers and prospective customers. They are between customers and other customers, customers and other companies. This is what makes social media a very difficult new channel for companies to deal with: the threat of bad reviews spread by word of mouth across the globe in minutes and hours. Conversely, it is a potentially great new customer channel: having positive reviews spreading in a similar manner. Monitoring and measuring the customer touch points in social media has become enormously important.

But it is also extremely difficult. In part, this is because the social media ecosystem consists almost entirely of unstructured data. In contrast, the interactions companies have with customers in survey research are structured; a customer fills out a survey consisting of well-formulated questions, ticking off boxes to answer the questions. The customer's opinions can be quickly gathered, processed, and analyzed.

The customer dialogue in social media channels is anything but structured. Customers aren't responding to surveys or to the questions of call center agents. Customers are sounding off on their experiences with companies—posting YouTube videos, typing comments on blogs and discussion forums, chatting with one another on Facebook or MySpace. Companies trying to monitor these discussions will be tuning in to electronic conversations that are difficult to collect. (It's not possible for a company to listen to every outpost on the Internet in which it is mentioned.) Even those conversations that a company *does* tune in to are difficult to analyze. Understanding the context of the data can be difficult—the reasons customers are discussing a company. It's like barging into the middle of a heated conversation at a party and trying to make sense of what other guests are talking about.

The second factor that makes it difficult for companies to measure what customers are saying to other customers through social media is that these interactions are at undefined points in the customer life cycle. And understanding where customers are in their life cycles with a company greatly affects how that company will treat them. When a customer calls the toll-free phone number for his cellular service provider, enters his phone number, and selects the menu option for billing, the provider already knows the caller is an existing customer with at least one cell phone account and that he has a question or issue regarding his billing. This set of steps takes hundreds of points in the customer life cycle and defines it into a narrow span. Although many other facts may remain unknown, when the agent picks up the phone, there should be enough context to hold a relatively efficient conversation.

Conversely, in social media, companies typically don't know who is talking about them via social media or in what context the conversation is occurring. The identification of the people tweeting or posting blogs has little or no correlation to the names or customer numbers in a firm's customer relationship management (CRM) system. In addition, because the firm doesn't have the context to interpret a comment an individual posted on YouTube, Facebook, Twitter, or a product review web site, it has no idea where the person is in the life cycle. Furthermore, it's often hard to discern positive sentiments from negative sentiments, or to determine whether a comment is worth responding to. For example, if a consumer electronics company finds one of its customers online researching flat-panel televisions after recently purchasing a flat-panel TV, it could mean many different things. It could imply that the consumer is unhappy with the product and a return is imminent. It could mean that she is so pleased she is looking for another one to put in a different room. Or she could be researching a gift purchase. Is this an average customer about to become a great customer or an average customer about to become unprofitable?

Understanding a customer's context is critical to trying to predict his next moves and how to respond (including spending money on fixing a problem). But it is exceptionally difficult to understand the context of customer dialogues in social media.

Why Social Media Provides a Whole New Tool for Understanding Customers

Despite the challenges companies face measuring the return on customer investments today, firms that can harness this new interaction channel can gain a far more complete picture of what customers feel about them and are likely to do next. The customer insights they glean from social media will be far more powerful, predictive, and actionable when combined with the insights they gather through traditional channels than what either of these channels can deliver on its own.

If companies can develop such insights, they will be able to measure customer sentiment with far greater accuracy and timeliness. They'll be much better at deducing what investments to make (and not to make) in marketing, sales, and service—investments to improve the way they attract and retain customers. Those investments will yield many more customers, more profitable customers, and long-term customer loyalty. Those that harness social media will be able to jump the curve in the hunt for customer insights and vault over companies that remain focused on gleaning insights through traditional channels.

But how can companies harness social media to measure customer sentiment and generate customer insights? Everything a company gathers, stores, analyzes, measures, and monitors about its customers to determine where to make customer investments is a surrogate for answering three questions:

1. **How do you truly feel about us?** This is not what customers said but rather how they truly feel about a company. What is the customer's current emotional state regarding a company?
2. **What will you do in the future?** This question is about discerning what the customer likely will do next. A telecommunications carrier wants to know whether a household will add cell phones to the account or consolidate them, or whether it plans to increase or decrease its landline usage.
3. **How can we address your unmet needs?** Answering this question enables a company to identify wants and desires it hasn't asked consumers about that remain unfilled—and are ones the company could meet.

Social media enables companies to "see" pertinent information about customers—information that has been hidden in the past, the dark matter, as we have referred to it. What companies know today about its customers is the tiniest fraction of customer insight. Most customer information resides in the dark matter.

To illustrate this, consider a customer who buys a flat-panel TV. He may spend an hour interacting with a company over the life of his relationship—filling out a product warranty card, calling the contact center to troubleshoot a problem, and so on. The company's knowledge about the customer, along with the knowledge gained at time of purchase, is trivial. But the dark matter—how the customer feels about the product, whether it's meeting his needs, which products he is likely to buy next—is far more important. The customer will spend hundreds or thousands of hours using the product. While he is using it, he is increasingly likely to use social media to tell other people about the product. The dark matter information he is providing online can provide a powerful means of discerning his next moves with the product and his unmet needs.

Social media allows companies to see much of the rest of that proverbial dark matter, the hard-to-see sentiments that drive customers toward or away from a firm. Companies that can see the whole customer—that can use social media to measure the unseen parts of their customer relationships and combine it with what they already know about a customer—will have superior tools for weighing investments in marketing, sales, and service.

We refer to this emerging customer performance metric as "customer health," which we explore in more detail.

Essence of Customer Health

Customer health is the holistic measurement of a customer's real and potential value to an organization. It consists of a customer's historic lifetime value, potential lifetime value, and social reach and influence. The next story illustrates what we mean by customer health. Consider Harley-Davidson customers. Some of these motorcycle purchasers are far "healthier" than others to Harley-Davidson. They would include the customer who purchases one bike at a full rate and says great things about the bike to friends and neighbors. This customer may be healthier than the customer with two Harleys in his lifetime but uses the social Web regularly to pan the company and has a large online following. Only by including and measuring what those customers are saying about it through social media can Harley determine the real impact of those customers. The fact that one spent $15,000 and the other spent $30,000 on Harley's products means little.

Just as customers are not binary in the value they contribute to the company, they are not binary in their overall health. Consider customer health as a spectrum. At the weakest (least healthy) end of the spectrum is apathy. At the strongest (healthiest) end of the spectrum, customers are profitable advocates. Companies must include what customers are saying about them through social media into their measures to understand where a customer is on this spectrum. The least healthy customer, the apathetic one, is actually worse than an angry one because she is occupying the investment of money, time, and attention while demonstrating no engagement. Worse yet, our experience shows that these customers possess the least amount of loyalty to the company.

On the other end of the customer health spectrum is the loyal advocate. Irrational loyalty is the objective most companies are trying to achieve. An insanely loyal Harley-Davidson customer not only buys Harleys, he owns the peripheral equipment—the accessories and clothes. He also might have a Harley tattoo, which makes him a walking advertisement for the firm even when he isn't riding his bike. That bike may be costing him big money. It may be a nightmare to maintain. But he has gone so far as to emblazon the brand logo on his skin. That is irrational loyalty.

For years companies have tried to identify and understand the characteristics of their best customers. They typically rely on how much money a customer has spent on their products, their income, their stage of life, and thus what they are likely to spend in the future. But without the data to determine how strong an advocate a customer is, they don't really have a good sense of her market influence—her ability to affect other customers. But if companies really want to build and nurture advocates, they need to understand how much more valuable such advocates are than those "best customers" (i.e., the ones who have bought the most and are likely to buy the most in the future).

Building advocates is not free, and it doesn't happen quickly. In fact, it takes a long time and significant resources. But without these investments, the health of a company's customer base won't improve. A company won't be shifting many currently apathetic customers to ardent advocates. When an organization can measure the impact of its advocates—how much total revenue and profit they generate on average among the entire customer base—it can begin to easily assess the worthiness of investments to boost advocacy.

Every company that is still in business has advocates. But to thrive, it must understand how many advocates it has, who they are, and what it must do to create more of them. Only through a metric such as customer health—a metric that incorporates the sentiments customers express to the world about companies through social media—will a company be able to survive and thrive in the new world. It is a world in which a company's reputation can soar or crash on the social media chatter about it that's winding its way around the world.

To be sure, companies weren't blind to measuring customer advocacy before social media became popular. Many used tools such as net promoter scores. However, for the shortcomings we noted earlier (it is based on the interactions between a company and its customers rather than the interactions among customers, it relies on the customer reporting truthfully, and it's a measure at just one point in time), the net promoter score now must be just one component in a much broader gauge of customer health.

Monitoring social media to determine customer health is important for another reason: It enables companies to measure a customer's more recent behavior far better than ever. What's more important for determining what a customer will purchase: information on her behavior in the past five minutes or the past five years? A few advanced customer-centric companies can quantify the profitability of a customer based on how much she purchased during those five years and how much the firm spent on marketing and providing service to her. With this information, these companies can predict that customer's future value—how much she is likely to purchase in the next five years. But what if a company monitored her comments on product review sites, the company's Facebook fan page, competing companies' product review pages, and other social media sites where she indicates her latest purchasing intentions? Isn't that more important to know than how much gear she has purchased from the company in the past five years? Absolutely. The company would have a far better opportunity to intercept her and direct her its way. For many customers, loyalty comes down to which company is the latest one to make them aware of the best deal or to fill an unmet need.

When it comes to data, we can sum up the issue thusly: The past five minutes of customer information gathered through social media is becoming more important than the past five years of information a company has in its CRM system. The clock speed of the customer relationship has increased dramatically in the past few years.

Four Predictors of Customer Health

Understanding where customers are on the spectrum from apathy to advocacy is now crucial. But how can managers gauge their customers on this metric? We have found four key predictors of customer health—vital signs that will indicate how customers feel about a company, what they will do in the future, and how the firm can best address those customers' unmet needs:

1. **What customers tell a company.** Feedback customers actually tell a company is not typically indicative of what they will do going forward. It tends to be far more positive or negative than what their behavior demonstrates. Rarely do comments correlate with behavior. For instance, a customer who fills out a survey at the checkout line provides information that may sound predictive ("The line was too long—I'll never shop here again!"). But his future behavior rarely proves out.

2. **What customers tell others.** The comments customers make about a brand to others tends to be much more predictive than what they tell the company. Customers are more honest and less reactionary (positive or negative) when telling their stories about the brand to others. When they are extreme in their comments, a company can take that to the bank. It tends to be real feedback, real perceptions that will stick and predict their future behavior.

3. **What customers show others.** What customers do with a company's competitors or adjacent organizations in the value chain tends to be very indicative of health. Customers are voting with their dollars when interacting with other companies. They are voting against a company when they purchase goods and services from its competitor and for a company when they purchase or interact positively with its business partners.

4. **What customers show a company.** This is the most accurate predictor of a customer's future behavior. It encompasses all the interactions a customer has with an organization: what she buys, what she rejects/returns, how she utilizes products and services, and the manner in which she interacts with a company on every channel.

Social media provides companies with an unprecedented lens on what customers are showing and telling others about it. The insights managers can glean from such online expressions are more important for predicting the health of a customer base than a company's traditional CRM data. Companies that monitor social media and compile an incisive measure of customer health can get much more precise in their customer-related investments. They can create far more effective promotions, advertising campaigns, sales processes, and service policies. They can capitalize on the treasure trove of information that customers are leaving behind on the social web to predict their purchasing behaviors.

Measuring the Four Predictors

First and foremost, measuring the four predictors of customer health must be manageable for the enterprise. As companies engage with social media, they begin to fuse existing metrics (customer CRM data) that are very pragmatic and actionable with new ones that actually give them a sense of the previously unseen dark matter. Along the journey, new and existing customer measurement coexists until an inflexion point where there is enough intelligence gained through social media data gathering and analytics that the company can fuse the two into a powerful new metric.

The important and crucial first step is to gather data effectively for the four predictors of customer health. A company need not gather all the data that is available, but certainly the relevant data. What customers show a company is the easiest data to assemble, yet many companies are still far behind in their efforts to create an integrated view of the customer. This data consists of a full accounting of what business a customer has done with the company over time across the company's entire range of products and services including how profitable that business has been. But it doesn't stop there.

Customers show companies other things in addition to purchases. Companies must understand when, how, and why customers interact with them. Doing this means such things as a detailed understanding of inquiries they have of the company, utilization of its products and services, issues they have raised, and customer service performed. The sources for this data come directly from the company's systems of record, such as order management, provisioning, account management, CRM, point-of-sale, e-commerce, and billing systems.

What customers tell a company is the next most easily obtained type of data. This information exists in comments and reason codes within customer service and contact center systems as well as e-mails from customers. Ratings and reviews are another source of direct feedback from customers. Finally, surveys and focus group data round out the existing sources of data regarding direct customer feedback. This data consists of structured and unstructured data. Although both forms are useful, categorizing the unstructured data is critical to preparing this type of data for customer health analysis.

What customers show others is basically competitive intelligence on where the company's customers are spending their time and money. It consists of the same general types of data found in what customers show the company directly. However, because companies rarely have access to their competitors' data, much of this information will have to be creatively gathered or imputed. Third-party data providers, such as Nielsen, IRI, Claritas, D&B, and Polk, are examples of data sources that can be used to estimate the business a customer is doing with competitors based on their estimated spend overall minus the company's share of wallet.

What customers tell others is the predictor of customer health that has been directly enabled or even created by the advent of social media. It consists of what customers are saying about the company's brand, products, and services to one another. It includes comments made on social media sites and blogs as well as customer advocacy forums. Customer sentiment monitoring is one way to get a view into this type of customer health data.

For example, Microsoft pays considerable attention to monitoring what happens in the community forums it sponsors for particular audiences. "Measurement is quite a bit more robust [in these forums] because we want to look at overall health from the standpoint of the customer experience," explained Toby Richards, general manager for communities and online support at Microsoft. "So we monitor growth and participation—not just [in terms of] people who come to the site, but actually growth of people either asking a question or the growth of people doing the answering."

Once data is gathered, the next step is to analyze these four types of information. Analysis at scale will depend on effective structuring of the unstructured data. Doing this will entail encoding the verbatim data and identifying the interaction reason, customer sentiment, outcome, and so on. The verbatim data should be stored as well for future reference. Analysis also will depend on integrating the various data on what customers showed and told a company and what they showed and told others. Analysis will be most effective when these four types all can be associated to individual customers. No method of integration and attribution will be foolproof; however, it is important to remember that "perfect is the enemy of good" in this regard, and the lack of 100 percent accurate matches should not deter companies from integrating 80 percent of the data. Both descriptive and predictive analysis will be required to generate insights from the data. Descriptive analysis is required to explore the data and search for value pools of untapped opportunity. Predictive analysis is required to cluster customers into behavioral segments and determine likelihood to buy or switch providers.

Just because a company can gather, integrate, and analyze customer data doesn't mean it can gain customer insight effectively. Generating insight is one of the most challenging activities for companies to perform on a consistent, operational basis. Generating insight entails finding intersections within the data sets that have been analyzed. For example, seeking out pools of low-value but high-potential-value customers, determining the behaviors that are limiting their current value, and the behaviors that would generate more value illustrates the intersection of value and behaviors. The final step of generating insight involves the definition of value propositions—the elements of the customer experience that ultimately will drive those more profitable behaviors.

Acting on Customer Health

Once the data for customer health has been gathered and analyzed, insight has been generated, and value propositions have been defined, companies must act on the insight in an attempt to increase the health of the customer base.

The first step in acting on the insight is to deliver the value propositions. The value propositions are elements of the overall customer experience that have been tailored to address unmet needs, thereby improving customer health. For example, a value proposition might be a new menu selection on the toll-free customer service number for automatically accessing loyalty points. Or it might be a specialized banker at a financial institution's new retail branch who is capable of handling everything from transactions to basic financial planning. Value propositions also can be as simple as promotions geared toward a certain customer segment whose health a company believes it can improve through the stimulus of a weekend sale.

Some value propositions require significant investment and planning to be executed, and others are simply automated via changes to configuration rules in a CRM system. Most tailored value propositions do require, however, the training of people—people in contact centers, the sales force, or in retail locations. The training of the workforce is instrumental in the delivery of the value proposition. Successful delivery will depend on employees having the context for the value proposition as well as the specific "says and does" required to execute the proposition effectively.

In addition to delivering new value propositions that will improve overall customer health, it is important to change aspects of today's customer experience that lead to poor customer health. "Dissatisfiers" are those moments of truth when the company has failed to deliver. First and foremost, these barriers must be fixed for those customers with good health. Removing the dissatisfiers will improve the brand perception and overall customer health. Common dissatisfiers include a return policy, customer service, or the process for resolving billing disputes.

Finally, insights into customer health must guide strategic prioritization of investments made in the customer base. This strategic prioritization includes overall marketing and promotion spending as well as investments in the sales force and customer service. Questions must be asked as to which business capabilities are the least developed today and which have the potential to drive the greatest customer health going forward.

New Processes and Roles for Customer Health

Even before the advent of social media, companies have been challenged to effectively measure the ROI of their customer investments. However, although it may have been possible to get by on directional information and intuition in the past, tomorrow's world full of the immediacy of social media will not be so forgiving. Just as inventory replenishment was transformed from a manual process based on the collective experience of lifetime inventory analysts to a data-driven process fueled by mathematical models, customer health measurements will be required to compete effectively in the era of the new normal.

But making customer health operational will take more than just defining it, gathering data, performing analysis, and generating insight. Process and organizational changes must be defined to ensure the measure is continuous and applied.

Continuous Health Improvement Processes

The company's customer base can never be healthy enough. There always will be new faces, new places, and new spaces for a company to address in the pursuit of growth and therefore new levels of customer health to aspire to. It is imperative that continuous customer health improvement processes are defined. These processes start with ones around the analysis and generation of insight that ensure the continual development of new, refreshed customer value propositions. But it is just as important to instantiate the processes that will continually ensure that the appropriate people, process, and technology changes are made to roll out these new value propositions. Today, customer-centric initiatives at many companies stall out after the initial round of value proposition deployment takes place. To compete in the new world, companies cannot afford to overlook these deployment processes.

Customer Health Maintenance Organization

One of the most difficult questions for companies to answer is: Who in the organization is accountable for customer profitability? It is challenging because overall customer profitability is a function of not just sales or the economics of a single customer transaction. It is the sum of all revenue and costs attributable to a customer over time. Although few companies can measure this in a meaningful way that does not simply spread costs evenly across the customer base, even fewer have accountability for this metric. So, customer health will be difficult to assign accountability for unless a customer health maintenance organization (CHMO) is established.

The role of this CHMO is to manage customer health. This organization must work across product and service lines as well as marketing, sales, and service functions. The initial focus of the CHMO will be to create a governance structure that can manage across the enterprise at multiple levels and clock speeds. Typically, most of the enterprise is geared to a monthly and largely quarterly management and reporting rhythm. On one level, the CHMO will have to be responsive to the daily and weekly requirements of customer health. On another level, the CHMO will have to be cognizant of the enterprise's long-range strategic objectives and profitable growth agenda.

Getting Started

No enterprise can perform the full transformation necessary to adopt and manage customer health in a single stroke. Like any fundamental transformation, the move to customer health must start with quick wins and pragmatic steps. Enterprises can take three actions to begin the journey toward measuring and managing customer health.

1. **Define the metric.** The first step is to tailor the customer health metric to meet an organization's needs and the dynamics of its industry. For example, "What Customers Tell Others" will have a different meaning in the business-to-business telecommunications market than it does for the consumer fashion footwear industry. Next, sources must be identified for each of the four components of customer health. Some sources will be internal and some will be external. Challenges in collecting and summarizing the data can exist with both internal and external sources. Where data is absent or elusive, surrogates can be developed that provide a directional substitute for the actual information. This way, the organization can begin using customer health as a compass even if it has yet to be tuned for more precise decision making.

2. **Assign accountability.** Equally important to tailoring the customer health metric for an organization is assigning responsibility for defining the metric, calculating the metric, and driving actions based on the metric. Doing this usually entails a new or modified governance structure as the applications of the metric likely will span organizational lines. Where accountability for customer health resides organizationally will vary based on the industry, operating model, and channel structure the company has for connecting with the customer. In general, responsibility for

customer health should lie within the organization that has the most holistic view of the customer relationship. Yet assigning accountability does not mean centralizing all decision-making authority or customer investment. It does mean ensuring that visibility is brought to the metric and the parties who have investment authority are brought together and are making decisions with full knowledge of the impacts to customer health.

3. **Create a customer health capability road map.** Making customer health an operational metric will almost certainly require new business capabilities. Changes to people, process, and technology will be required to calculate and apply the metric in an ongoing, sustainable manner. In addition, the customer health metric should be refined and improved continuously. As data becomes available through new internal capabilities or new external sources, surrogates in the customer health metric should be replaced with more accurate information. All of the capability transformations and continuous improvement work should be prioritized and mapped out on a customer health capability road map. This way, investments in the capabilities can be more logically staged and communicated throughout the enterprise. The road map, like the application of the customer health metric itself, should be overseen by the same governance body.

Measuring the return on customer investment always has been a difficult challenge. It's even more difficult now with the advent of social media. However, social media offers the opportunity for a much richer, more accurate, and more actionable measure of the health of customer relationships. Companies now can holistically measure a customer's real and potential value to an organization: a customer's historic lifetime value, potential lifetime value, and social reach and influence. Capitalizing on this opportunity to measure and manage against customer health will require change—not just technology change, but real organizational change substantiated by new capabilities.

4 Selling Social Media within the Organization

Robert Wollan

CHAPTER HIGHLIGHTS

Organizations do not naturally gravitate toward social media, as the senior leadership and C-suite are the least likely to use, and therefore understand, social media potential.

Generally, they need a champion who can capture the initial flicker that engages the leaders of the company; translate that flicker into a "North Star" that will resonate with the rest of the leadership team and encourage it to follow suit; and navigate toward it by shoring up support across multiple leaders.

Selling the case requires appealing to both the heart and the head (both potential and hard benefits) to generate enthusiasm for social media across functional boundaries and maintaining momentum as social media execution expands across the company.

Social media is a disruptive and growing phenomenon; its reach and influence increasing exponentially every year. So why is it so difficult to get companies energized about it? We think there are four main reasons.

The first is that social media often is triggered in one area of the company (for example, should we launch commercials via Twitter?) and quickly becomes associated with just one application or leader, thus creating tunnel vision and stifling the perceived applicability across the enterprise. In other words, individuals tend to associate social media with a specific application or functional use rather than seeing the full cross-enterprise impact social media can and will have.

Another reason is that, despite the increasing use of social media, it has yet to spark a true sense of urgency in companies who contend with more traditional options to reach customers and/or to grow revenues. Instead, social media is viewed as something executives need to deal with over the horizon—several years in the future. It isn't seen as a here-and-now issue because there are few examples of how social media is driving business growth in mainstream companies and because only portions of the company's customer bases may be using social media. (Just what percentage of the customer base is active in social media is often well below the C-suite radar screen.)

The third reason is that social media touches a muscle that many companies haven't flexed: the ability to sense, capture, and analyze day-to-day market data. Social media is just that: the daily marketplace "noise" about a company coming from all directions and around the world. To use an earthquake analogy, the customer comments that arrive via social media are merely tremors that most executives cannot, or do not, sense. Executives are far more used to reacting to earthquakes than to tremors.

Perhaps the biggest reason involves the makeup of senior leadership teams. In most organizations, we find a great divide in the ranks over social media. Senior executives in general don't use social media regularly, and thus they don't realize how extensively it is used by a younger generation of customers, business partners, and employees. Many managers and workers on the front line do understand and use social media, but these individuals generally lack the power to make the large-scale operational changes needed for a company to fully embrace it.

For example, in the United States, only 13 percent of people 55 years and older were using social networking sites in early 2010.[1] The leadership teams of many companies are dominated by people who are least likely to use social media every day: The average age of a Standard & Poor's 500 chief executive officer (CEO) in 2009 was 55.7; the average board director was 61.7.[2]

The real distinction among age groups, however, is how they use social media. Most people age 50 or older generally use social media such as

Facebook simply to stay in touch with family and friends.[3] They generally are not familiar with how customers and competitors are using social media, nor are they fully versed in the multitude of social media types and applications. In fact, according to a recent study, only about 13 percent of companies had executives who supported and were actively engaged in social media.[4] When one gets to the CEO level of big companies, social media usage drops even more. According to Forrester Research, not a single CEO of the 100 largest companies in the world participated in social media.[5] Forrester further notes that among the world's 1,000 largest companies, only one CEO grew up during the personal computing revolution, which further makes the concept of interacting with others via social media very foreign to them.[6]

Clearly there are obstacles to widespread support and adoption of social media. But this situation can't—and won't—continue. We see three objectives for the executive in charge of driving this adoption forward: getting the executive team to acknowledge (emotionally and academically), embrace (see the opportunity and potential), and amplify (mobilizing the organization to deliver results) via social media. Based on the experiences of companies whose senior management team has gotten behind social media, we know this can be done. We explain how in this chapter.

All on Board: Getting Senior Management behind Social Media

C-suite executives get to the top of an organization by being experts in their fields. However, that can make it hard for them to unlearn the things that got them there. Changing such entrenched mind-sets requires a deliberate approach, one that requires a unique blend of engaging both "the heart" and "the head" of the executive team to succeed. In other words, a leader who wants to capture the attention of senior executives needs to make an emotional connection with those executives around social media while demonstrating the return on investment social media can generate for the business. Failure on either count will make it virtually impossible to convince senior executives to get fully behind social media.

How does a leader engage both the heart and the head of senior executives? we believe there are three steps: (1) capturing the "flicker" that will engage the leaders of the company; (2) translating that flicker into a "North

Star" that will resonate with the rest of the business and encourage it to follow suit; and (3) navigating toward that by shoring up support across multiple leaders. Let's examine each step.

Capturing the Flicker

A leader looking to sell social media to the rest of the senior executive team needs much more than statistics on how much customers and competitors are using social media. Facts and figures about broad trends alone are unlikely to convince executives to act. In our experience, top management needs a visceral case—a personal interlude with social media—to recognize its importance. Thus, the first thing a leader should do is to pause and ask the critical question: What exactly sparked the initial motivation to consider social media? What emotional connection did social media make in her that inspired her to believe in its power and potential impact on the company? Whether the initial flicker came from a competitor's actions, a board member's insight from another company, or a personal connection with another brand, all give valuable starting points for the conversation with the rest of the executive team. This step often is overlooked, yet we find it to be one of the best starting points to build on when engaging the broader leadership team for support. It's critical to not skip this step.

Best Buy's chief marketing officer, Barry Judge, caught the Twitter bug after marketing employees urged him to start using the microblogging service. "I'm now a big participant in Twitter, and I think that's turned me into a big fan," he said in a video for *Forbes* magazine's web site.[7] Judge's experience with Twitter has been a big spark for him. "Twitter made me realize that transparency is one of the huge social trends that we all need to figure out. It's about opening up your brand to other consumers, which in the end builds trust."

Turning the Flicker into the "North Star"

After sparking social media interest in a champion on the executive team, the next step is to get other executives on the leadership team on board the journey. This requires turning the flicker into a "North Star"—that is, a mechanism that will connect with others who are critical to social media success in the company and broaden the base of support to move forward.

Once again, appealing to both the heart and the head is necessary to bring others on board and maintain momentum as social media is engaged in multiple functions.

There are a number of commonly used ways to create interest and attachment among the broader executive team. The first is personal connections. Start with polling the senior executive team about recent experiences they've had on Facebook, LinkedIn, or other social media sites with which they're familiar—a situation in which they've either complained about or complimented a company, and then ask, "What if someone did that to our company?"

If an executive or board member with such a personal experience can't be found, try to create one. Companies for many years have alerted top management to customer problems by getting them directly in front of customers. More than a decade ago, one large retailer asked senior executives to spend a day in a call center so they could hear customer complaints firsthand. That ushered in a new appreciation for the important role of customer service (not just a backroom cost) and an overhaul of service at the company. The same thing today could happen with social media. Leaders can point out what customers are saying about their company in any number of discussion forums, online communities, and broader media to bring the current social media environment to life. Some of the more insightful programs have included customer-developed content from You-Tube, real-time feedback on customer experiences on Yelp, or more broad examples mined from chatter across the Web.

Far less cumbersome may be getting executives to listen to panel discussions of social media–savvy employees or younger customers who can discuss how they use social media to engage, interact with, and buy (or not to buy) the company's products. (By the way, that's often better than asking executives to talk to their children about social media. Their children may be loath to share complete perspectives of the company in the dynamics of social media circles or, worse, a narrow interpretation that may shut down the conversation entirely.) In any event, such live discussions are far better than forcing executives to sit through PowerPoint presentations that drone on with statistics about the wonders of social media and lose people after the third slide.

Appealing to executives' heads requires compiling a fact base—an engaging business case for why a company must launch a comprehensive social media initiative and where it will have the most impact. Successful business cases provide the financial and competitive justification for diving into social media—with combinations of traditional business case inputs and unique areas that social media can amplify. Getting key players whose functions will be affected most by social media (typically marketing, customer service, sales, human resources (HR), information technology (IT), and product development) involved in shaping the business case is important. It will help enlist them in the initiative and reduce the chances of a fragmented and reactive social media strategy.

There are at least three layers of a fact-based, social media business case:

1. **Start with target areas that executives value highly and easily understand.** Most managers realize the importance of the functions that create demand for the company's offerings—sales and revenue growth—as well as cost reduction. Therefore, making a case for how social media could dramatically improve the way the company identifies and captures new customers is one of the most common starting points. Also, many companies value the retention of existing customers, so showing how social media could improve customer service and boost loyalty quickly follows. Other companies will pay attention to social media initiatives that help them penetrate new geographic markets. Because social media such as Facebook, LinkedIn, Twitter, and YouTube have users around the world, they can be a key tool for creating awareness outside a company's primary markets. Two anecdotes we cited in Chapter 1—IKEA's Facebook photo-tagging experience and Nokia's Beta Labs—are just a few tangible examples of how companies use social media to help them cost-effectively enter new geographic markets.

2. **Add benefits for downstream opportunities.** This is about using social media to improve activities that are farther away from the front lines of customer sales and service: developing new products, creating brand extensions, and improving the way the organization engages with employees, for example. Companies that compete on the basis of product innovation are likely to embrace social media initiatives that generate better insights into customer needs and wants. VitaminWater, for instance, used a Facebook page to have customers post their ideas for the company's newest flavor. A customer from Illinois ultimately came up with the winning entry, netting herself $5,000 and giving VitaminWater a fresh new taste.[8]

3. **Broaden support by linking the social media initiative to broader corporate initiatives.** In some companies, ongoing initiatives crowd out all others for resources and mindshare. That may not necessarily be a problem for social media enthusiasts who are able to show how social media can help the company achieve those bigger goals. For example, many companies are going through complexity-reduction initiatives to reduce or eliminate costly programs such as customer loyalty points. Other companies are focused on high-value customer segments—for example, Baby Boomers becoming senior citizens or emerging-market customers. Social media, of course, can help a company reach those customers. Organizations that place employee satisfaction as high as they do customer satisfaction also will be interested in how social media can be used to increase worker feedback and boost the number and quality of internal ideas for improving products and processes. Accenture's "innovation grapevine," for instance, uses wiki technology and crowdsourcing to solicit ideas from around the organization on how to address critical challenges a company faces. The concept has been used successfully by a variety of businesses, including U.S. banking giant Wells Fargo, which employed a pilot of the innovation grapevine as part of an effort to generate new ideas from employees on how to further improve the customer experience (which we cover in more detail in Chapter 7).

Every solid business case contains a new set of facts and insights about competitive threats, top-line and bottom-line projections of impact, and the like. In competing against a horde of other internal initiatives, social media strategists must have such facts in hand or else risk being quickly eliminated from C-suite consideration. They must bring several types of facts forward in the North Star.

The first set of facts involves the social media activities of direct competitors. Social media strategists must gather information on what competitors are doing with Facebook, LinkedIn, Yelp, smart phone applications (for example, for Apple's enormously popular iPhone), and how their initiatives are helping those businesses. A great amount of information has been written about many social media initiatives in trade publications, social media blogger sites, and other corners of the Web. Managers running these initiatives often speak at industry forums, and their presentations can be secured or purchased from conference organizers.

In addition, much of what competitors are doing with social media can be observed firsthand: looking at Facebook fan pages, LinkedIn groups, and other sites. For example, every convenience store chain in the United States—and perhaps every retailer, period—should be following what northeastern convenience store operator Wawa has done on Facebook with its customers. Wawa, a $4.5 billion, privately held convenience store operator known for its hoagies and devoted fans, has attracted about 400,000 Facebook fans (www.facebook.com/#!/wawa), about 40 percent more than one of its competitors.

Learning what customers are doing with social media is as important as knowing what competitors are doing. Social media strategists must gather facts on how much of the customer base uses social media and what it represents in revenue, profit, service usage and other key metrics. Many companies will find that customers who are rabid users of social media are also more valuable customers.

Understanding the value of customers who use social media is critical. Conducting market research is invaluable. If a manager doesn't have data on the demographics of the company's customer base that uses social media, the company's operations teams may be able to provide clues on the social media habits of those customers: In the contact centers, how many agents are hearing from customers who heard other customers complain through Facebook, YouTube, or some other social site? The experiences of front-line workers are just as important at the statistical research that can be gathered.

Once a manager establishes the percentage of customers who use social media, how valuable they are, and how they use social media to interact with or talk about the company (for example, are they comparing bad customer experiences with other customers?), it's critical to monitor the total life cycle of these customers. Do they have a high propensity to switch to competitors? How much sales, service, and other resources do they consume? The idea is to extrapolate the financial impact of the company's social media–savvy customer segment to determine how much it is worth to retain them, and to attract new ones like them, through social media. These numbers will help a manager engage the chief financial officer early in the social media discussion.

Gathering such facts is critical to creating the case for social media in an organization, to building its North Star. A number of research companies have cropped up to conduct research on the social media-savvy customer. For example, Peanut Labs[9] provides research on the under-24-year-old customer segment. It conducts surveys of social media users and gives them "virtual" credits for participating. It posts surveys on social networks such as Facebook and more than 200 other social networking applications and communities, some of which have collected tens of thousands of responses in hours.

Even if a manager doesn't have perfect customer data, collecting some of this new, more dynamic data is important. For example, if it is difficult to pinpoint which customers use social media, a good proxy can be the company's multichannel customers—the ones who use the Web, stores, phone, and other means to do business with the organization. Multichannel customers tend to be higher-value customers: They have larger market baskets, higher profitability, and greater purchasing frequency (the three big levers of lifetime value).

Today, many companies don't know how many customers use social media and the value of social media users to the organization. But even if they turn out to be a small slice of the customer base, they are likely to be growing fast as the millennials age. Knowing how many customers are using social media and how valuable they are have become critical data for every company.

One final note about the business case: To be compelling, it must be written in language that all relevant parties can understand. This is a challenge for many social media enthusiasts because the jargon and shorthand terms of this rapidly evolving field will be bewildering to executives who have not been following it. Many managers are not familiar with words that have become standard vocabulary for social media followers: microblogs, social networking sites, RSS feeds, and wikis, to name just a few. Managers involved in creating the North Star must explain such terms in language and points of view that the uninitiated understand.

Shoring Up Support across Multiple Leaders

After capturing the flicker of interest and the North Star plan that sizes and defines the opportunity, the final step in selling social media in an organization is shoring up support among multiple supporting leaders to broaden the support and staying power of the initiative during learning periods. This may sound like overkill. Why not just hand the business case to the head of sales or marketing and hope for a positive response? Getting a function or department within a function to jump on social media will be a mistake because the company will then apply social media far too narrowly. To be sure, marketers need to create social media campaign plans. But sales, customer service, product development, HR, and other functions must respond to social media too. To have large-scale beneficial impact, a social media initiative must be a cross-functional initiative. That means the creators of the North Star need to sell multiple executives in the C-suite. They need a broad number of advocates. And that, in turn, starts with two key selling roles: the champion and the sponsor.

The champion is the person charged with pushing the initiative forward on a daily basis. Generally, the best person for this role is *not* a member of the C-suite because he or she isn't involved in the day-to-day sweep of activities in an organization. The champion must be able to see the integration points of a social media initiative—where marketing and sales, or sales and service, or HR and product development, need to collaborate in social media. A manager a level below the C-suite is a better candidate for filling the role of social media champion. Why? This person is more likely to be in tune with what's really going on in the organization and how the functions work together on a daily basis. Furthermore, a member of the C-suite is apt to be pulled into attending to other pressing priorities while the company gets real with social media.

Successful sponsors often are heads of functions that will be affected by social media—for example, the chief marketing officer and head of sales, or the head of service. Sponsors must be devoted to the firm's social media strategy. That means they must be willing to remove obstacles and provide resources to make it happen. They will be the chief beneficiaries of the social media initiative, and, as such, they must be willing to exercise their authority to secure those benefits.

Having additional sponsorship outside sales, customer service, marketing, and product development is important—for example, the chief financial or information officer, or head of strategy and HR are commonly some of the more important supporters in keeping the social media approach moving forward. They add credibility, operational rigor, and integration with the broader business strategy to the initiative.

Keeping sponsors engaged and satisfied requires giving them concrete measures of progress. The social media champion and his or her team must supply a range of traditional metrics to show the initiative is having impact (for example, on revenue, the conversion rate of prospects to customers and so on). Many metrics will be traditional ones used to gauge the health of any corporate initiative. But, as noted in Chapter 3, other metrics will be new ones that social media interactions can provide, such as level of customer engagement with a brand.

In either case, it is important for the social media team to establish metrics that cross functional boundaries. The reason is that such higher-level metrics are likely to reflect bigger improvements in operating performance. For example, reducing the time it takes to acquire customers requires both marketing and sales functions to do something new with social media. Showing just how leads are coming in faster would be insufficient.

The three steps that we've laid out in this chapter provide a high-level road map of how to get senior executives on board the social media train. As with any major change with which they have little personal experience, gaining top management's attention and getting them to provide the resources for a major social media initiative won't be easy. However, the process described in these pages has helped get some of the most recalcitrant executives engaged in social media and has unlocked the door to seizing the opportunity.

Marketing and Sales in Social Media

5

Social Media and the Voice of the Customer

Chris Zinner and Catherine Zhou

CHAPTER HIGHLIGHTS

Social media takes voice of the customer to an entirely new level because it gives organizations true insights into customer behavior—in their own environment—not just their transactions. In doing so, it gives companies access to a greater diversity of data than they ever could generate before and, consequently, enables companies to group customers into ever more granular levels of segments against which they can mobilize.

Social media has exposed, once and for all, the shortcomings of traditional customer research: slow, expensive, and inaccurate.

Organizations around the world pay homage to the "voice of the customer," and rightly so. The feedback customers provide daily, both solicited and unsolicited, helps companies continually improve their products, services, policies, image, and overall customer experience. Such rapid improvements have become elemental, given that every large company now competes with organizations around the globe, which customers can find in seconds just by typing a few words into a search engine. In this environment, the stakes are high for any company that doesn't respond quickly to customer needs and complaints.

Customer feedback traditionally has come in many forms—phone calls to call centers, e-mail, and regular mail letters, discussions with sales and field support personnel, customer surveys, and more. Regardless of the source, all of it provides important clues to the way customers perceive a firm today and whether they will buy from it in the future. As a result, voice of the customer data (VoC for short) can be an incisive leading indicator of a company's future performance.

VoC data is the foundation of customer insight—that is, a company's deep knowledge on what customers think and feel about issues relevant to its business. Such insights articulate key customer needs, attitudes, preferences, and perceptions about a product or service. They also explain customer behavior—that is, how customers interact with a company and how they would prefer to buy its offerings. Insights on customer behavior are critical because what people *say* can be much different from what they *do.* Understanding customer behavior can yield very provocative insights, ones that may force a company to revamp its products and services as well as the processes through which it sells, delivers, and supports them.

Possessing such knowledge is the first critical step to delivering offerings that are on target and to creating buying and postsales service experiences that delight customers. Many company leaders make investments in their offerings, service, and selling processes based on intuition—what they *think* customers want and need. Not enough companies base their decisions on listening intently to customers through all the ways they provide feedback and then collaborating with them to arrive at the best answer.

An effective VoC program enables companies to answer with certainty two sets of questions, which most have difficulty answering today with any level of certainty:

1. What do our customers want? How do we know this and how can we prove it?
2. Which investments for improving our offering and customer experience would have the greatest impact on our most important customers? Which improvements would boost their loyalty the most?

To shift from a product-centric to a customer-centric world, managers must answer these questions. By better understanding customer needs, wants, and behaviors, companies can more easily develop the right products and services and market them through the right channels. They are also more likely to deliver those offerings to the right customer segments and at the right point in the customer life cycle.

However, dealing with today's online customers poses new opportunities and threats to companies. Customers use the Internet to give feedback in entirely different ways: through social media such as online networking sites, discussion forums, blogs, videos they produce and post on sites like YouTube, and other public places where their comments can seen by hundreds, thousands, and sometimes millions of other customers. They engage strongly in social media as another feedback channel because it empowers them, helps them share experiences (good and bad) with peers, and makes the companies they buy from more transparent and responsive.

This forces companies with even the most successful VoC programs to rethink the way they develop and respond to the insights they gather on customers. But before we go into this, let's quickly review the traditional methods of understanding customers and the shortcomings of those approaches.

Shortcomings of Traditional Approaches to Listening to the VoC

One of the primary methods of the past for gathering customer feedback was research, both quantitative and qualitative. Quantitative research tools, such as phone, online, or in-person surveys, can generate substantial insights on customer needs and wants. Qualitative research tools, such as customer focus groups, field interviews, discussions with call center reps or store representatives, and panels with "trusted" customers on call to provide feedback on different ideas, have helped companies add texture to their quantitative feedback, to better understand why customers feel or behave a certain way.

Although research data has been crucial, in today's fast-evolving world it has several shortcomings. One is that it can be very expensive to gather and analyze data, especially through qualitative research techniques. Getting customers to participate in focus groups and for research firms to analyze the discussions can cost significant sums, which forces many organizations to do it infrequently. That, in turn, increases the risk that a company pays inadequate attention to its customers. Another drawback is getting sufficient customer input. Enticing consumers to take part in focus group meetings or surveys is increasingly difficult; "survey fatigue" is now commonplace. Furthermore, such research typically takes a long time to conduct. A company can spend weeks or months designing surveys or focus group questionnaires, getting customers to participate in research, and learning from their input.

As a result, by the time a company has conducted quantitative or qualitative research to answer a pressing customer issue, the problem may have spiraled out of control—or an opportunity to capitalize on an unmet need may have passed.

New Ways to Listen to the VoC: How Social Media Changes the Game

The shortcomings of traditional customer feedback channels now are much more apparent because of the arrival of social media. The Internet gives companies as a far more effective and efficient way to tune in to the voice of the customer. If they don't, they risk being besieged by swarms of angry consumers spreading reputational poison over the Web.

Social media is a powerful source for understanding the VoC for four reasons.

1. **Social media can give companies a torrent of highly valuable customer feedback.** Every day, millions of people around the world are blogging, participating in social networking sites like Facebook and LinkedIn, and providing opinions on products and services on sites like Epinions.com, Amazon.com, and ConsumerReports.org. In fact, one researcher estimated that 82.5 million U.S. consumers created content on the Web in 2008.[1]
2. **Such input is largely free.** Unlike focus groups and surveys (which often must pay consumers to participate and often require the services of a market research firm), consumers give feedback at no charge.
3. **Customer feedback issued through social media is qualitative data, just like the data that market researchers derive from focus group and in-depth interviews.** Such data is the best type of customer feedback because it gives companies a better chance to get inside the customer's head—something that structured surveys, which force consumers to choose from predetermined answers, simply can't do as effectively.

4. **Such qualitative data is in digital form—in text or digital video on a web site.** The advent of text-mining tools—software that combs through voluminous customer comments to find patterns and problematic issues—means companies now can analyze huge amounts of qualitative data much more efficiently than focus group discussions or one-on-one interviews. In the past, companies would have been overwhelmed had they asked 10,000 customers to each write several paragraphs about their feelings about a product. It would have been too time consuming and expensive for an analyst to determine what the collective input really meant. Text-mining tools enable a company to easily "quantify" qualitative feedback.

As great as those opportunities are, the risk of not paying attention to what customers are saying through social media channels provides companies with even greater motivation to get involved. With the tools now at their disposal to spread negative feedback about a company quickly and beyond geographic boundaries, many consumers do not hesitate to take their frustrations with a company to a worldwide digital audience—a situation we call "aggressive consumer activism." Thus, a company's ability to listen to what consumers are saying about it and intervening when necessary is critical. We discuss aggressive consumer activism in more detail in Chapter 9.

Social Media: A New and Very Different Kind of Listening Post

The time has come for companies to plug into the numerous conversations that customers are having about them via social media. However, managers must realize that this feedback is very different from the type they get through traditional channels. And while it doesn't supplant traditional customer feedback—quantitative and qualitative research as well as input from e-mails, correspondence, and call center phone conversations are all still important for providing important customer insights—social media feedback is an entirely new breed of data.

How so? First, social media feedback is usually more emotional—that is, strongly slanted toward an opinion. In comparison, traditional customer service channels typically generate less temperamental feelings. Thus, social media feedback makes it easier to discern how consumers really feel about an issue (so-called consumer sentiments).

The intended "receiver" of social media feedback—other customers, rather than a company—also makes for a much different type of data. Customers get on YouTube, Amazon.com, Facebook, Twitter, or LinkedIn to let other customers know about their experience with a company, in contrast to a consumer's call to a contact center to complain directly to a company about a product or policy. Customers thus use social media to talk "about" a company rather than "to" it. Because social media feedback poses much greater and more immediate reputational risk, it is even more important for companies to listen to it than to call center or other traditional customer service interactions.

The third way in which social media feedback differs from traditional customer data is focus. Customer research is designed to generate feedback on a specific issue. The data that comes back is "structured"—it is about the issue at hand. That makes survey results easier to analyze than the results of open-ended questions in which customers can more freely speak their minds. However, the time and expense of consumer research forces companies to constrain their conversations with consumers. Customers may not talk about what is most important to them if it falls outside the lines of the researcher's questions. Thus, traditional customer feedback channels promote very little "unstructured" responses. In contrast, social media data is nearly all unstructured. It does not come in the form of point answers to point questions. A blog post, YouTube video rant, text box, or other form of consumer feedback may be about anything—and many things. And because it comes over the Internet, it can be collected in large volumes and analyzed rapidly (with the right technology).

Three other big differences relate to data quality, authenticity, and predictability. Social media can produce "dirty" or "garbage" data—inappropriate language, rogue advertising, and other unhelpful content slipping in. New technologies can sift out much of this, but some still slips through the cracks.

But even if the data is usable, it can come from questionable sources. Is a real customer or a competitor complaining about a product? Although many companies require customers to log into their web site before posting reviews and other comments, most social media outlets cannot prove the authenticity of the author. Companies must take the anonymous nature of social media into account when they decide how to respond to what they hear. However, too many executives dismiss the negative feedback from social media.

Whether such feedback is accurate or not, it will be seen by customers. In fact, 70 percent of consumers online trust the recommendations of other online consumers whom they don't know.[2] Thus, it requires some type of response.

Last, the data from social media is unpredictable; a company doesn't know when or how this data will come in, as it does when fielding a survey or running focus group. That makes social media feedback harder to prepare for.

Capitalizing on Social Media: Tuning in to the Voice of the Internet-Savvy Customer

As we mentioned earlier in this chapter, companies shouldn't abandon their traditional customer listening posts in favor of the new social media feedback channels. Many customers continue to use traditional channels such as e-mail, call centers, and the postal service to talk back to their suppliers. Those channels are not likely to lose favor soon, if ever. Instead, managers need to incorporate social media channels into the rest of their voice of the customer listening posts. In fact, we argue that our traditional model for collecting and acting on VoC data still applies to social media.

Accenture has developed a SLOPE model which has five basic steps. (See Figure 5.1.)

1. Synchronize.
2. Listen and Learn.
3. Optimize and Operationalize.
4. Personalize and Propagate.
5. Expectations and Execution.

We review each step and how it pertains to social media.

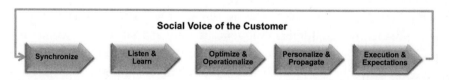

Social Voice of the Customer

Synchronize → Listen & Learn → Optimize & Operationalize → Personalize & Propagate → Execution & Expectations

FIGURE 5.1 Accenture's SLOPE Model for Listening to the Social Voice of the Customer.

Synchronize

The Synchronize phase is the one in which a company determines its strategy and approach to collecting and synchronizing customer feedback data across all its "listening posts": customer research (surveys and focus groups) and traditional customer service channels such as call centers, e-mail, instant messaging, hard-copy correspondence, field offices or stores, and so on. Social media outlets are the newest set of listening posts, and they can be categorized as "on board" and "off board."

"Onboard" social media outlets are ones a company hosts on its web site or the microsites that it controls. An increasing number of companies are instituting sophisticated software on their web sites that allows Web viewers to post product ratings and reviews. There's good reason for this: Good reviews can boost sales. In fact, USAA, a financial services firm, attributes an year-over-year increase of nearly 16,000 auto insurance loans to launching the ability for its members to rate their auto insurance on the USAA web site.[3] Many companies are using social media software from such firms as Bazaarvoice, PowerReviews, and Customer Lobby to let customers discuss and rate their offerings. Bazaarvoice's software, along with similar products from Lithium and Get Satisfaction, also lets customers ask questions of other customers in discussion forums, thus enabling them to share their customer experiences through personal stories. Bazaarvoice's products have become highly popular; numerous retailers, consumer goods, financial services, and other companies are using them. Since 2005, the company has worked with more than 700 companies worldwide and has grown to more than 500 employees.[4] PowerReviews has sold similar technology to companies such as Staples, Walgreen, Brookstone, and Mountain Gear. Consumers' embrace of product review Web pages—one of the key early success factors of Amazon .com—shows how intent people are on interacting with other consumers and their suppliers.

"Offboard" social media channels are those outside of a firm's control and external to its web sites—that is, the other web sites that its customers and prospective customers frequent. If onboard sites are a company's private Web, offboard sites are the public Web. But where on the public Web should companies be listening for their customers' voices? From our experience, we believe managers should focus on six types of public web sites:

1. Product ratings and reviews (e.g., tripadvisor.com and epinions.com)
2. Customer discussion forums (many industry research firms have them now, for example, Edmonds.com in the automotive business) or popular community question-and-answer sites such as Yahoo! Answers
3. Multimedia sharing sites such as YouTube
4. Social network communities such as LinkedIn and Facebook
5. Microblogging services such as Twitter
6. Industry- or product-specific blogs, vlogs (blogs that mainly publish videos), and podcasts

Web sites in the preceding categories could easily number in the thousands. The Web is strewn with many potential listening posts, and new ones are emerging weekly. So where should companies begin? How do they prioritize? Companies should start by determining where the greatest number of people will be—specifically, the ones who could be talking about them. From a defensive posture, for most consumer-oriented companies, the sites with the great number of Web viewers are a good place to start: YouTube, Facebook, Twitter, and Amazon.com are the biggest. From an offensive posture, a company should focus on industry-specific forums. For example, a hospitality company firm might want to closely monitor sites such as TripAdvisor.com, where consumers provide feedback on hotels and travel destinations. Or an automotive-related firm might want to follow online consumer banter at *Consumer Reports'* web site (consumerreports.org) or Edmunds.com.

Best Buy, for instance, has a number of clearly defined social media outlets that it deems most important to monitor and participate in:

- *Online forums.* "We get about 5,000 dialogues a week," said Tracy Benson. "In our forums, we can actively participate in a conversation and understand how our customers are engaging, what they think about us, and how they feel about Best Buy."
- *Facebook.* "We have about 1.3 million fans and we actively talk to them," Benson noted. "We actively survey those folks and they give us great feedback."
- *Twitter.* Best Buy uses Twitter in three ways: to communicate deals to customers, send out brand-reinforcing messages, and facilitate service and support. The company also regularly surveys customers about the effectiveness of Twitter.

- *Reviews and ratings.* Benson said Best Buy has focused on reviews and ratings for several years. "We know [ratings and reviews] play well into intent and influence."

Once a company knows which social media listening posts to dial into, it must be prepared to monitor and analyze the feedback. Given that the feedback may be substantial, that firm should be ready to scale up its listening capabilities. It will face three choices doing so:

1. *Build such capabilities internally.* Doing this will require investing in technology that conducts Web crawling (also known as spidering)—software that roams the vast Web (and especially the listening posts that a company targets) much the way a search engine like Google combs through millions of documents looking for key words. Companies like Kapow Technologies, Fetch Technologies and SAS sell technology that crawls and "scrapes" content from the Web and then organizes it into a repository that can then be analyzed.
2. *Outsource capabilities to a company that specializes in collecting and consolidating consumer feedback on the Web.* Many firms are letting agencies such as Radian6, Alterian and Nielson BuzzMetrics monitor and analyze their social traffic.
3. *A hybrid model.* Such a model uses a third party to collect data but then lets in-house analysts pour through it using text-mining and sentiment analysis technology from companies such as Clarabridge or Attensity.

Which option is best? It comes down to this: How critical is social media monitoring and analysis to a company's success? This can vary dramatically from industry to industry and even company to company. Those that do much of their business online, face off against many competitors, and have customers with low switching costs are prime candidates for making significant investments in an internal analysis capability. A substantial portion of their customer base is online, and Web-fueled critiques may easily drive their customers to rivals. In contrast, companies that largely sell their offerings offline, to a narrow customer base, and have few competitors and high switching costs would be more likely to outsource such social media monitoring and analysis. For example, a business-to-business (B2B) company whose sales force sells construction materials to wholesalers probably would not need to make social media monitoring a core competency.

Many companies should begin by dipping their toes in the water. They can manually track a few web sites where customers spout off, then draw conclusions on what topics they focus on and what issues they complain about the most. A number of companies can help here, offering free services to analyze the social web: Social Mention, Attentio (TrendPedia), Nielsen (BuzzMetric's BlogPulse) and Twentz (Twitter feeds), among them. One step up from these firms are fee-based services, such as Lithium's Scout Labs and Nielsen BuzzMetrics, which possess more advanced dashboards and analytics.

Companies that need to build in-house capabilities must be careful not to lock themselves into proprietary technologies. In deciding what to buy, they need to use an open technology architecture, one that lets them incorporate emerging social media monitoring and analysis tools into their mix. These tools are in their infancy, and so today's popular tools may be not be so popular (or may not even exist) in a few years.

Listen and Learn

After an organization has synchronized its listening posts and its data collection and analysis strategy, the next step is to Listen and Learn and make sense of the consumer noise that a company collects on the social media sites it is monitoring. With substantial feedback data in hand, what insights can be drawn about how customers think about a firm, its offerings and ways of doing business? Managers need to go beyond making observations on this; they must determine the root causes of critical customer issues so their organizations can act on them.

But acting only on what customers are saying is inadvisable. Many customers will complain about a company, but not all are ready to desert that firm. For example, a mobile phone company may find a small group of customers complaining online about a certain feature of a rate plan. However, it also may find that the majority of customers do not feel the same way and that the complainers continue to use the plan even though they are no longer under contract.

Ferreting out the idle gripes from the important concerns requires collecting data on customer behavior, not just customer feedback, and then comparing the two. Behavior data comes from transactions—for example, purchases, web site visits/click streams, customer service inquiries, interactive voice response usage (IVR), and other sources. Correlating behavior data with explicit feedback data from social media and traditional customer research can reveal important actions to take: product design enhancements, customer service process and policy improvements, and enhancements to customer interaction channels such as web sites, to name a few. If poor customer reviews of a company's product are followed by substantial sales declines, it may well signal a causal relationship—one that requires immediate attention.

The best companies look at both explicit customer feedback and customer behavior rather than one or the other. That gives them a more complete picture of their customers' mind-sets and intentions and lets them assess the return on investment to correct an issue. Because social media can give companies a heavy dose of negative feedback, it is quite natural to want to respond to it all. But companies need to compare what customers are saying with what they are doing. As our parents taught us, "Actions speak louder than words." (We present some frameworks for how to assess, prioritize, and respond to negative feedback in Chapter 10.)

Nonetheless, much of what customers say through social media—positive or negative—is important for companies to pay attention to. Fortunately, a number of technology advances allow companies to analyze huge volumes of customer feedback data and gain deeper insights into customer beliefs and potential actions. In fact, these technologies make it possible for companies to learn much more about their customers than they did through their service interactions of the past.

One set of advances is making it easier to "read" key listening posts. Optical character recognition (OCR) and automated speech-to-text conversion have become robust, enabling companies to convert customer correspondence (letters) and calls into digitized text. When text is digitized, computers can be set up to process and analyze it.

Recent advances have brought text mining—technologies that can recognize patterns in digitized text—out of the world of academia and national security and into the world of business. Companies now have unprecedented opportunities to quickly determine how their customers feel about them, even if those customers number in the hundreds of thousands or millions. Leading text-mining companies, such as Clarabridge, Attensity, and Overtone, provide tools with two basic capabilities:

1. **Categorization.** Understanding what topics people are talking or writing about in the unstructured portion of their feedback
2. **Sentiment analysis.** Determining whether people have positive, negative, or neutral views on those topics

How do text-mining technologies actually work? Consider a customer who writes this review on a travel web site:

> I loved this hotel. The lobby and pool areas were brilliant, the staff was on top of their game, and of course it was sparkling clean. The only issues were that the beds were too soft, the pool a bit cold, and there were children running up and down the hallways at night.

The goal of the categorization function of a text-mining tool is to dissect this review and decide what topics it referred to. Advances in text mining save companies from trying to figure out all the possible keywords customers use to describe a topic. If a hotel only used simple keywords, one topic the company could believe is important to listen for—noisiness of rooms—would not show up on this review. However, advances in text-mining systems would associate the statement "children running up and down the hallways at night" with the noisiness of rooms issue that the hotel is sensitive to.

But what about topics that customers are talking about that a company hasn't anticipated? Text-mining techniques such as natural language processing (NLP) and unsupervised clustering help firms to begin to "know what they don't know."

How would a computer analyze the hotel reviewer's sentiments about the place? The text-mining software would be programmed to figure out that the word "cold" is bad when used next to the words "swimming pool" and that too much softness in a bed is a negative thing too. "Children running up the hall," already tagged to room noisiness, would be flagged as a third strike against the inn.

Such advances in categorization and sentiment analysis have drastically reduced the time and cost to process and analyze the key conclusions from massive amounts of qualitative, unstructured customer feedback. Companies now can draw deep insights on customers at a rate never before possible by quantifying the qualitative. That's a big breakthrough.

Through such techniques, social media can help companies understand their customers' perceptions much better than they can through call center, correspondence, and other traditional customer service interactions. Customers use social media to talk about specific issues they are having with companies, and their postings are almost always more opinionated—positive or negative. That makes social media feedback in many ways more fertile for helping determine how to fine-tune their products and processes.

Although social media is a prime source of new customer insights, we do not believe that social media alone can lead to huge new findings about customers. Doing this requires combining social media insights with those from traditional customer research and service channels. The biggest insights come from integrated findings across all VoC channels, not from one or two data silos. The U.S. intelligence community learned this a while ago: the need to gather numerous types of specialized data and analyze it rapidly across silos to detect national security threats.

Companies likewise need to move from "single-source analysis"—where analysis (e.g., customer surveys) is completed in silos and results are not integrated and correlated with other forms of analysis (e.g., text mining of customer e-mails)—to "all-source" customer intelligence, where the output of each of these critical functions is integrated in a single "Voice of the Customer." Some companies already have begun to formalize their sources, creating groups that handle primary customer research (quantitative and qualitative), behavioral analytics (propensity modeling, multidimensional analysis, simulation and optimization, using customer transaction data, contact history via the call center, Web, field offices and so on), and—more recently—feedback analytics of social media and traditional customer service interactions (i.e., categorization and sentiment analysis). Combining and integrating the insights these groups generate gives an organization much more data on which to draw conclusions, allowing outliers to be put in their proper places. That increases the likelihood that managers make the right investments based on customer feedback—investments that focus on primary, not secondary, drivers of customer satisfaction. Companies that integrate their insights across data sources will be much more likely to develop big and more profitable insights on customers, and do so much faster.

Understanding a growing online sentiment about a company and its products or processes is one thing. Being able to predict customer behavior is another. The onset of customer feedback through social media gives companies a way to improve their predictive capabilities. How so? The immense volume of unstructured customer feedback from Twitter tweets, blogs, discussion boards, and social networking site discussions provides the opportunity to glean much sharper insights into how customers think about specific aspects of a company's brand and its offerings. The unstructured feedback from social media is a treasure chest of data that companies can use to predict how customers will act to new pricing, product, packaging, marketing, and other moves.

New techniques have been developed to make predictions more accurate. These techniques capitalize on text mining of customer opinions voiced through social media outlets. Although social media data can increase the accuracy of a company's prediction model, even this can fall short when only categories and sentiment data are used in a model. The next frontier in analyzing customer data is running predictive analytics directly on unstructured customer feedback where all available data—including customers' writing styles and choice of words—feed into the predictive model. This could be applied, for example, to predicting a customer's propensity to churn based on the unstructured content within a product review that they write. Companies must go beyond just categorizing and evaluating the sentiments people are expressing through social media and other channels. They need to connect how customers "feel" about "what" and tie it to "what will they do next?"

After analyzing all the voice of the customer data they collect—social media, customer service, and other—managers will be far better positioned to understand how customers view their organization on multiple levels:

- **Brand.** What do customers think the firm's brand stands for? What do they see as its "brand promise"? Its core competencies? Its core values?
- **Products and services.** Do they meet customer needs? What aspects of them drive satisfaction and dissatisfaction? What improvements are necessary? Are they priced correctly? What new offerings do customers want the firm to bring to market?
- **Channels.** How could the company improve the way customers interact with it—the web site, call centers, field offices/stores, and so on? What actions would markedly improve the customer experience?
- **Competitiveness.** What do customers think about a firm versus its competitors? What should it change or not change?

Optimize and Operationalize

After they understand what customers are saying about them, companies must decide what to do about it and then create a plan to do it. Doing this requires putting the actions a firm must take into a form that gets the right parts of the organization to make the changes they need to make. We will not discuss such actions in depth here; the topic is covered in subsequent chapters. Rather we will provide an overview of how companies need to optimize their response (or nonresponse) and operationalize that response into reactive or proactive changes that span from strategic to tactical.

How can a company know when to take action and when not to? How can it prioritize the insights it gleans from social media and the potential actions to respond to the customers based on such insights? A rigorous model to assess the right data, filter and prioritize the insights gleaned, and prioritize and optimize its response is critical to maximizing the return on investment of a VoC program. Figure 5.2 illustrates a commonsense approach to validating objective issues and analyzing subjective issues and opportunities to make changes that positively impact the customer experience. Balancing responsiveness with limited resources and capacity for change, high-performing companies look at the volume and sentiment of customer feedback for a particular idea or change before dedicating resources to

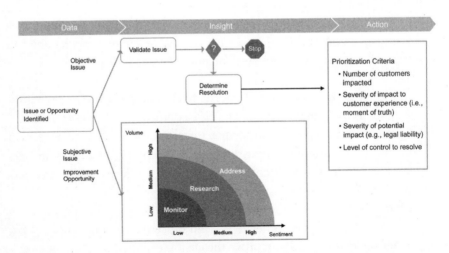

FIGURE 5.2 An Approach to Evaluating Objective and Subjective Issues to Determine the Appropriate Actions.

respond. And even in those cases where it is determined that change is appropriate, all changes must compete with and be evaluated against other corporate priorities.

The key to managing customer perceptions in a world of limited resources is transparency: being clear that the company has heard the customers' feedback, that it cares about customers' satisfaction, and that it values and seriously considers customers' opinions. A great example of this is the "Ideas in Action" blog on "My Starbucks Idea" (http://mystarbucksidea.force.com), where Starbucks responds to and keeps customer updated on progress on various ideas.

When making process, policy, or experience changes in response to negative customer experiences that are shared on social media outlets, companies must look at the nature of the negative feedback and assess the risk and value of responding or not responding. Companies have found, over time, that customers and the general public tend to be more concerned and less forgiving in certain situations than in others. Figure 5.3 depicts a simple framework that highlights the fact the customers are more forgiving when it comes to operational issues where there is some question as to the control of the company (such as one's home Internet connection going out for a brief period of time) than they are when encountering negative customer service

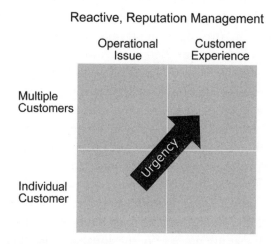

FIGURE 5.3 Customers' Opinions About Operational versus Customer Experience Issues.

experiences where the perception is that the company has more control over the situation (such as being brisk and non-empathetic when explaining why a bill cannot be credited).

And in both of these cases, the broader the impact across the customer base, the more deserving of a response or the need for some change and a corresponding communication of that change.

The question is whether or when a company should insert itself into the conversation to react to something negative or to proactively stimulate something positive. Our research shows that having insight on the "social amplitude trend" is critical to determining whether and when to step into a heated online public discussion or to risk attempting to amplify positive but latent messages about one's brand. Some emerging process models and enabling technology can help companies quickly identify the social amplitude (or "loudness") of a social media posting and the speed at which it is trending up or down as well as measure the impact of actively responding to such posts.

Social media can quickly generate many fans or enemies for a company. Thus, managers must be able to operationalize their response rapidly—regardless of whether it is reactive or proactive. Reactive capabilities are especially important. Social media is a 24×7 public channel. There are no "hours of business"; Facebook never "closes." At all times, companies must be prepared to identify emerging problems that could billow into something bigger, as in the case of Domino's Pizza in response to the disgusting video posted on YouTube by two rogue employees. It took Domino's 24 hours to post its own video response, even in an environment where the video went viral and received more than 250,000 hits within the same time period. What about the emerging customer experiences that most companies come across that never go viral? How do companies create operating models to nip these in the bud before they get posted as viral videos on YouTube? Maintaining such vigilance requires having technology that can detect issues earlier, the ability to determine the root cause of a customer problem rapidly, to get such issue and uncovered root causes to the right people in the organization (and, if necessary, escalate things if it isn't resolved), and then communicate quickly back to customers that the issue has been resolved. These issues are not new in the annals of customer service. However, social media now greatly exacerbates them.

As an example, one leading big-box retailer provides for all employees who interact with customers (perhaps the best listening post) an online portal to submit any issue they identify that could worsen the customer experience for some or all of the customer base. Headquarters personnel constantly monitor employees' comments in the portal. When necessary, they dispatch "tiger teams" to create a coordinated response. The company launched this portal before the advent of social media. It's become even more important now.

The dawn of social media forces companies to start making proactive moves as well. Leading companies do not sit back and wait for panicked calls at the eleventh hour; rather they proactively listen to and even solicit customer feedback and ideas to improve the customer experience. However, one of the biggest challenges to responding effectively to customers airing their frustrations through social media is getting the relevant parts of an organization to act quickly and in concert. Product developers, call center and web site management, and many other functions play major roles in improving a company's offerings and processes. Just because a function responsible for listening to the voice of the customer sees a problem or opportunity doesn't mean that manufacturing, distribution, product development, or another function will do something about it. As a result, one emerging practice is an account management model, in which the integrated voice of the customer program assigns dedicated resources to produce actionable customer insights—from social media and other listening posts—tailored to the downstream business functions that will make changes. Another emerging model is pushing the access to real-time VoC data and insight products out to the edges of the organization through enterprise VoC portals, which empower downstream business functions and increase the likelihood of customer insight–driven business decisions. When it comes to the customer experience, knowing beats guessing every time.

Personalize and Propagate

Before executing the change, companies must take the time to understand the impact of their actions on target customer segments as well as the "halo effect" on closely related segments.

Near the bottom of the recent economic downturn, a multiproduct financial services firm picked up signals from various listening posts (including social media) that its customers were worried about their investment strategies and were criticizing the company for "not doing enough" to protect their retirement nest eggs. In an attempt to calm the customer base, an executive communication was sent out to customers encouraging them to be prudent in their investment strategy. Unsynchronized with marketing's message that "now is the time to consider investing when stocks are low," the executive communication caused customer confusion and alienated one of the company's primary growth strategy and target segments: young investors.

Starbucks, however, through its mystarbucksidea.com web site, has implemented ideas that are personalized toward and meet the needs of its target segment of gourmet coffee drinkers who are often highly educated with disposable income. Examples of these are the Starbucks minicard and the recycling program recently implemented based originally on customer-submitted ideas. However, the jury is still out on another of Starbucks' recent decisions: to offer free "one-click wi-fi" in its stores. Will this attract new, lower-value customers and change the "intimate" experience that high-value customers appreciate so much?

Once the actions have been personalized toward target segments and the possible unintended consequences have been identified and mitigated, a company must ensure that the change is propagated sufficiently across the organization to all impacted functions. The extent of impacted functions typically depends on the nature of the change, as the company's actions can be categorized as strategic and tactical. Some actions must be taken at the top of the company: the keepers of the strategy or brand strategy, the designers of the customer experience, product development and marketing campaign heads, and so on. Such actions impact a large portion of the organization, and it is critical that they are coordinated. Other actions, however, are more tactical; they focus more on individual customers and fall on the front lines of an organization—on customer service reps, field personnel, salespeople, and others. For example, a customer service rep could be forewarned through their call center application about the sentiment of a customer who calls a week after posting her ire about the firm on its product review site, or a field technician visiting a homeowner to address cable television service trouble could be informed of the homeowner's history of online rants against the company before he arrives. Such tactical actions depend on standing process, policy, and technical infrastructure, and can be executed with much less coordination across the organization.

Execute and Expectations

Having lots of insights about customers and their sentiments is worthless unless a company can execute on those insights. Organizations that can do something quickly and effectively with the information they collect from social media will possess a major competitive advantage over those that don't or can't.

When executing, it's also critical for companies to continually set expectations and monitor perceptions along the way. Does a company's actions convince customers that it is listening? Although not everything a company hears will result in changes that are obvious to customers, it is important keep them informed of the actions it is taking. Especially with issues communicated via social media, telling customers the issue has been resolved—or that an issue wasn't even an issue—is crucial. Consider a recent airport incident in the United States. A popular blogger recently assailed the Transportation Security Agency (TSA) for "taking my son"—removing her infant from her view while conducting additional screening on her. Public reaction was swift and harsh. But TSA used its own blog to respond and YouTube to post the actual security video footage of the incident from multiple angles. It clearly showed that the accusation was false and that the child remained in arm's reach of his mother. Another example: On its IdeaStorm web site, Dell keeps an updated status of each individual customer idea posted, publishes metrics of how many ideas have been implemented, and maintains a corporate blog on which the company occasionally recaps the suggestions that have been put into action.

After it responds to a social media incident or suggestion, a company must determine how well it resolved the issue. That means measuring customer opinions about the firm—about whether the company heard customers and took sufficient action. Why is this so important? It's important because of the public and transparent nature of social media. So many customers in so many parts of the world can get a negative impression of a company so quickly. With social media, a metaphorical fire can rage out of control rapidly. Companies need to make sure they have extinguished it or, at the very least, kept it from spreading.

How does a firm know when the flames have died down? Traditionally, a company would poll customers and compare their purchasing behavior before and after an incident. Social media allows a company to do this at scale—to compare opinions and sentiments of numerous customers before and after it takes specific actions.

All investments for improving the customer experience that a company provides should be measured—both before and after they are made. Leading companies use a "test and learn" model. They listen to the voice of the customer to determine which investments would most profitably improve the customer experience. After making those improvements, they measure the customer impact by assessing what customers say and do. This model creates a virtuous loop that helps companies get smarter as they learn, creating more and more valuable customer experiences.

Key Hurdles to Using Social Media to Understand the Voice of the Customer

Every large company today must get closer to its customers, especially as more of them share their experiences with the world through social media. But tuning in to what customers are saying over the Internet is not easy. From our experience with numerous companies, six challenges loom larger than any others, yet all can be overcome.

The first hurdle is all the things that prevent managers from acting rapidly to counter the social media chatter. Social media feedback comes instantaneously. Hitting "save" on a blog post publishes it to the world in seconds; in contrast, an irate letter to a local utility company can take a week to arrive and months before a person in a position of power ever sees it. Real-time complaints require real-time intervention. Rapid response requires accelerating the process by which a company listens, understands, acts, and measures the adequacy of its actions. Sony, Southwest Airlines, United Airlines, Domino's, and TSA didn't have the luxury of taking months to respond to their customer experience issues. They needed to respond the same day, maybe even within hours.

The second challenge is dealing with the sheer volume of information. The amount of customer feedback that companies received in the past (letters, call center hotlines, e-mails, surveys and the rest) was relatively predictable. That made it easy to schedule the right number of people to respond. Social media channels can generate exponentially higher volumes of customer feedback, and the surges are unpredictable. United Airlines and Southwest couldn't anticipate the Internet videos of the angry guitarist and the tweeting of the disgruntled film director. They couldn't staff up that day to prepare for incidents they couldn't predict. This fact poses difficulties not only for companies' staffing policies; it also bedevils their computer systems. The technology architectures of many companies are designed to process gigabytes of information every day. Now with the emergence of social media, they need to sort through terabytes of data in hours or minutes. Companies such as Yahoo! are increasingly appointing chief data officers to grapple with this—managers knowledgeable about the strategic value of data and skilled in understanding how to rearchitect systems to handle immense volumes of it in little time.

Managing the diversity of customer opinions is the third barrier. Whose nuggets of information are worth acting on, and which ones are just distractions? If someone like the film director with the bad flight experience is tarnishing a company's reputation and can trumpet his feelings to more than a million people in minutes, the company has to deal with it quickly. But if another person privately provides an opinion on a new product design, that opinion doesn't count for much. To sell it to as many people as possible, a firm needs to gather many more opinions. Determining whose opinions to respond to isn't easy.

Also not easy is creating the right capabilities to incorporate social media into traditional VoC data, the fourth big barrier we've seen. Determining what new skills, processes, and technology tools are necessary is not straightforward. The tools are particularly perplexing, given their nascent state of development (unlike, say, the Enterprise Resource Planning software world). What tool should a company standardize on (if any)? Which technologies will still be here in three years? And how can multiple types of data be integrated with which tools into an enterprise information system? (We explore the issue of technology tools for social media in Chapter 12.)

The fifth challenge is one we call segment generalization. This involves making assumptions about the customers who are voicing their opinions through social media. Who are they? What are their demographics? What customer segment would we put them in? With the anonymous nature of social media, it's very hard to put people in a segment. And if they can't easily be put in a segment, it's hard to generalize whether other similar customers may feel the same way. Of course, segmenting and attributing customers into specific segment is easier with traditional VoC data. If a customer phones the call center, the company knows who that customer is and how to deal with him. Sending the customer a survey also comes from a place of knowledge: That customer is part of a segment, and how he responds to the survey can be compared with how other similar customers responded. It isn't so tidy with customers who provide feedback through social media.

The last major challenge is about the precision and recall of today's text-mining technologies. To varying degrees, some are more accurate than others at capturing the essence of online chatter correctly (precision), including whether they are the customer's real sentiments. And some are better at flagging all the comments on a topic (recall). Too many companies perceive the technologies as immature and hold back on investing in them. Others require unnecessary levels of reliability. Although national security requires a technology that captures a very high percentage of troubling online comments, does a company need the same level of proficiency? What percentage of all the negative comments on the Internet does a firm need to capture to put stock in what's being said? Certainly it does not need 100 percent recall (gathering all the comments) or anywhere close. Companies should lean toward more precise technology tools—ones that will categorize customer comments the right way rather than those that are better at recall. In any case, the imprecise and imperfect recall rates of the tools are no longer valid reasons for staying on the sidelines.

Moving Forward

The social media revolution has just begun. YouTube and the popular social networking sites are less than a decade old. Hundreds of millions of customers are already using them, and their usage keeps growing geometrically. Companies need to move aggressively to track social media and respond effectively if for no other reason than it is becoming the favorite hangout of their favorite customers.

But social media can't be looked at as a necessary evil. There's so much more that companies can learn about their customers in the world of social media—if those companies learn how to listen, understand, and act on what customers are saying.

6 Integrating Social CRM Insights into the Customer Analytics Function

Rayid Ghani and Sarah Bentley

CHAPTER HIGHLIGHTS

The customer analytics function plays a key role in enabling a company to "listen and learn" in the social media realm. The data available for this function is growing faster than ever, is becoming more complex, and is not all under the control of the company. As a result, organizations must wrestle with making sense of this data and integrating it into their customer analytics function. This requires fundamentally changing the process of analyzing customer data and taking full advantage of the new insights that social media offers. The integration of social media has numerous implications for the technology, organization, culture, processes, and data governance policies of a company's customer analytics function.

Social media has dramatically changed the requirements for the customer analytics function. Not only are there different types of data (and a greater amount of it) to inform the analytics functions, but the customer is also more influential in the process and the outcome. This new rich data source provides organizations with an excellent opportunity to Listen and Learn with their customers. For customer centric companies the insights derived from social media, if harnessed effectively, can provide great opportunities to develop new product ideas, new market opportunities, and resolve (or even prevent) customer service issues. However in order to capture these insights, companies must refresh their processes and systems for collecting and analyzing data.

Data collection and analytics processes are no longer linear in progression, historically focused, or project-oriented. Analytics that leverage social media must be more iterative, real-time, predictive, fine-grained, and collaborative.

With increasing use of social media among customers and consumers, companies don't control information in the same way as they have historically. Customers can easily voice opinions and pass judgments on products, services, brands, and companies. Take, for example, how eBay enables purchasers to rate sellers and vice versa. Amazon, Yelp, and a multitude of other web sites encourage customers to rate books, products, and businesses across numerous categories. And any individual is free to blog or tweet opinions about brands, products, and service experiences.

Through ratings, votes, and independent analysis, customers have significant influence over the success or failure of a company's actions, whether that be a product launch, marketing campaign, acquisition, or handling of a corporate crisis, such as a recall.

Organizations must now deal with more volume and complexity of data. Social media generates more data than other customer interactions simply by its conversational nature and by virtue of it including dialogue between consumers without any involvement of the company itself. Conversations take the form of unstructured (natural language) text that is often difficult to use directly in traditional customer analytics tools. The data is generated faster, and it changes faster. The "shelf life" of social media data is highly variable as threads can meander, gain rapid momentum, or trail off without a lingering impact depending on the source, reliability, and type of insight it generates. Therefore in order to effectively Listen and Learn, companies need to find new ways of absorbing the data, generating meaningful insights, and responding to them. There is also the challenge of the changing nature of the analytics cycle. Before the availability of data from social media, a company typically sourced and analyzed information with a specific purpose in mind, such as informing a new marketing campaign, developing a new product, or improving service performance. Now the company is receiving massive volumes of often-unsolicited data from conversations which it has not had access to in the past. The actions a company takes based on that data are going to be highly subjective in terms of whether it chooses to do anything or not, at what point it intervenes, and where or how it intervenes. In essence, the purpose of the analysis is often unclear prior to gathering the data.

As a result of these factors, the nature of customer analytics has fundamentally changed. In this chapter, we review more specifically how social media insights can be generated and integrated into the customer analytics function and how the analytics function must change to gain maximum benefit from the more timely and predictive insights it enables. Considering the SLOPE model described in Chapter 5 (Synchronize, Listen and Learn, Optimize and Operationalize, Personalize and Propagate, and Expectations and Execution), this chapter focuses in more detail on the "Listen and Learn" steps in the process.

New Insights and Social Media Analysis Techniques

The conversational, free-flowing, and unstructured nature of social media data requires companies to define new metrics and use new kinds of techniques to analyze this data and measure the new metrics. Analyzing social media data requires techniques from machine learning, data mining, text mining, information retrieval, natural language processing, and social network analysis. Here are some examples of social media–driven metrics and technologies that need to be used to measure them and provide insights about the consumer base.

Volume (Buzz)

Volume is the most basic metric and gives an indication of the issue's interest to the public. Measuring the change (and rate of change) in volume after a certain event or campaign can provide more meaningful insights. For example, the number of mentions a brand gets before the release of a new advertisement versus the number during and after can be used to measure the reach and impact of the campaign. Comparing the buzz generated by different customer segments can also give actionable information for better targeting. Measuring the rate of change of volume tells a company if a new issue is emerging and what trajectory it could take in the future.

Measuring this volume may seem simple at first glance, but can be quite complex due to the unstructured nature of social media. Take, for example, the buzz around the name of an organization. You can easily measure the volume for unique names (such as Accenture, Pfizer, Walmart) using a simple keyword search. But the effort is much more complex when dealing with names such as Sun (Microsystems), Apple, and Sprint, which commonly occur in social media referring to entities other than the target organization. Text-mining techniques must be used to disambiguate each mention of the terms in question. This step is known as *entity disambiguation* in the text mining world and involves analyzing each mention of an entity (say Apple) and deciding which object it belongs to (the company Apple, the fruit, or the person Mr. Apple). Entity disambiguation is critical during the data collection stage to filter the social media an organization analyzes. For instance, a comment about *an apple keeping the doctor away* later can result in spurious correlations between Apple products and medical problems.

Double-counting is another concern to keep in mind when measuring volume in social media. Should a single blog post or news story forwarded, re-tweeted, or copied in 100 places count as a single instance or 100 instances? Someone asking a question on a forum and the people answering that question while including the original question in their response can skew the volume metrics as well. In some cases, each instance must count on its own. In others, it's important to unify all instances. These cases are further complicated when the same content is paraphrased in multiple places making detection and unification more difficult. The right decision can vary by the business purpose of seeking this insight, but companies need to have technologies that are capable of supporting the entire spectrum.

Topics

Measuring the volume around certain words, such as the name of an organization, is only the first step in social media analysis and provides only limited actionable insights. The next step is to analyze which topics are being mentioned and measure the volume (as well as change in volume) around each of these topics. Several techniques (and tools) exist to track known topics as well as discover new topics in streaming unstructured text data. The simplest of them require the user to predefine a set of inclusion and exclusion words for each topic. For example, if a company is tracking the topic *Apple* (the company), it might use *Apple, ipod, iphone, imac, mac* as inclusion words and *fruit* as an exclusion word. The software then scans each piece of social media to assign it one or more topics using this list of keywords (or phrases).

This manual keyword-based approach is simple to implement but has several drawbacks. It relies on the user not only to create this exhaustive list but also to update and maintain it over time. Generally, people are not very good at exhaustively making a list of words that belong to a topic. This problem gets worse as the number of topics that must be maintained often range from tens to a few hundred. In addition, this approach does not allow a company to discover new topics that might emerge in social media. Techniques from machine learning, such as text clustering and classification[1], allow a company to both discover emerging topics and to automatically tag new content with existing topics. These technologies help make the process of analyzing topics in social media less human-intensive, cheaper, and more scalable. A typical classification algorithm works by taking sample articles, documents, or keywords for each topic from the user. Machine learning algorithms are then used to learn statistical classification models for each topic. These classification models are used to take new articles and automatically assign topics to them. For example, if a company wants to track messages about customer service, it could start by manually tagging some small set of messages (blog posts, Facebook status messages, tweets, e-mails) as belonging to the topic *customer service*. This set is then provided to the machine learning tool which learns a classification model for *customer service*. It can then take new incoming messages and tag them with the topic *customer service* if appropriate.

Even though standard machine learning algorithms have proven to be cheaper to build and maintain than keyword-based tools, they still require some human effort to build. The past few years have witnessed the development of more interactive machine learning approaches (collectively known as Active Learning) have been developed recently in academic research that are extremely accurate in detecting topics while requiring a fraction of the user's time compared with the keyword-based approaches. It will probably take some time for them to become part of mainstream off-the-shelf tools, but free research prototypes are often available for companies to experiment with.[2]

Sentiment

Measuring the sentiment of customers' discussions can be immensely valuable. Identifying the sentiment toward a company's brand, products, and services can provide insights into what part of its business customers like, dislike, and are neutral about. Strategically, the company then can emphasize elements that are popular and take steps to mitigate the unpopular ones.

With current text-mining technology, fine-grained sentiment analysis is fairly inaccurate but aggregated measures are reasonably reliable. Most of the products available today rely on a predefined list of positive and negative words along with some natural language processing techniques to account for various forms of negation (such as *not good* or *too fragrant*). Using these word lists to detect sentiment works in certain industries but is often inaccurate in a variety of cases. Differences in how sentiment is expressed in different industries is difficult to capture using a global set of words. This leads to the challenge of customizing off-the-shelf sentiment models to a company. For example, *small* might be a positive word in the context of describing the size of a mobile phone but negative when describing a hotel room and neutral when describing a *small difference*. Word lists are typically brittle, not context sensitive, and perform poorly in new domains. The key is to combine natural language processing techniques with statistical machine learning algorithms and build sentiment classification models much like topic classification models described in the previous section. Like classification models, they need training data in the form of documents, sentences, or words tagged with sentiment. Once this tagged set of content is provided, the machine learning algorithms learn sentiment models that can be used to detect the sentiment in future data. Statistical approaches are very accurate in detecting sentiment at an article (document) level but may not work as well when dealing with short pieces of text (sentences, text messages, tweets). An advantage of statistical approaches is that they provide a confidence score when analyzing sentiment. Companies can use this confidence to decide how aggressive or conservative they want to be in bringing a particular piece of data into the customer analytics function. There are research and development efforts going in academia and corporate labs (including Accenture Labs) to create the next generation of these technologies. The next few years will bring new technologies combining statistical and linguistic techniques to accurately detect sentiment in short, ungrammatical social media that can be cheaply (and reliably) customized to new domains and can adapt to the fast-changing nature of social media and improve over time.

Topic Sentiment

Topic volume and overall sentiment are useful measures by themselves, but the combination is often what provides more actionable insights. "Topic" in this context doesn't refer only to concepts we typically think of as topics (sports, news, economy, etc.); it also refers to features of products or services (screen size of a phone, weight of a laptop, friendliness of a customer service agent). Sentiment alone might tell a company that its brand has 78 percent positive sentiment, but knowing that the negative sentiment is mostly about its television advertisements should lead to a more focused investigation and potential corrective actions.

Text-mining techniques today are not accurate enough to reliably provide sentiment analysis on short pieces of text such as *Coooool*. The longer the text, the more reliable the sentiment measure. However, the longer the text, the more topics it typically contains. This results in uncertainty about which topic is associated with which sentiment. Shorter pieces of text are often about single topics but are harder to detect sentiment in using statistical techniques. Linguistic techniques are better at this fine-grained analysis but are not generally scalable and require users to spend considerable time building and maintaining them. Any useful system needs to contain technologies that combine statistics and linguistics to achieve a robust system that is both effective at detecting sentiment at a granular level and efficient to maintain.

Beyond Sentiment

Positive and negative sentiment metrics are one class of metrics that can be used with social media. Social media also can be categorized into narrower categories, such as compliments, suggestions, requests, and complaints. Breaking down customer feedback into these categories allows companies to take more targeted actions that are specific to each category. On the other hand, going beyond simple sentiment requires more effort and more sophisticated algorithms. Before investing in more sophisticated tools, companies first need to analyze small samples of their social media data to decide whether the insights generated are worth the extra effort.

Social Influence

Influence is measured by ascertaining the originator of a comment or section of prose and determining the number of people influenced by it. Often the number of people reading a comment is used as a proxy for influence; however, a more accurate measure takes into account what action a particular writer or poster influences the readers to take. The actions can range from repeating the post (forwarding it to others), voting on it (either positively or negatively), citing it in another post, responding to it, or maybe even buying a product that it mentions.

Identifying the most influential people online is immensely powerful for a company. It allows attention to be focused on those with the most influence and at the expense of those who have little or no influence. The intelligent targeting of a key influencer can fundamentally change the way the world thinks about and discusses a topic because individuals who have built up reputations as being reliable sources of information online are trusted far more than companies broadcasting the same message to conventional media.

Influencer analysis uses social network analysis techniques and looks at which online personalities affect most people. This analysis can be done agnostic of the topic, but influence sometimes can vary across topics. An influential digital photography blogger may or may not carry over that influence capital when blogging about gardening products. Influence analysis quantitatively shows who has the most power and influence in the online arena and therefore should be afforded the most attention when attempting to influence the online community. "Influencing the influencer" is now possible.

Although influence is commonly measured for people, it isn't necessarily restricted to them. Certain blogs, web sites, or groups also have influence and should be included when performing influence analysis.

All of these metrics require companies to invest in technologies such as machine learning, data mining, text mining, information retrieval, natural language processing, and social network analysis. All of these are areas that are changing very quickly, with new vendors emerging frequently, new public domain software being released, and new algorithms being developed by researchers in universities and industrial labs across the world. It's not only important to invest in the technology, but also in people who understand the technology, can keep up with the changes, and can experiment with the latest and greatest to stay ahead of competition.

Companies serious about social media insights must develop and continuously maintain internal data sets of manually annotated social media data. They must sample the social media, manually annotate it with topics and sentiments, and then run it against current tools as well as new and emerging techniques. This is critical not only for measuring how current tools are performing, but also for creating benchmarking metrics that will help in new product evaluations.

Changes to the Customer Analytics Function

The customer analytics function must change to take full advantage of the new insights that social media offers through the use of new metrics described in the previous sections. The integration of social media into the customer analytics function has numerous implications for the organization, culture, processes, and data governance policies of a company.

Changes in Organization

The types of analytical skills that organizations need for social media and the technologies required to analyze this data are new and unique. Such analytical resources are currently in scarce supply. In addition, significant cost can be incurred if data collection and analytical tools are duplicated across distributed or fragmented analytics teams. For these reasons, most organizations recognize that the most beneficial organization structure is to centralize the social CRM and customer analytics functions. This central function gathers and analyzes data in a single team and distributes insights on sentiment, volume, and other measures to different groups that use the insights for different purposes.

However, in many organizations for many reasons, this centralized approach may be impractical. If an organization finds itself unable to fully centralize and staff the function, the best approach is to focus on critical business areas. Start with a pilot program to get core resources onboard, systems integrated, and processes defined. Find the most relevant parts of the organization where social media can make the largest impact, focus resources there, and build out the function over time. For instance, if in social media strategy development a company identifies product innovation or marketing or service as an area highly impacted by social media, it should start with providing analytics support there, prove the value, and then build out a shared customer analytics function.

Regardless of organization structure (but especially critical to a distributed approach) is creating an oversight role for social media data and customer analytics. For instance, some companies have a chief data officer who handles data governance including that generated by social media—dealing with such concerns as how specific types of data are handled, how much data should be stored and archived, and how much should be sensed on behalf of the business so that it can act on the data. (Chapter 16 covers the role and responsibility of this position in more detail.)

Changes in Culture

Prior to the social media revolution, CRM was becoming increasingly analytics focused. Now this analytics-intense trend has accelerated and is on a much broader scale. Data is changing much, much faster. And, therefore, analysts must be able to change the focus of their analysis much, much faster and in turn, leaders must be able to effect the decisions they are making much, much faster. Cultural agility is a business imperative in leveraging social media insight.

Analysts must be able to deal with uncertainty—in both the data and the insights it offers. *Test and Learn* can and should be part of the enterprise culture. For instance, leading online retailers regularly use controlled experiments using multivariate or A/B testing to optimize what gets shown on their web site to customers.

Understanding and acting on customer insights requires collaborating with customers instead of managing customers—a significant change for the culture of many organizations. Because the customer is far more influential in the analytics process and the analytical outcome, companies must establish a culture of collaborating with both customers and employees. Social media is a two-way dialogue. It's no longer a linear process: and so just listening to consumers and employees, conducting analysis and taking action is no longer enough. It's about listening and interacting with them, and collaborating with them as well.

Changes in Decision-Making Processes

The customer analytics process and approach will vary by usage. How social media data is analyzed and integrated into an organization will depend to a degree on the specific need of the department using the knowledge. For instance, a marketing department may be analyzing insights for campaign performance. In this case, the process would closely parallel the process used prior to the integration of social media data but would incorporate these new insights. Analytics for product innovation will be much more fluid and collaborative. And the analytics process to support a customer service function likely would be integrated into the customer service work flow to provide additional information for self-service or call center service.

However, a significant shift in the customer analytics decision-making process is to define the process and guidelines that enable analysts occasionally to make immediate decisions. Because of the real-time and interactive nature of social media, there are times, when scanning social media data, that an analyst must take immediate action as opposed to waiting until the best decision can be made.

Last, analyzing and acting on the insights regarding influencers will be an increasingly important part of the analytics process. Organizations must figure out, through analysis, that, for a particular problem, there are certain specific individuals (inside or outside the company) who are the best to respond via social media. Action could be taken to encourage them to respond or to increase the odds that they will respond.

Changes in Data Governance and Analytics

Many data governance issues require policy decisions to be made by the customer analytics function. For instance:

- How reliable is the data? Is it spam or real data, or data generated to intentionally manipulate the decisions?
- How reliable is the insight generated by the data? If the data was initially in the form of unstructured text, could the insight be incorrect due to errors made by the text mining tools? Are there confidence measures generated by text-mining tools attached to each insight?
- When can this data or insight be used and for how long? A company can't possibly use every piece of information, and every insight gained from social media, all the time. There is a governance issue around how long the data should be included in the process and to instruct the

technology (as well as the people) embedded in the data warehouse on those parameters.

Beyond the challenges of data governance, data analytics takes the volume of information produced every hour and mines it to provide reports that analysts then can manage to provide clear and unbiased strategic guidance. Customer analytics now must incorporate unstructured data, conduct text analytics, and integrate with other unstructured data and broader enterprise analytics. Decisions that typically relied on customer segmentation and forecasting analytics now have to incorporate text mining, natural language processing, and social network analysis.

Insights generated from all of the traditional ways of listening to customers (via solicited surveys, unsolicited call center conversations, or e-mails that are coming in) must combine with social media insights to create a more robust view of the customer. Multimodal data analytics incorporates structured, unstructured, temporal, and network data. Analysis can be done separately and combined together or done jointly. Because the data coming in from social media is noisy and sometimes incorrect, the analytics must be robust and probabilistic.

Analytics also must be predictive. The focus is not on describing what has happened but on predicting what's going to happen and then determining how to manipulate what's going to happen to shape the future.

The analytics need a systematic way of conducting trial-and-error iterations and adapting accordingly. Most companies find they need to have an analytics infrastructure for continuous experimentation that allows them to generate lots of candidate decisions and automatically select the best performing ones.

Toward the Next Generation of Customer Analytics

For years, companies have been moving toward a more analytical approach to CRM. All of these traditional and evolving data-mining and analytical techniques still remain appropriate and relevant today. The integration of social media requires new analytical techniques and provides new metrics and insights which allow improved and more robust customer-focused decision making.

As companies look toward the future of their customer analytics function, the focus must be on the integration of social media insights with enterprise insights (traditional customer sources as well as insights from finance, sales, marketing, service, supply chain, and Enterprise Resource Planning [ERP] systems). Through such integration, leading organizations will deliver an improved multichannel customer experience and enhance enterprise-level decision making.

Customer Analytics within Microsoft's Online Service Division

Microsoft's Online Service Division represents an example of how one organization has structured its customer analytics capability to deal more effectively with social media–generated data. The Online Service Division includes the Bing search engine, MSN portal offerings, and products.

The Divisions marketing analytics groups analyze large data sets—both internal and third-party data from subscription services and panels. They also use third-party services to crawl different types of web sites for user-generated comments. The service provides a sentiment measure (positive, neutral, not favorable) and a volume level. The team then monitors sentiments on a regular basis and compares metrics from period to period.

In addition to ongoing monitoring, the groups do an increasing amount of analysis using third party research companies who manage opt in research panels of consumers who allow these companies to track their internet usage and to conduct market research (surveys). This allows the research groups to study not only what these users do online, but also merge that with attitudes and perceptions to create a number of different consumer segmentations or ways of looking at how people interact with search engines, portals, and with social networking products and services. Intelligence on these different consumer segments is then shared with other functions within the Online Service Division to inform their various strategies and programs.

7

Using Social Media to Drive Product Development and Find New Services to Sell

Adi Alon and A.J. Gupta

CHAPTER HIGHLIGHTS

By using social media in product development—not only in ideation, but also in product piloting and refining, a company can increase customers' emotional attachment to it and its products or services. If customers feel more engaged with the development of an offering, they're more likely to embrace and champion it.

Companies using social media as part of their innovation efforts should expect the unexpected—both good (learning about demand or usage of which they previously were unaware) and bad (getting negative feedback about products or services that are available for the whole world to see).

Social media typically is thought of as an important tool for creating demand, but it also has become critical to helping a company *satisfy* demand. In fact, innovative companies already have experienced considerable success in using social media to help them address three long-standing product development challenges:

1. Expanding the sources of innovation—particularly those outside of a company's formal research and development (R&D) organization—necessary to develop a complex product or service
2. Ramping up product development efforts to keep pace with ever-shortening product life cycles
3. Bolstering a company's ability to understand and target narrow customer niches with relevant new offerings

How have leading companies done this? We have observed that companies with the greatest success in using social media to propel their product development efforts have been adept at deploying social media across three key "spheres":

1. The company's own employees
2. A "trusted network," or a prescreened network of consumers, suppliers, partners, academics, and others
3. All potential contributors and collaborators around the world

Such companies also excel in identifying how social media can be used to improve each of the steps of the product development process—from ideation and concept testing to the retail experience and postsales.

In this chapter, we discuss what companies can learn from these leaders as they consider how to deploy social media to improve their own product development efforts. We also offer a framework for companies to use as they design their approach to applying social media to their product development processes.

Social Media and the New Era of Product Development

The value of social media to a company's customer service and marketing functions are inarguable. Social media enables a company to tune in to thousands or even millions of previously inaccessible customer discussions and try to influence them in a positive manner. Yet the impact of social media on the product development function may be equally significant.

Why? It's because social media creates a whole new way for customers to form an emotional attachment to a company's offerings. Social media enables a company to stimulate and then tap the collective passion and insights among its customers, identify new needs, test solutions to meet those needs, create customer buzz, and get customer acceptance—even before a new product or service hits the market. Social media also helps companies harness additional resources and expertise to complement and bolster their internal development capabilities—in effect, making the world a potential rich (not to mention low-cost) source of new ideas. (See Figure 7.1.)

To be sure, product innovation has never been more important—or more difficult. From pharmaceuticals to high tech, more and more companies are spending huge sums on product development and getting smaller—and less predictable—returns.

For instance, a recent study found that just slightly more than half (55 percent) of 1,600 companies globally reported being satisfied with their return on innovation spending.[1] This figure is astounding, especially when considering

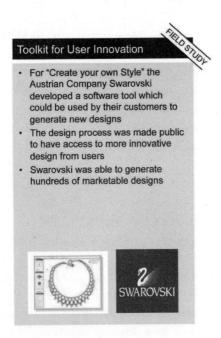

FIGURE 7.1 Social Media Enables Companies to Engage Customers to Generate New Product Designs.

how much money is dedicated to innovation efforts—which, according to the Battelle Institute, a science and technology research organization, will top $1.1 trillion globally in 2010.[2] How many other business investments yield as much certainty as a coin toss?

What's the problem? Three forces are conspiring to make life difficult for a growing number of product development managers:

1. **Because the rapid commoditization of products results in shorter product life cycles, the need to accelerate the product development process is paramount.** Consumer products of all types—from cars and televisions to jeans, cell phones, and even packaged goods such as food and toothpaste—have experienced rapidly decreasing life spans in the past decade. Thus, although in years past, companies had many years to reap the benefits of its R&D investments while working on their next big ideas, they no longer have that luxury. They must, as the adage says, strike while the iron is hot to capitalize on marketplace needs while keeping their foot on the product development accelerator to stay ahead of competitors eager to one-up them with their next release. Today, a sluggish and slow-to-respond product development process is a major hindrance and, in many industries, can deal a fatal blow to a company's prospects.

2. **An expanding range of expertise and competencies is required to introduce highly complex products to the marketplace, some of which are beyond an organization's knowledge and skills.** This is due in part to the increasing digitization of products and services. An automobile today demands deep expertise in a wide variety of electronics, wireless communications, computer hardware and software domains than it did 20 years ago, even 10 years ago. Genetics expertise and many more types of knowledge and skills are required now to develop new pharmaceuticals than was required in days past. Even formerly low-tech products, such as drink dispensing machines, now come with embedded software and communications systems for reordering product. But the proliferation of technologies also adds to the challenge. For example, cell phones have at least three major software operating systems, making it difficult for an organization to achieve critical mass in all relevant platform technologies. In short, it's extremely rare for any company to have in-house the full range of product development expertise and skills that are necessary to excel in today's environment.

3. **Increasing microsegmentation exists.** Most companies today are confronted with an ever-more-fragmented customer base (both consumers and businesses) that has diverse and hard-to-predict needs—and that now expect more personalized and customized offerings enabled by technology advancements. From cereal makers to cellular phone providers, companies are slicing their customer bases into increasingly smaller segments: for example, from breakfast offerings for teenagers, to simple-to-use cell phones for senior citizens. Getting to know what the needs of these microsegments are, let alone profitably fulfilling them, is a major challenge for companies in all industries.

A growing number of product development executives are using social media to deal with the three mega-challenges of shrinking product cycles, the need for greater expertise, and narrower customer segmentation. They realize that traditional approaches and tools won't get them there. They know they cannot afford to hire all the various technical expertise they need. They recognize they can't make major improvements in their ability to predict consumer reaction to new products just by fine-tuning their traditional forecasting methods. They're turning to social media to make quantum improvements in product development.

Companies such as Procter & Gamble (P&G), Best Buy, Dell, and Starbucks have been early pioneers of using social media to conceive, design, develop, and test new products. What common threads run through these companies? What approaches, tools, methods, and mind-sets do they share?

In our research and consulting work, we have found that these and other leaders use social media both internally to facilitate the flow of ideas among employees and externally to tap in to customers, suppliers, partners, and others outside the organization. They also use social media across all aspects of the product development process, not just in the most obvious one (i.e., gathering customer suggestions for new products).

Three Spheres of Involvement

One of the central tenets of social media is that it enables people and organizations to interact with each other in real time. Of course, this opens up huge possibilities for companies to gain insights into what kinds of products and services would strike a chord with potential customers—and avoid a lot of

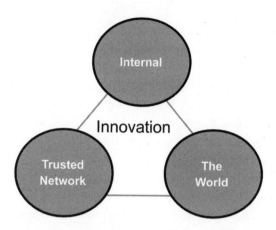

FIGURE 7.2 Social Media Can Help Orchestrate Three Spheres of Influence to Boost a Company's Innovation Efforts.

expensive and time-consuming trial and error while enhancing the chance that resulting offers will have the features and functions customers want.

The companies that have been most successful in leveraging social media in product development are those that recognize social media's power to connect not only the people within their organization but also those outside of the company who could serve as rich sources of ideas that could lead to the next big (and profitable) product or service. There are three such "spheres of involvement": internal, trusted network, and the world. (See Figure 7.2.)

Internal Sphere

The first sphere is internal. Inside a company, social media can be a useful tool to harness the ideas of people around the organization, especially front-line employees who interact with customers daily. Such interactions—most notably, customer complaints—can be great pointers to new product and service needs. Social media can shorten the communication cycle between the bottom and top levels of a company, thus getting an intriguing idea born out of a customer complaint to the top of the R&D function in minutes. In the past, such ideas were not likely to climb their way up the corporate ladder quickly, if at all. And, in an era where many companies have diversified workforces spanning the globe, social media can help bridge the "horizontal" divide.

Furthermore, social media can help marketing, service, product development, finance, supply chain, and other experts inside a company to better pool their ideas. Domain specialists can be found easily through a company's internal Facebook pages or a wiki. Employees also can be a good provider of feedback on new products. A growing number of companies are running internal contests for best new product ideas. Those with a large payroll—10,000, 50,000, or more employees—can become a great source of new ideas and test bed for others.

For instance, U.S.-based banking giant Wells Fargo—long admired for its sterling customer service—implemented an initiative designed to create further differentiation and drive innovation in its customer experience. As the financial services industry and its products have become more complex, companies like Wells Fargo can struggle to deliver a consistent and high-quality customer experience. To meet this challenge, the bank launched an enterprisewide program to identify solutions and strategic change ideas to improve the customer experience and, in the end, ensure customer loyalty and retention.

Wells Fargo created an "innovation network"—a means of connecting and tapping in to the insights of the bank's employees to identify and address the main threats to customer loyalty. An organization can accomplish more by mobilizing this type of broad horizontal network of participants than it can by leveraging a small group of experts, such as corporate development or strategy.

As part of the effort, the company piloted a new system called Accenture Collaborative Innovation Solutions. This system is based on the principles of crowdsourcing and uses Web 2.0 technology and rich Internet applications to effectively source and develop ideas from diverse audiences. (For more on the system and how it works, see the sidebar titled "Heard It through the Grapevine" further in the chapter)

The success of Wells Fargo's innovation network was twofold.

1. It generated a pipeline of more than 50 ideas highlighting specific product and process issues as well as ideas for improving the end-to-end customer experience.
2. Implementing the innovation network fostered higher levels of employee engagement and awareness for the customer loyalty program. More than 250 Wells Fargo employees—representing more than 21 U.S. states and 90 job titles—submitted substantive ideas, resulting in seven high-quality innovations for the company.

Following this initial success, Wells Fargo is creating ongoing collaborative networks as part of a broader innovation capability that will support the transformational and cultural changes needed for the company to achieve sustained high performance.[3]

Trusted Network

The second sphere of involvement with social media is something we call the trusted network. A company's trusted network consists of external parties who advise on everything from product concepts and key materials to prototypes and manufacturing processes. Members of the trusted network can be customers, such as the network that Nike is building for golfers who use its products. The company hopes to use the expertise of its customers to build better golf equipment.

But network members can go beyond customers to product tinkerers. P&G's Connect + Develop network is a great example. Its online portal solicits ideas for products and processes that can turn into big new ideas for the $76 billion company. By 2006, with the help of Connect + Develop, more than 35 percent of P&G's new products consisted of external ideas—more than double the 15 percent level in 2000. Today, about half of P&G's new products were shaped by external input from the Connect + Develop process. P&G says Connect + Develop has boosted its success rate at product innovation more than 100 percent despite lower product development spending.[4]

Data storage solutions provider EMC is another company that is using social media to help support open innovation efforts with trusted networks. The EMC Innovation Network is an organization through which the company's researchers collaborate with each other and with other research teams around the world to discuss and explore promising new ideas. The company's trusted network includes researchers at a number of universities worldwide as well as several influential industry trade groups.

The World

The third type of sphere of involvement that companies can gain through social media is one that is open to the world. Social media allows companies to reach out to the large numbers of outside contributors worldwide—people who can offer ideas on product concepts, test products, troubleshoot packaging and manufacturing problems, and make other contributions to innovation.

Dell Inc. for years has used online tools to solicit ideas from customers, which has helped improve its computer hardware, software, services, and customer service. (See Figure 7.3.) The computer manufacturer was one of the early adopters of the crowdsourcing concept with the launch of its IdeaStorm web site (www.ideastorm.com) in 2007. According to the company, IdeaStorm was created "to give a direct voice to our customers and an avenue to have online 'brainstorm' sessions to allow you the customer to share ideas and collaborate with one another and Dell." Dell reports that three years after the launch of the site, more than 10,000 ideas have been explored and nearly 400 implemented.[5]

Similarly, Starbucks' web site called "MyStarbucksIdea" (http://mystarbucksidea.force.com) solicits ideas for new products, improvements in the customer experience, and ways the company could improve the communities it operates in. By June 2010, the company had received more

Community Innovation at Dell

- Dell rolled out an innovative project called IdeaStorm, which **allows customers to contribute new ideas**
- The company **monitors all mentions** of Dell online (RSS, searches) and ultimately **implements the best ideas**
- Since 2006, when Dell launched its major online community initiative, **online mentions of Dell have decreased from more than 50% negative to only 20% negative**
- Due to the success of IdeaStorm, Dell **created further Dell forums** (e.g. Direct2Dell, Studio Dell)

FIGURE 7.3 Dell Has Been a Leader in Harnessing Social Media for Community Innovation.

than 20,000 ideas for coffee and espresso drinks. The company has launched dozens of new concepts based on such social media–generated customer feedback.

A company called InnoCentive provides another good example of how social media can open a company's innovation processes to the world. The firm has a network of more than 200,000 people—including engineers, scientists, inventors, and businesspeople with expertise in a variety of industries and disciplines—whom companies can tap for help in solving their innovation challenges. InnoCentive's Open Innovation Marketplace, based on a crowdsourcing platform, pairs "seekers" (those looking for help) and "solvers" (individuals with the answers). Solvers who submit the most innovative solutions earn compensation that could reach as much as $1 million. According to InnoCentive's web site, major R&D-driven companies including P&G, Avery Dennison, Eli Lilly, and SAP have submitted "innovation challenges" to the network.

Using social media to open up an organization to a world of ideas allows it not only to tap concepts from everywhere but also to have a large pool of customers ready to assess those ideas. Such early feedback on new product concepts has become crucial: It helps companies avoid costly mistakes in products that have insufficient numbers of customers or are markedly deficient in price, features, or other key elements. Social media gives a company real-time customer reaction to new concepts or prototypes.

Tapping the ideas of outsiders has become critical to many companies that can't afford all the technical expertise they need these days to bring a new product or service to market.

Using Social Media in Steps of the Development Process

The preceding section illustrated how leaders understand the *who* aspect of applying social media to product development. But that's only half the battle. Equally important is recognizing the *where* and *how*—in other words, determining the precise points in the product development process in which social media can help.

When people think of social media and product development, most think of the front end of the innovation process, or the ideation stage. As the Dell and Starbucks examples showed, social media can be very effective in gathering and brainstorming new ideas to be explored further. But what about the other steps in the process? We've found that companies that are truly leveraging the power of social media to super-charge product development are using social media in many steps of the process, not just in ideation.

For example, some companies are using social media to more precisely understand the demographics behind a certain customer segment or better divine their needs—that is, to listen better to the "voice of the customer." This is important in trend-driven markets where needs change rapidly due to peer interaction.

Other companies use social media to hasten and improve the step of getting feedback on product prototypes. T-shirt company Threadless (www .threadless.com), for example, uses online tools to quickly test customer reactions to new design concepts. T-shirt fads change abruptly; it's very hard to predict what graphic image or words will resonate with fickle consumers. By using social media to get people to submit designs and vote on those that appear to have promise, Threadless can substantially reduce risk and maximize its gains on a current (and fleeting) trend. In faddish, high-risk businesses like fashion, social media can be a powerful tool.

Another example of using social media to test prototypes is the campaign recently conducted by Marmite, a Unilever-owned brand famous for its yeast spread (similar to Vegemite, the version sold in Australia) that incites either lust or disgust, depending on one's palate. Looking to create a new "more mature, extra strong" version of its standard spread, Marmite identified a set of customers who were extremely active and passionate about the brand on social networking sites. The 200 lucky individuals, dubbed "Marmarati," then were given beta versions of the new product and asked to give their views on various aspects of the samples. Their feedback was sent along to the product development team to help determine the formula of the product that ultimately went on sale.[6]

An often-overlooked part of the product development process is the experience that customers have in purchasing and using a new product. Companies traditionally have collected feedback on the customer experience through surveys—phone, in-store, and online. In all cases, the data may not be timely. Social media lets companies acquire customer feedback on the buying and postsales experiences in real time and begin to assess and correct

FIGURE 7.4 HP Uses Social Media to Improve Testing of Printers in Real-Life Environments.

potential issues immediately, before they become problems. Furthermore, social media allows companies to hear or read consumers' unvarnished, real words and get an appreciation of the emotion and context involved, unhidden by a survey firm's interpretation of them.

A great example: In the days immediately after the launch of Apple's iPad, hundreds of thousands of tweets were sent containing the word "iPad." Was this just meaningless chatter? Quite the contrary, as an editor at *Harvard Business Review* discovered. Scott Berinato, working with software developer Jeff Clark, evaluated the more than half a million tweets containing "iPad" during the product's launch weekend and found that while some proportion of the tweets certainly had no value, the vast majority of them, if analyzed correctly, offered a gold mine of insights that Apple could use to improve various aspects of the product and the company's support of it. From a product development standpoint, for instance, the tweets offer an unflinching look at users' experiences with the product. By pairing up attributes of the iPad (such as "keyboard," "display," or "weight") mentioned in the tweets with positive and negative words in the same communications, Apple's product development team can quickly pinpoint what's turning users off and, thus, prioritize fixes they should consider for future releases.[7]

Microsoft provides another example of how a company can use social media to prioritize service and product problems—and, in particular, how social media data can be used to get the attention of the product development team. In the days before social media, the company had two major sources of feedback on product issues: phone calls to the call center and data coming into the company via product instrumentation. "Both of those are valid, but they're difficult to rationalize," noted Toby Richards, general manager for communities and online support at Microsoft. In other words, when issues from the call center were passed on to the product development team, the latter team members were dubious because often they were not seeing evidence of the issue in the data they collected via product instrumentation. "Now we'll use the tone and volume of social media to help to validate issues we're hearing about," said Richards. "We can say, [for example], 'In the past two weeks there were 80,000 Twitter posts and 10,000 questions on this particular issue.' Social media has really helped to battle the perception gaps between what product engineering thinks is an issue versus what sales, marketing, and service thinks is an issue. It's really helped to create a more objective customer-centric conversation."

A company's ability to collect feedback in these three steps in the product development process can accelerate time to market and increase the chances that a product is in tune with customer needs. Furthermore, every customer who participated in the development process will feel better connected to the product that eventually hits the market. In this way, the marketing and selling of the product has begun even before it reaches retailers' shelves.

Put Social Media to Its Own Innovation Test

We believe the best way to begin incorporating social media in product development is to put the technology to the test—but quickly. Take a new-product concept, create a plan for soliciting ideas internally and externally using social media, and start soliciting feedback. The information gained is likely to be substantial—not just about that product but, more important, for how a company's product development process must use social media for its new-product pipeline in the years ahead.

It's also important to note that there is no one-size-fits-all approach to social media for all product development organizations. How a company uses social media to launch new products will depend on what industry it is in, the spheres it decides to activate, and the steps in its development process that can derive the greatest benefit.

Social media promises to transform product development. The companies that thrive on product innovation in the future will be those that exploit social media across the entire product development process and use it in all three spheres.

Heard It through the Grapevine

By Michael E. Bechtel and Lauren M. Chewning

How does a company—especially a large one—distill a multitude of raw ideas into value-creating innovations? One key is to tap the imaginations and experiences of the entire workforce, which, in turn, becomes not only the source of the ideas themselves but also a critical element of the evaluation process that separates the great thinking from the merely good.

That's the idea behind the Accenture Innovation Solutions Network, a "mass collaboration" technique for managing the innovation process. Known inside Accenture as the "innovation grapevine," the tool begins with a "seed," as it were—a strategic challenge or business idea. Something like, "How can we improve our operations to deliver world-class customer experiences?" Or, "What recruiting programs might help us compete more effectively in the war for talent?"

The next step is to find fertile ground for the seed among the people of the organization (or business partners, or even customers) who are knowledgeable about the topic under discussion and who might be able to contribute breakthrough, value-creating ideas based on their

(continued)

(continued)
own experience and on their collaboration with others. People contribute their input to a central electronic repository, so ideas aren't lost and so their origin can be tracked.

So far, so good. But as demonstrated in the accompanying article, merely having a colossal electronic suggestion box really won't help the innovation process much. Who is going to sift through all the ideas, and based on what criteria? Who is going to separate the good grapes from the bad ones, and then turn the whole thing into fine wine?

That's where applied wiki technology and crowd sourcing come into play. The innovation grapevine uses a wiki concept—a shared composition and editing environment like Wikipedia—but inverts it. Instead of asking a crowd of people to come back with one synthesized bit of thinking about a topic, it gives people one idea and asks them to come back with as many applications and variations as possible. Call it a "divergent wiki," rather than a convergent one.

Now the branching aspect of a grapevine becomes more than just a nice metaphor. Because it is in fact the branching of ideas, and the morphing and improvement of an idea as it moves from one person to the next, that offers real potential for creating a value-generating innovation.

Often it's not the original invention that turns out to be the moneymaker—it's the subsequent one, which takes the first idea to a new level. The classic example is the steam engine, which seemed to have limited commercial application until the invention of the mechanism that converted the up-and-down motion of a piston into rotary motion.

The grapevine then asks those same contributors to evaluate the ideas that reside in the general repository—much as a web site such as Amazon.com uses its huge customer base to generate product ratings. Think of the TV show *Who Wants to Be a Millionaire?* When the contestant polls the audience for an answer, the crowd produces the correct one more times than not (indeed, statistically, more often than the "call an expert" option).

So imagine executives who have put out a request on the innovation grapevine for ideas in support of a new strategic initiative. When they monitor the results of the process in a couple of weeks or so—open up the wine cask, so to speak—they will find not only a bunch of ideas but ideas evaluated and ranked according to the collective wisdom and experience of the entire organization.

By putting ideas through this process, informed and shaped by people currently involved in leading-edge and frontline experiences, a company increases its chances of generating value-creating innovations.

Source: This sidebar originally appeared in the article "How to Capture the Essence of Innovation," by David Smith and Craig Mindrum, in Accenture's *Outlook* journal (January 2008), www.accenture.com/Global/Research_and_ Insights/Outlook/By_Issue/Y2008/captureinnovation.htm.

8

Social Community Marketing and Selling

Robert Wollan and André Trochymiuk

CHAPTER HIGHLIGHTS

The decline in traditional marketing channel effectiveness has challenged chief marketing officers to adjust both their spending and focus in driving growth. Social Community Marketing provides an attractive new discipline for capturing the attention of growing numbers of customers and prospects.

The speed and dynamics of social media are blurring the lines between marketing and sales, requiring greater levels of integration and coordination. Multiple successful approaches to drive growth have emerged in the market—with different levels of customer engagement that is tailored to the product involved.

There are three levels of social media marketing and sales maturity—each increasing both the impact of social media on company revenue and the level of commitment of the organization to execute.

Most, if not all, marketers at major companies will agree that it's never been more difficult to reach consumers effectively.

Although there has been a substantial increase in technologies, media, and channels available to marketers that offer greater variety, they also make it difficult for companies to send messages effectively and consistently.

Complicating matters is the fact that customers increasingly are using these new channels to, in effect, become "head of programming." As head of programming, customers now dictate how and when messages reach them, instead of being at the mercy of the medium.

Companies have been slow to adopt to the new reality, with many reluctant to give up on traditional marketing efforts because they were uncertain how to use these new channels most effectively. However, that is now changing, as evidenced by the increasing use of online advertising. According to a recent study, online advertising totaled $22 billion in 2009 and is expected to grow by nearly 3 percent in 2010.[1] In some markets, online ad spending has overtaken spending on some traditional advertising channels. For instance, one report noted that online ad spending likely will surpass all other media for 2010 new-vehicle advertising in the United States—driven by e-mail, social networking, and especially streaming audio and video campaigns.[2]

But such moves still will only get companies so far. Although never seen as entirely virtuous, advertising has become virtually persona non grata among today's consumers, who are likely to be more suspicious of advertising than ever and see it as a major contributor to the marketplace clutter and noise that turns them off. Consider the following statistics (see Figure 8.1): Sixty-five percent of consumers believe they're bombarded with too much advertising, 86 percent do not trust the information communicated in ads, and

Landscape Trends		Effects	
Online advertising channel shift	• In certain markets online ad spending has **overtaken spending on some** traditional advertising channels (e.g. print, radio)	65%	Proportion of people who believe they are **constantly bombarded with too much** advertising
		82%	Proportion of **TV advertising campaigns** generating **negative ROI**
Proliferated media fragmentation	• Tremendous **increase in available technologies, media and channels** • New channels offer greater variety but make it **difficult to send messages across effectively**	90%	Proportion of people who **can and then do skip TV ads**
		86%	Proportion of people who **do not trust advertising information**
Customer as "head of programming"	• Customer increasingly use new communication channels whereas traditional media use declines • Customer decide **how and when messages reach them**	30%	Proportion of people that **look for comments from internet users before entering a contract** with a business
		56%	Proportion of people who **avoid buying products** from companies who they think advertise too much
Decreasing marketing effectiveness	• The **impact** of classical advertising formats **is decreasing** • Despite a decreasing effectiveness advertising and sales promotion costs rise	80%	Proportion of people that **use the internet to conduct comparison shopping** for major purchase

FIGURE 8.1   Trends Affecting Traditional Marketing Initiatives and Their Impacts.

Channel	Not effectively (1&2)	3	4	5 Very effectively
In-person contact with front-line employees	3%	25%	30%	37%
Encouraging customers to recommend our products/services	17%	28%	31%	25%
Corporate web site	17%	35%	29%	19%
Print, TV or radio advertising	29%	31%	26%	14%
Online advertising	31%	33%	24%	13%
New digital marketing	34%	32%	21%	13%
Direct mail and telemarketing	37%	28%	25%	10%
Online communities	43%	29%	18%	11%

FIGURE 8.2 How Effectively Companies Use Key Marketing Channels.

56 percent avoid buying from companies they think advertise too much. Perhaps these figures help explain why 82 percent of television ads are generating a negative return on investment.[3]

The net result is that most companies have experienced a substantial decline in marketing effectiveness. In fact, chief marketing officers (CMOs) participating in an Accenture survey acknowledged as much, indicating that their organizations have substantial room for improvement in the area of marketing channel usage. As shown in Figure 8.2, only about 2 in 10 CMOs surveyed said their companies very effectively use most channels to reach, influence, or interact with customers. In-person contact with front-line employees and encouraging existing customers to recommend their products/services were seen as the most effective channels, with 37 percent and 25 percent of respondents, respectively, indicating they use these channels very effectively. Beyond those, however, fewer than 20 percent of CMOs said they effectively use digital channels (the corporate web site, online communities, online advertising, and mobile and location-based marketing), traditional advertising (print, television and radio), and direct mail and telemarketing.[4]

Impact of Social Media on Marketing and Sales

Of course, one of the major drivers of the challenges marketers face today is social media. There's no doubt that social media is increasing the velocity of the buying cycle—from marketing through consumer research to the sale and use of goods and services. Consider, for example, a consumer's purchase of a major appliance. In the old days, simply learning what's available was a time-consuming process that involved sorting through newspaper and magazine ads and trekking to various retailers to "touch and feel" the products and get a sense of pricing. After that came the "asking around stage"—conferring with friends and trusted associates for their opinions (and experiences with the candidate products, if available) to help narrow down the list of models. Then it was back to the retailers to negotiate prices and, ultimately, to make the purchase. Along the way, appliance manufacturers had ample time and opportunity to directly influence the consumer's decision through ads and point-of-purchase brochures. In essence, companies had greater control over access to information (especially reliable information beyond company-provided advertising) as a gating factor. Independent testing services, such as *Consumer Reports*, helped fill the gaps but were published infrequently.

In today's world, that transaction—which often took days or weeks to complete—has been compressed to hours and is far more convenient for consumers. With a few clicks, consumers can enter specifications for the appliance (e.g., features, functions, price range, and brands) and be presented with a list of everything that's available. Consumers can compare prices instantly among retailers and read about other consumers' experiences with the products through their reviews. If a consumer needs more advice, he can post a request among his friend networks on Facebook, tweet what he's looking for to a broader audience, or engage in a discussion with other consumers in an online forum dedicated to the appliance in question. Armed with all the information needed to make a decision, he completes the purchase online. Importantly, throughout this process, the manufacturer's ability to influence the decision has been greatly reduced and replaced with the insights from a wide range of consumers who presumably have real-life experiences with the products in question.

This increase in both speed and unpredictability in the buying process, in turn, is making it necessary for companies to more tightly integrate marketing and sales so they can respond to consumer needs in an acceptable time frame. Indeed, 70 percent of the CMOs in the Accenture survey said they thought their marketing organization needed to be better integrated with the sales function.[5]

Social Community Marketing as a New Discipline

To increase their marketing effectiveness and be better positioned to quickly identify and respond to customer needs, companies should begin adopting an emerging online communication discipline called Social Community Marketing as a new approach to creating an ongoing dialogue with customers. At the heart of Social Community Marketing is the notion that brand building moves from a mass-marketing model in which the goal is to acquire as many customers as possible to a more targeted, tailored approach in which the aim is to start a conversation with customers and increase the richness and depth of those conversations over time.

In the past few years, there have been myriad examples of how leading companies have embraced the concept of Social Community Marketing to support their demand-generation activities. For instance, Amazon.com's pioneering use of user reviews helped make customers more comfortable not only with purchasing from the company but also with the product itself. Dell's use of crowdsourcing helped the company identify promising new product and service offerings quickly and inexpensively, and also encouraged individual consumers to form buying consortia to take advantage of group volume discounts. And many companies' use of Facebook and Twitter to communicate new or special offerings to a devoted fan base helped generate greater loyalty and stronger sales.

Becoming an effective social community marketer, however, requires some new thinking and innovative strategies that essentially blend the marketing and sales functions to drive growth. The strategies that have emerged for actually selling via social media are broad. However, companies must consciously choose a specific strategy to follow—one that enables social media enthusiasts to engage with a company's brand while also providing for ways that social media can coexist and integrate with other traditional selling models for non–social media consumers.

In our experience, three broad strategies that have emerged with multiple sales approaches for companies to capitalize on new social media selling opportunities. (See Figure 8.3.)

Strategy #1—"Accessing Social Consumers": Use Social Media as a New Channel to Individuals

- User reviews—trust others like you
- Social media wildfire
- Creating urgency/spontaneous selling

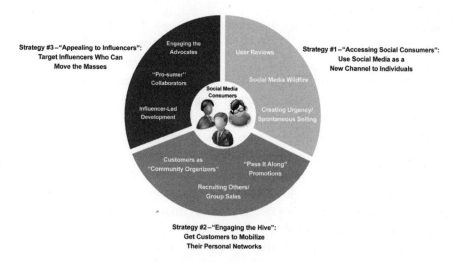

FIGURE 8.3 Examples of Social Media Selling Strategies in the Market Today.

Strategy #2—"Engaging the Hive": Get Customers to Mobilize Their Personal Networks

- "Pass it along" promotions
- Recruiting others/group selling
- Customers as "community organizers"

Strategy #3—"Appealing to Influencers": Target Influencers Who Can Move the Masses

- Influencer-led development and selling
- "Pro-sumer"—product development collaboration
- Engaging the advocates

Strategy #1—"Accessing Social Consumers": Use Social Media as a New Channel to Individuals

User Reviews—Trust Others Like You

One of the earliest examples of the social media phenomenon was the advent of user reviews posted alongside a company's or manufacturer's product information. Such reviews created the opportunity for others to share and view content that is much more widely accepted by consumers who are researching product or service purchases.

Early adopters of online user reviews included Amazon and Best Buy; however, reviews now have become a standard consumer expectation and are highly valued by consumers. For instance, one study found that one-fourth of Internet users (24 percent) reported using online reviews prior to paying for a service delivered offline and nearly all (97 percent) who had purchased something after consulting a review indicated their purchase accurately reflected the review. Those in the study who use reviews also believed consumer-generated reviews were more influential than those provided by "professionals" and were willing to pay a minimum of 20 percent more for a product or service that was rated "excellent" or received five stars than for one that was cited as "good" or received four stars.[6]

Given these facts, it's not surprising that most major retailers and consumer products manufacturers offer some type of review mechanism for consumers to express their opinions.

Social Media Wildfire

This strategy involves using social media–only content to spark interest in a product through a combination of unique applications or placements. The idea behind the strategy is to create something that is so engaging and interesting that it catches the fancy of the target audience so much that they are compelled to send it to others and promote the content for the company. In time, if successful, such campaigns take on a life of their own and result in immeasurable publicity for the company.

One of the best examples of this strategy in action is the campaign launched by Stride gum, a unit of global confectionary manufacturer Cadbury, featuring Matt Harding. Harding had gained a modest following on the Internet for his videos of him dancing a "farmer's jig" in various places—famous and pedestrian—around the world. Looking for a unique way to promote the launch of Stride in 2006, the company's agency thought a collaboration with Harding would provide the perfect vehicle to spread the word about the gum. The two parties struck a sponsorship deal, and Harding proceeded to film more dancing videos in far-flung locales—all bankrolled by Stride. Interestingly, although the Stride logo appears occasionally in the videos, Harding does not wear Stride-branded clothing or mention Stride. For the cost of some plane tickets, meals, and hotel rooms, Stride has gotten its name in front of the millions of consumers who have watched the Harding videos, and has done so in a highly memorable way.[7]

Creating Urgency/Spontaneous Selling

One of the major advantages of social media is its immediacy: Anyone with an idea can broadcast it instantly to people all around the world and do so regularly. Many companies capitalize on this advantage by using social media to promote limited-time or special offers that appeal to niche customers, thus providing a heightened sense of urgency to "buy before they're gone."

For instance, JetBlue uses its Twitter account to alert its followers of special fares it calls "Cheeps." The blurb on its Twitter account says it all: "Watch for great deals on last-minute flights every Tuesday. Cheeps are offered for a limited time and limited availability so act fast!" Similarly, United Airlines offers its own version called "Twares," or special fares made available exclusively to its Twitter followers.

One company that is built exclusively around the urgency model is Woot (www.woot.com), which bills itself as "an online store and community that focuses on selling cool stuff cheap." The company sells one and only one product every day until 11:59, then replaces it with the next one. When an item is close to selling out, the company goes into "Urgent Mode" and a bouncing "I Want One" button appears on the site. Woot accompanies its products with a robust community—in which customers post comments, opinions, and experiences as well as share technical knowledge about Woot's products—and a blog in which all products are described in detail and related articles and links are posted. And Woot offers an RSS feed that enables customers to receive updates of all new items and blog posts as they go live.

Strategy #2—"Engaging the Hive": Get Customers to Mobilize Their Personal Networks

"Pass It Along" Promotions

Programs based on a "pass it along" strategy use individuals to begin chain reactions among their personal network. For example, United Airlines held a ticket giveaway contest on Twitter. The catch to be entered? It required individuals to retweet the sweepstakes rules to their followers.

Another example involves the hugely successful Old Spice Man campaign, one of the most daring and innovative social media campaigns to date. The campaign is built around the character The Man Your Man Could Smell Like, portrayed by actor Isaiah Mustafa, whose exaggerated humor and swagger made him instantly likable. As of this writing, the original ad attracted more than 19 million views across all platforms,[8] clearly striking a chord with consumers. However, the creative team behind this campaign was far from finished. To engage customers and encourage them to spread the word of the campaign to their networks, the team began choosing their favorite comments posted by viewers and, in real time, created personalized video commercials in response to them directly. Some of the people were famous, some not. But by speaking directly to fans in this way, Old Spice was able to get these people to, indeed, spread the word about the campaign by telling all their networks that they got a personalized response to their post from the Old Spice Guy.[9]

Recruiting Others/Group Sales

As the old saying goes, there's strength in numbers. And that's precisely the concept behind this strategy, which enables customers to team up to make volume purchases and receive prices that none of them could achieve individually. In essence, a company employing this strategy is giving customers the ability to benefit from the same type of discounts that large business customers enjoy—and, in the process, boosting revenue as well as loyalty.

One of the best examples of this strategy in action is DellSwarm, whereby Dell customers recruited other customers into their "swarm" to make purchases. The larger the group became, the larger the discounts for the group. DellSwarm was piloted in Singapore in 2009 and was so successful and well received that Dell quickly decided to roll the program out globally. Interestingly, in the case of DellSwarm, aspects of two other strategies come into play: Urgency and Pass It Along. A swarm has only 72 hours to complete its purchase, and Dell encourages people in the swarm to use all their social media tools to promote their experience.

Another popular example of a non–product company is Groupon.com, which selects local companies who opt in to provide a deep discount for a "Deal of the Day" coupon in multiple cities. Groupon is similar to Woot in that it offers only one good or service each day. But it takes the model a step further by, as the company says on its web site (www.groupon.com/about), "leveraging [its] framework for collective buying," which enables Groupon to offer better deals to customers.

Customers as "Community Organizers"

If social media consists of online communities, then every community must have its organizers. Savvy companies are using social media to create opportunities for customers who value the chance to act as "organizers" of their network of friends and colleagues—and are driving incremental sales in the process.

Dunkin' Donuts' "Dunkin' Run" campaign is a great example of engaging an individual to organize her community—in this case, to purchase coffee, donuts, or other goodies. Using a computer, mobile device, or application on an iPhone, a person starts a "run" for Dunkin' products by selecting the people she wants to include in the run and providing their e-mail addresses or mobile phone numbers. The "runner" then places her order from the Dunkin' menu, and Dunkin' contacts the runner's friends to have them do the same. The company compiles all the individual orders, which are ready for pickup at the store by the runner. The result is both higher sales per "run" for Dunkin' and "hero status" for the runner among her community.

Strategy #3—"Appealing to Influencers": Target Influencers Who Can Move the Masses

Influencer-Led Development

Similar to the pass-it-along approach, this strategy specifically targets individuals who have both significant followers as well as demonstrated "weight" in their communities. It's based on the notion that an overwhelming percentage of audiences typically are swayed by the influencer in the group—and that if a company can "influence the influencer," it is more likely to have success in that community. Indeed, a study by Columbia University found that 90 percent of an audience is influenced by an opinion leader and that word of mouth rates are tightly linked to sales growth: The more positive the word of mouth, the stronger the growth. What typically happens is that influencers use information gleaned from media campaigns as word-of-mouth ammunition to influence individuals in their personal networks (which, according to a study by Northeastern University, average 62 people). Thus, advertisers can

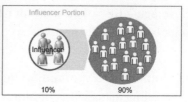

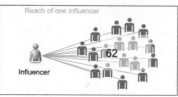

FIGURE 8.4 Companies Can Use Social Media to Effectively "Influence the Influencers."

boost campaign return on investment by targeting those with outsized influence in a particular group. (See Figure 8.4.)

Sony Corporation employed this strategy to great effect in marketing its massively multiplayer online (MMO) games. (See Figure 8.5.) The company monitored forums and generated reports based on general player feedback

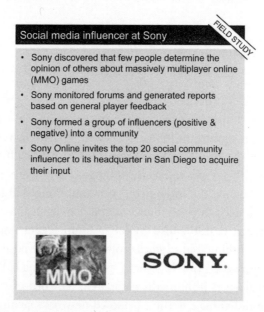

FIGURE 8.5 Sony Uses Social Media to "Influence the Influencers."

and ultimately formed a group of influencers into its own community. Sony invites the top 20 social community influencers to its American headquarters in San Diego to get feedback on how the company can improve its offerings and ways of interacting with customers.

"Pro-sumer" Product Development Collaboration

Although we discussed this in Chapter 7, it's worth touching on again in the context of social media sales and marketing strategies. Engaging passionate niche customer bases to shape new products and/or product extensions is a recipe for successful products and loyal customers. These overly engaged product users ("pro-sumers") hidden in a company's customer base bring a unique perspective on broad uses for a product, exactly what differentiates the product from the next one on the shelf, and what new products or features would appeal to members of their group. Most often, finding them can be as simple as asking them to identify themselves via a company's web site or social media community sites.

Toy manufacturer LEGO, for example, runs several online communities geared toward different customer bases. One is the "ambassadors' forum," which comprises customers between the ages of 19 and 65 from more than 20 countries who provide feedback on LEGO products. The most interesting and promising ideas from the group are fed to the company's new product development team. "We obviously don't have big social platforms with millions of users like Facebook or LinkedIn, but our LEGO brand communities are definitely an important complement to our research and development programs," notes Tormod Askildsen, head of LEGO community development.[10] In one instance, a community was requesting a more advanced product. Inspired by its customers' ideas, LEGO created a sophisticated model, priced at $300, which sold out in five weeks.

The yearlong campaign by Mountain Dew also demonstrates how involving customers via social media in the development of new products can incite fierce customer passion. Under the banner "DEWmocracy 2," Mountain Dew enlisted its social media fan base to help develop and roll out three new flavors. The company issued a request to all fans for proposals on why they should be chosen to be a part of the team. The top 50 applications were given instructions to test seven different flavors and shoot videos chronicling their tasting adventures. Mountain Dew then selected the top three flavors—Mountain Dew® Distortion™, Mountain Dew® White Out™, and Mountain

Dew® Typhoon™—and created what it called Flavor Nations for each of the three. Each nation then was put fully in charge of branding and promoting its respective flavor—including label design, color, agency selection, and creative approval. Each nation has its own community on Facebook and Twitter to help them spread the word.[11]

Engaging the Advocates

Advocates differ from influencers and pro-sumers in a subtle but important way. Although influencers are looking for the "best" to pass along to their followers and pro-sumers actually are engaging a company primarily on their own behalf, advocates represent a constituency—consumers, buyers, sellers, patients, citizens, and so on—looking either to effect change or to protect themselves from change. They serve as lightning rods between organizations (e.g., companies, governments, and political parties) and networks of concerned or vulnerable people. Recognizing these lightning rods, engaging them, and managing them can be just as important to a successful social media strategy as seeking out and appealing to influencers.

The earliest examples of this involve fundraising—most notably, Barack Obama's 2008 U.S. presidential campaign. The Obama campaign clearly understood the power of social media to organize supporters to spread Obama's message—and used social media to much greater effect than his opponent, Senator John McCain. Consider that by the time the election rolled around in November 2008, Obama had 5 million "friends" across 15 different social networks.[12] He had some 3 million supporters on Facebook—nearly four times as many as McCain—and 23 times more followers on Twitter. Furthermore, Obama's YouTube campaign videos were seen by 50 million viewers—four times as many as McCain's—to the tune of 14 million hours. Many pundits have credited this mobilization of advocates in the social media arena as one of the keys to Obama's ultimately winning the election, and it since has served as a blueprint for many subsequent campaigns.

This practice also has cropped up in niche social communities that blend advocacy and contemporary business practices. For example, xigi.net touts itself as "the creative commons where people who want to be involved or learn more about investing for good will hopefully come together to house their collective market intelligence and thinking." In other words, xigi.net provides a forum for advocates of capital investments in "good" programs, with "good" being defined by their communities.

In short, appealing to advocates has a major ripple effect, potentially increasing the social status of a company or creating business opportunities on a far broader scale.

The preceding examples show how leading companies are tapping in to social media to build bonds with consumers that heretofore were difficult or impossible to create. But the only risk greater than assuming these examples can be copied quickly is the risk of getting started without a clear plan in place to integrate the marketing and sales teams.

Putting the Plan in Place

Although the marketing and sales strategies can vary, we believe there are three common levels of maturity that any company should follow to "join the conversation" and begin using social media for marketing and selling. (See Figure 8.6.) Each level is dependent on an increasing level of customer insight but also results in deeper and more profitable customer relationships.

Level 1: Leverage—Listen and Respond!

At the outset, a company is best served by listening to the conversations being held in social media outlets. By joining existing social communities,

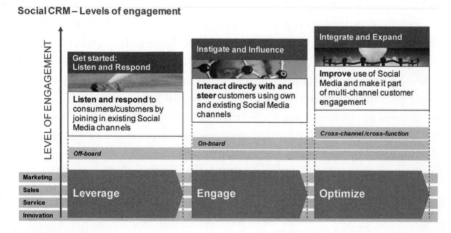

FIGURE 8.6 Three Levels of Maturity that Companies Go Through to Join the Conversation.

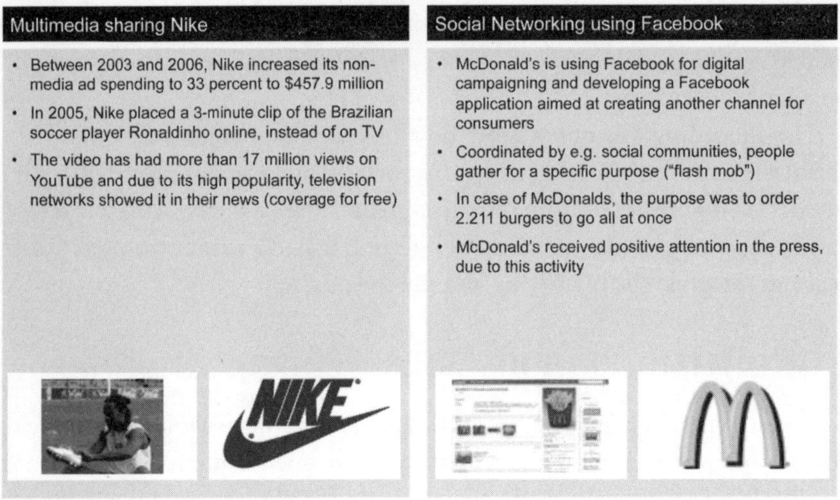

Multimedia sharing Nike

- Between 2003 and 2006, Nike increased its non-media ad spending to 33 percent to $457.9 million
- In 2005, Nike placed a 3-minute clip of the Brazilian soccer player Ronaldinho online, instead of on TV
- The video has had more than 17 million views on YouTube and due to its high popularity, television networks showed it in their news (coverage for free)

Social Networking using Facebook

- McDonald's is using Facebook for digital campaigning and developing a Facebook application aimed at creating another channel for consumers
- Coordinated by e.g. social communities, people gather for a specific purpose ("flash mob")
- In case of McDonalds, the purpose was to order 2.211 burgers to go all at once
- McDonald's received positive attention in the press, due to this activity

FIGURE 8.7 Nike and McDonald's Use Social Media to Broaden Their Reach to Consumers.

companies can benefit from an inexpensive method of gaining base-level, but still highly valuable, customer insight.

A company first should identify and monitor customer platforms that already exist, where the company, products, or brands are being discussed (such as communities, blogs, or forums), then analyze data or statements gleaned from those conversations. Using these early insights, a company can pinpoint initial opportunities for service or product improvement initiatives.

Once it is comfortable listening, a company can begin interacting with existing communities. A good starting point is to join relevant discussions (on, e.g., a blog) to which the company can add information that enhances the conversation. At this point, the company also should create a presence on one of the major social networking communities, such as Facebook or MySpace, and upload videos (especially company ads) and photos to relevant communities including YouTube and Flickr. (See Figure 8.7.)

Level 2: Engage—Instigate and Influence!

In Level 2, a company is ready to build its own network—to establish its own customized community to learn from customers and actively promote products and brands. (See Figure 8.8.) In creating such a community, a company

Social Community Network on eBay
FIELD STUDY

- eBay established a social community network on their corporate website that is made up of eBay members, buyers, and sellers, as well as eBay staff
- The eBay community encourages open and honest communication among all its members (respect and communication are the cornerstones of the dynamic community)
- The community page serves as a valuable information hub and provides several resources (e.g. chat rooms, answer center, discussion boards, eBay blogs, etc.) to help members to be informed about the latest events, programs, and news
- Therefore, many issues or enquiries can be solved directly without engaging the customer care department
- However, eBay does not use any available data to analyze customer needs in an appropriate manner

FIGURE 8.8   eBay Has Established a Robust Online Community for Its Buyers, Sellers, and Staff.

either should integrate it with the corporate web site or create it as a stand-alone site with a link to the corporate site. Once the community is active, it's critical for a company to interact with it—publishing content, executing activities, polling community members, providing new services, and the like. A tool kit for analyzing and monitoring data from the community is important for gauging how effective the community is and whether it's meeting the needs of members.

With its online community up and running, a company then should turn its attention to identifying and influencing the "lead dogs"—those members who wield the most influence and respect in the group. Applying social community analysis can help a company find these individuals and determine their relations and interactions with the community. These influencers can be identified via sophisticated analysis tools that scan and analyze existing online forums, responses to product or service requests, and quality of user reviews, or by simply tracking the ratings by members of the community. (Online communities are very effective at policing themselves.)

Once a company identifies the influencers, it should use them to seed the company's messages in the community and should create special marketing campaigns targeted specifically at influencers.

Level 3: Optimize—Integrate and Expand!

At the third level, a company is ready to use its social media presence to make it part of multi-channel customer engagement—developing strategies that engage and empower customers and business partners to participate in the company's day-to-day business operations. As part of this effort, a company starts by linking several platforms and integrating them with their digital and CRM applications. Next, they definine/execute a consistent cross-channel strategy, interactions, and customer experiences. Finally, they connect Social CRM with other functional areas (R&D, HR) as discussed in the opening chapter. This increasing level of integration across the enterprise provides the backbone for truly tailored experiences that will stand out from competitors.

Conclusion

As businesses everywhere have painfully recognized, consumers today clearly are in control of the buying process, and they're not afraid to let companies know it. They are making it increasingly difficult for companies to reach them, and when they do interact with a company, they want to call the shots—or, at minimum, feel that they have a voice in what the company is selling them and how it is selling it. That's why the marketing and sales approaches we laid out in this chapter are so important. They are proven ways for companies to engage consumers, to break through the physical and virtual walls that many consumers have erected around them and entice them with something that's meaningful and compelling *to them personally*. Would the Old Spice Guy have become such a sensation if he was just another pitch-man on television commercials? Would Mountain Dew have mobilized a rabid fan base to contribute ideas for flavors via magazine ads alone? Would Amazon have experienced such strong customer loyalty if it had only posted product information provided by manufacturers? It's difficult to answer these questions with certainty, but our experience and instincts say absolutely not.

We close this chapter with four actions companies should consider as they determine how best to use social media to improve their ability to strongly connect with consumers.

1. **It's critical for companies to pick a strategy before a strategy picks them.** A company must set the tone of its approach to selling via social

media instead of being forced into action by a competitor's approach or having to reset marketplace expectations as a result of random, failed pilots across the organization.

2. **Companies must consciously select the level of engagement they are starting with (e.g., listen, engage, influence, lever), and then rally the marketing and selling organizations around that level.** Clear alignment will provide a basis for what social media consumers can expect from a company while beginning to build trust and engagement.

3. **Companies must focus marketing and sales on the same outcomes.** As we discussed in Chapter 3, having agreement on what the company wants to achieve from its social media efforts, and then putting in place the appropriate metrics to gauge performance toward those goals, will help keep trials, pilots, and campaigns focused and consistent while minimizing the chances of marketing and sales working at cross-purposes.

4. **Companies should nurture ideas in the market that may take longer to reach payback while expecting some failure along the way.** Just as a strong friendship between two people does not happen overnight, it will take time for a company to build credibility and trust among its social media fans and followers. But when it does, the rewards will be worth the effort.

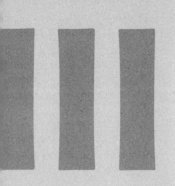

Customer Service and Support with Social Media

9 Using Social Media in Customer Service and Support

Stephanie Sadowski

CHAPTER HIGHLIGHTS

As customers increasingly expect service on their terms, customer "flare-ups" in social media are most likely to involve some aspect of a company's service and support. As many well-known examples show, these "flare-ups" are a ticking time bomb that must be dealt with proactively.

The ways in which customer service is being delivered via social media—for example, customers helping other customers in online forums—can enrich the customer experience. However, to do so, it must be tightly integrated with a company's traditional service and support functions.

Imagine this scenario: A friend buys a new car that she is very excited about. Just two days later, several mechanical problems emerge. She calls the dealer and demands a different car, not a repair of the one she bought. The dealer says no. She argues with the person who sold her the car, takes it to his boss (who is just as uncooperative), and then calls the regional manager of the auto company. No help there either. The traditional customer service channels have failed.

Not happy with what she's heard, she turns to Facebook. "Does anyone know anyone who works for this car company and who can help me get what

I want (a different car)?" she writes in the "What's on Your Mind" box atop her Facebook "wall." Sure enough, she gets lots of responses—several dozen, in fact, since she has more than 1,000 Facebook friends. The most important advice is from a friend of a friend who works for the automobile manufacturer. Although he isn't in customer service, he offers to help. "Oh my gosh! I am so embarrassed," he says on her Facebook page. "Let me see if I can get it taken care of for you." Within a week, the issue is resolved. The dealer swaps another car for the one she had driven off the lot.

This is a real story. But how real could it be for a company? How many companies can respond as fast as this automaker did to an irate customer who uses social media to vent her venom? Those that can't should beware and prepare to get tarnished by numerous customers who can air their frustration with dozens, hundreds, and sometimes thousands of other friends and online acquaintances with just a few keystrokes. Social media has changed the face of customer service and support forever. Every company must be prepared to respond effectively yet without giving away the store.

With social networking sites like Facebook, product review pages on a growing number of retailer web sites, video sites such as YouTube that allow consumers to poke fun at the companies they buy from, and other social media tools, customers have a louder voice now. That is good for the consumer and often bad for the companies that sell them products or services. Before social media, customers had little choice but to go through the customer service channels that a company established: the phone, e-mail, its web site, and so on. Its processes for requesting service or filing complaints (or compliments, we must add) were rigid. If the customer failed to get the relief he was seeking, that was typically the end of it—unless the customer wanted to register a complaint with the Better Business Bureau (BBB), file a lawsuit, or take the issue to state authorities. Most do not. In fact, the U.S. BBB received only 26,019 complaints on new cars in 2009.[1] That translates to complaints on approximately one-half of a percent of new cars purchased that year.[2]

But social media changes all that. Customers have the digital equivalent of a soapbox and a megaphone at their disposal—and, in many cases, an audience of hundreds or thousands. And they can get on their soapbox and talk into the megaphone easily and quickly. If a company's prescribed service resolution process doesn't satisfy the customer, she can take a very easy escalation path to the masses—thus becoming an "aggressive consumer activist."

Before the advent of the Web and social media, consumers' ability to spread negative feedback about a company or its products/services was very limited—that is, to the people they came in contact with. Creating a groundswell of consumer opposition to a company was very difficult. At the very least, it took a lot of time. That didn't change all that much in the 1990s, the early days of the Web. The Internet did give consumers a new way to vent their frustrations with companies—but only if they were tech-savvy enough to set up their own Web pages. But even if they could, getting people to those Web pages wasn't easy. Any individual's e-mail contact list is only so long.

Today's Web is much different. Plenty of services allow even the most technically deficient person to set up her own web site. And consumers don't have to create their own platform and e-mail campaign to rail against companies. The three biggest social networking sites—LinkedIn, Facebook, and Twitter (all launched in the past decade)—give consumers a ready-made soapbox from which to air their grievances. And the more memorable they make their complaints—for example, through entertaining videos, presentations, or podcasts—the more likely those complaints are to "go viral." That's word of mouth on steroids.

Companies that don't act quickly to contain consumer outrage fanned through social media can watch their brand reputations get tarnished rapidly. In 2007, a video gamer's song that trashed the Sony PlayStation 3 game console ("How to Kill a Brand") became a heavily watched YouTube video (5.5 million views). In February 2010, an irate airline passenger took Southwest Airlines to task through Twitter. Kevin Smith, a heavyset Hollywood film director, was kicked off a Southwest plane parked at Oakland International Airport because his body extended over more than one seat on a packed flight. (Smith often books two seats when flying.) He railed at Southwest through more than 200 Twitter posts and a podcast. The problem for Southwest was that Smith had many Twitter followers—1.6 million by one estimate. At first, the company kept its response to Smith private. But soon it was forced to use its own blog and Twitter account to explain its seating policies.

Both of the preceding companies have survived these social media flare-ups. And, no doubt, they're better prepared for the next social media consumer attack. However, being unprepared is no longer an option. Companies must now play "defense" against the "offense" of such aggressive consumer activism. But they can't if they aren't listening to the social media chatter.

(We explore in more detail how organizations can learn about and respond effectively to negative customer sentiments in Chapter 10.)

For companies that have been scrambling to tap in to social media to hear the voice of the customer, this is not new. And although many companies are doing so to respond to customer complaints as well as to collaborate more extensively with customers in designing new products and new web sites, these are the early days. Social media has ushered in a world of transparency and collaboration. Managers are only beginning to transform the cultures of their organizations to deal with it.

The now-famous story of the Canadian country musician (Dave Carroll) whose YouTube video rallied against United Airlines for damaging his guitar in 2009—one year later, 8.7 million views and counting—should be a chilling reminder to every organization. When customers can share their stories with millions of other customers in hours or days, companies must be able to react competently. The potential to damage even the strongest of brands is now immense.

What's even more interesting about the Dave Carroll experience is that initially he didn't set out to chastise United in an open, global forum. Rather, he began simply by "following the rules" and adhering to the established protocol for trying to get attention to his plight. However, doing so got him nowhere. Thus, it was only after a nine-month odyssey of placing calls to the airline and speaking to increasingly "more important" people there—and ultimately receiving a final no to his request for compensation for his loss—did he turn to social media. And unfortunately for United, the company had no way of predicting his action—or the actions of similar customers out there who are social media "ticking time bombs" like Carroll.

Emboldened by the Dave Carrolls of the world who have taken to the social media "airwaves" to file their grievances, more and more customers are casting a wide net to see if anyone will respond to their concerns. Customers increasingly expect enterprises to be responsive to the things said about them in Facebook, Twitter, and other social media outlets. If companies are well prepared to respond to these social media channels, they can address issues quickly and effectively. In fact, a well-designed response delivered quickly through the same channels can enhance a firm's brand.

However, too many companies aren't prepared as an increasing number of customers use social media as their service channel of choice. They stand by as customers gain online allies in frustration and erode a firm's reputation.

The Early Going: Days of Missteps and Missed Chances

Social media sites such as Facebook, Twitter, and LinkedIn have generated massive audiences in the past few years. Thus, it might be unfair to expect corporations to be totally prepared to handle the barrage of customer complaints that are filling up the Web these days. However, even many companies that were the first to respond to social media often have stumbled.

Why? The first reason is that they have applied a one-size-fits-all customer service model across every customer segment and response channel including social media. They view social media in the same way as they view the phone, fax, e-mail, or their web site. They see it as just one more way for customers to contact them. And, as a result, these companies use the same complaint-handling processes for social media, and that's where the struggle begins. Companies quickly find they can't respond fast enough or appropriately without dramatically increasing their resources. The one-size-fits-all model doesn't factor in the speed with which the social media complainant wants an answer. People who use Twitter, Facebook, or another social channel regard timeliness as far more important than getting a polished answer. The complaint-resolution policies of most companies are anything but speedy.

In addition, the one-size-fits-all model typically means that each channel is offered the same information. Some companies have a philosophy of making all the capabilities for one customer feedback channel available to all their channels—call centers, e-mail, regular mail correspondence, and so on. This makes adding a new channel expensive and time consuming because everything must be accessible for all people. It often forces customers to plow through volumes of information and options that cover all possible service issues to register a complaint. Maintaining all channels equally becomes expensive and onerous, and often is not necessary; many customers don't need it.

The second reason why many companies are floundering with social media is they have tried to handle the burden of responding effectively themselves. They become daunted by the expense and number of people they believe they must hire to respond to thousands or even millions of customer messages coming through social media. And yet they don't realize that outsiders may be as capable as their own employees in answering customer questions. These companies shy away from using as part of their service capability the people who spend time on social networks and love their brands. They worry about the risks to security, corporate culture, and brand reputation from enlisting the help of outsiders.

Other companies fall down in responding to the social media chatter because their left hand doesn't know what the right hand is doing. In many organizations, sales, marketing, and service are autonomous functions that don't work closely with one other. For example, customer service employees may be on top of a product quality issue that customers are sounding off on in Facebook, and yet marketing may continue to operate as if there is no problem at all, running ads that don't address the issue. One major bank's human resources function made a big splash on Facebook and other social media sites about what a great place it was to work. But unfortunately, at the very same time the economy soured and the firm was beginning to lay off thousands of people.

In this way, social media shortens the time companies have to respond to a product, service quality, or other issue, and it heightens the need to take a coordinated response. With social media threatening to expose hypocritical corporate policies, the functions of service, marketing, and sales must get on the same page.

Learning from the Best

Despite the numerous missteps in the marketplace, a number of companies have successfully incorporated social media into their customer service models. From our research and consulting experience, these firms share seven common practices:

1. Defining a unique customer service channel strategy for social customer relationship management
2. Understanding the investment period to build this channel
3. Getting marketing, sales, and service to bring a unified channel
4. Creating online communities that enable customers to help other customers
5. Allowing many employees be a face to the customer, not just a few
6. Continually improving their social CRM channel
7. Using the social channel to surprise and delight customers

In exploring each practice, we use real-life examples of companies that have put them to work.

Defining a Unique Social CRM Channel

The best companies at using social media in service carve out a special channel strategy for customers who use the technology to talk about and interact with their suppliers. These companies intimately understand which of their customers use social media, what they value, the type of information they seek, and what kinds of transactions will have an impact on them.

Consider a retail bank. The kinds of service issues that customers who use social media will take to the bank are likely to be different than those of customers who don't use social media. For example, senior citizens are less apt to use Facebook or Twitter to complain about the bank than are customers in their twenties. Furthermore, the types of transactions that a senior citizen might call the bank about are not necessarily the same ones a 22-year-old would conduct through Twitter. Companies need to first understand what types of customers interact with it through social media. Then they need to determine what kinds of transactions will have the greatest impact on those customers.

Managers may find that some types of customer complaints or inquiries should be addressed through social media while others may require a different service channel. For example, it may be entirely acceptable to let a service agent handle a Twitter request through a return phone call. For instance, when Carnival Cruise Lines receives a tweet from a travel agent asking about promotions or discounts, its customer service team redirects the conversation to e-mail or phone to provide follow-up information. If a social media request is fielded through another channel, the request must be handled quickly and responsively. The fact that it came through a social media channel determines the speed with which it must be resolved: fast. A great example of this is JetBlue, the $3 billion, fast-growing U.S. airline. The company's reservation agents are largely work-at-home mothers. The airline recently has incorporated Twitter into their duties. Agents immediately follow-up on complaints via Twitter and get customer phone numbers and e-mails for response where appropriate. They also tweet information on flight delays ("Air Traffic Control is regulating the volume of incoming and outbound flights at JFK and weather is playing a part"), and help promote specials ("The Tour de France starts tomorrow & we're waiving bike fees until 7.30.10").

Investing to Build the Social Media Service Channel

Managers who hope they can save money by shifting call center, e-mail, and other customer traffic to a social media service channel are likely to be disappointed, at least in the short term. Most companies will need to invest in a social media channel without expecting other channel costs to fall. In fact, at first a company's social media channel probably will increase the number of service transactions it handles. In fact, we believe the approach taken by Joe Marchese, president of SocialVibe, to resolve a bad experience with JetBlue's rewards program is a typical one:

> The first thing I did was call JetBlue's customer service, where, after going through a phone automated system, I was put on hold to wait for a customer service rep. While on hold, I submitted my problem through JetBlue's online form. Still on hold, I turned to Twitter. I sent a tweet out with my issue, and before I got through to a customer service rep on the phone, I had two responses. One was from @JetBlue; the other was from a Twitter connection who didn't even work for JetBlue, suggesting that I send a note to @MatrySG, JetBlue's digital-savvy senior vice president of marketing.
>
> Still on hold with customer service, I was already discussing my issue with @JetBlue and giving someone the details of my situation. When I finally got through to phone customer service, I already knew what the issue was, and the phone rep wasn't able to help me. In the end @JetBlue was actually able to help me resolve the issue and turn a very negative situation into a very positive experience. Even if they hadn't been able to help me (because the situation was totally my fault in the end, for not fully reading the rewards policy when I first signed up), the detail and speed with which they were able to address my problem would have made a huge difference to my perception of how JetBlue values me as a consumer. The best part is I was able to go about my Sunday watching the World Cup in Manhattan's East Village with friends, while getting updates from @JetBlue over Twitter DM and having a conversation with Jet's Blue's Marty—who was poolside himself.:-)"[3]

At the same time companies must continue to deal with customers who don't use social media the traditional way, they need to build a social media channel to attract and retain customers from the "Net Generation"—people who are Web savvy, social media literate, and allergic to traditional contact channels. For companies with lots of Net Generation customers, creating a social media channel is not optional. Social media channels are a natural extension of how this generation communicates. Those customers expect it and will defect to competitors if it's not available.

We've seen this kind of behavior before. In the late 1990s, many established companies were forced to create Web channels for customers who preferred dealing with a web site to e-mail or call centers. They built quite elaborate web sites with self-service capabilities (the ability to order products, log in maintenance, repair, and other service requests, post questions, etc.). It took one to two years before some of them began to see lower traffic at their contact centers. Some haven't seen any reductions at all. In these companies, the web site channel has merely increased the number of customers who contact them, and the number of contacts. We predict social CRM will follow a similar path.

Ultimately, the rate of customer adoption of social media channels will depend on how aggressively a company attracts people to the new channel and how satisfied they are in using it the first time. An organization can build the greatest social media channel in its industry. But if customers don't know about it, they are not likely to use it. Organizations have to *market* their new social CRM capabilities.

If a company makes customers aware of its new social media channel but isn't prepared to deal with the crush of traffic, customers will become frustrated. That could erode the company's brand. In contrast, if customers have a positive experience in the social media channels a company builds for them, they will return. Eventually, a company will be able to build a predictable model for staffing and support, for both social media and contact center channels.

Unifying Marketing, Sales, and Service

We said earlier that social media requires getting marketing, sales, and service on the same page more than ever. To create a unified channel to the customer rather than autonomous silos, managers must take three actions. The first is keeping customers "in the know" in real time. A company must market new products, new service policies, and the like through social media. The $3 billion fast-food chain Chick-fil-A, whose 1,500 restaurants generate an average $3 million a year[4] (more than the average McDonald's outlet), used Facebook in a new product launch to increase store traffic. (The firm had more than 1.7 million Facebook fans as of July 2010.) It created a marketing campaign for people who were Facebook fans of the firm, enticing them to come in early and try its new spicy chicken sandwich. The Facebook campaign created a strong buzz that got younger customers in the doors. The campaign was done entirely through Facebook, text messages, and other social channels.

Several companies have addressed the real-time demands of customers who complain through social media by creating agents who are empowered to resolve such problems. These agents are able to take more action than the typical contact center employee who creates a "ticket" and hands it off to someone else to investigate. Empowered agents have the tools and authority to resolve many problems on their own. An agent position created by Comcast, a $35 billion provider of television, Internet, and other services in the United States, to handle Twitter traffic is a case in point. Comcast's "Twitter Man" (Frank Eliason) was successful because he could resolve customer complaints, many of them on the spot.[5] Something similar has been going on at Wells Fargo & Co., one of America's largest banks. Given the secure nature of the financial transactions being discussed via Twitter, many requests get referred to direct e-mail or phone calls for resolution. Nonetheless, Wells Fargo's social media agents have access to a higher level of tools for resolving customer issues than traditional bankers have. The company also has the right checks and balances to provide agents with more access and authority when necessary and yet still maintain security, privacy, and control.

Creating Online Communities that Let Customers Help Other Customers

Companies that see themselves as the only source to help customers solve their problems are setting themselves up for unnecessary expenses and headaches. This is especially the case in industries whose products or services need high levels of technical support (e.g., computer software) or in companies whose seasonal products result in being bombarded with questions in a concentrated period of time (e.g., barbecue equipment manufacturers in May and June with hundreds of customers wrestling with how to assemble the product). The problem with such companies' tech support—particularly those whose products are forever changing—is that the average contact center employee can't keep up with all the technical changes.

For these companies, social media can be a godsend. Companies that set up online communities enabling customers to talk to other customers can direct many questions to their knowledgeable users. In many cases, these people have more expertise than the own contact center agents of many firms. What's more, they often get more kicks out of helping fellow customers: They like feeling empowered, helping others, and getting the recognition that comes with being regarded as an expert. Social media is a tool that enables such power users to help others get fast response.

Power users are clearly something to capitalize on. However, they must be managed; a company doesn't want customers to provide bad advice, of course. But a number of companies have found ways to control their power users and help them provide good advice. One is Intuit, the $3 billion provider of tax software TurboTax. Intuit's contact centers are besieged with calls at tax time (January through April). Call center agents used to feel that they had to know everything. But the flurry of calls during tax season meant an increased risk that too many calls didn't get through or that quality went down and response time went up. One of Intuit's engineering leaders conceived the idea of embedding a user forum into the TurboTax product itself. Just five weeks into the initial test, one-third of the questions posed already had answers. Intuit founder Scott Cook noted that "crucially, our internal tax experts were pleased by the quality of the answers, which seemed to be self-correcting as other users refined them. TurboTax Live Community, as it's called, was the kind of clear success I'd been seeking. Live Community systems have spread to our other divisions and are inspiring more contribution experiments."[6] The firm has found that its power users are often more knowledgeable than its own agents and that they respond quickly. And like its own agents, the power users take pride in helping others.

As the Baby Boom generation continues to retire, the pool of power users will grow significantly. Retired people want to remain intellectually engaged—to solve problems (if not at 40 hours a week). Pharmaceutical giant Pfizer realized this in 2008 when it launched a crowdsourcing tool, Idea Farm, to gather input on a variety of research, manufacturing, and engineering challenges. The company uses the tool to solicit ideas from thousands of employees and outside partners whose brains it wants to tap. In some cases, Pfizer solicits free help. In other cases, it pays for weightier advice.

In another example, researcher William Dampier of Drexler University is taking a novel approach to HIV research. He is hosting a bioinformatics competition, which requires contestants to find markers in the HIV sequence that predict a change in the severity of the infection. The prize for the best idea is $500 and a publishing opportunity. More than 75 individuals and organizations from around the world submitted ideas.[7]

Expanding the Face to the Customer

The fifth hallmark of companies that have excelled in using social media in customer service is an expansive view of who can deal with customers. In these companies, the customer service "face" includes anyone who works for the company and participates in social CRM. These tend to be employees in influential positions—that is, managers who stand to be the most embarrassed by a service failure.

It doesn't just have to be the head of customer service, product development, or marketing. It can be any employee who is knowledgeable about a certain issue and can get something done about it quickly. Consider, for example, a recent service experience that put UPS on *BusinessWeek*'s 2009 "Extreme Customer Service" list. The *BusinessWeek* writer ordered an oversize product from Target that was to be delivered via UPS by 9:00 one evening. As it approached 9:00 P.M. and the package hadn't arrived, he posted on Twitter about waiting for UPS and mentioned how he couldn't walk his dog as a result. The writer got a message from Tony Hsieh, chief executive of Zappos, who happened to follow the writer's tweets. Coincidentally Mr. Hsieh was having dinner with UPS's president for the western region. The UPS executive called within five minutes and then got in touch with a UPS operations manager to arrange for a delivery the next morning at 9:00 A.M. The doorbell rang promptly 9:00 A.M. The UPS delivery people had the package, flowers, chocolates, and treats and toys for the dog.[8]

Companies need to embrace the likelihood that customer service issues can be fielded by anyone in the organization who uses social media to stay connected to friends, relatives, and acquaintances. That means companies need an escalation process that every employee can use to get a customer's issue resolved. If it manages such grievances well, a company can markedly improve its reputation.

Continually Improving Social Media Monitoring and Resolution

Competitors continually raise the service bar. A one-day response to a problem becomes obsolete when rivals offer a two-hour response. Sixty-minute call waiting times become onerous when competitors guarantee five-minute times. It's no different for customer service delivered through social media. A company can design the best process for handling Twitter messages, and it will last only a few months before a competitor offers something better.

Managers not only need to watch how competitors are upping the ante in social CRM. They need to keep their eyes on whether customers are bypassing their traditional service channels and going straight to Facebook, Twitter, or some other social channel to be heard. If that's happening with increasing frequency, it could mean that call centers, e-mail response teams, or other traditional service channels need to be improved. If a company can close the gaps in performance, it will have fewer customers who are escalating issues through social media and exposing their ire to the world. Those who contact the company through social media will simply be those who prefer this channel of communication.

According to Microsoft, the key is reducing what the company calls *customer effort*. "The faster I can get a solution to the customer, the better," explains Toby Richards, General Manager for Community Support Services and the MVP Program. "That might be time to response or better search optimization to [reveal] the right answer. Customer effort is a whole category of measurement that we are looking at, both for the phone and for our online and social media techniques. And we've actually been [working] on establishing some baselines on the topic of improving or reducing customer effort because if you reduce customer effort, it's statistically proven to improve company loyalty."

Surprising and Delighting the Customer

The companies that are mastering social media in customer service are going beyond damage control. They are proactively warning customers about pending issues, alerting them so they can change their plans. Informing customers in real time what they need to do can smooth out peaks in customer service calls. It can also give the company a loud and positive voice in moments that could turn greatly negative.

This is about using social media to surprise and delight customers. Several airlines have taken the lead here. They offer texting services that notify people of changes in their flights and gate information before the flight departs. Rather than having customers travel to the airport only to find their flight has been canceled, airlines are notifying passengers through text messaging and making suggestions on new flights.

Every company has the same ability to do this through social CRM channels—the barbecue equipment manufacturer with a defective product, the tax software company with a fix to a product bug, or the cable TV operator that issues a text message about when service will be restored. The goal is to proactively inform customers so that they know what's going on in real time, especially when an unexpected event will change their plans. Increasingly, with cell phones, smart phones, and other mobile devices becoming ubiquitous, there is no better way to reach customers wherever they are than through social media that connects to such devices.

Managers who create effective social media channels will indeed increase customer satisfaction. But the biggest gains in satisfaction, and the biggest sources of operational efficiencies, require getting out in front of service problems. Social media provides a highly effective early warning system of customer issues before they become full-blown crises. Insurance company USAA for years has done a great job of anticipating customer needs before they surface. For example, through Twitter (http://twitter.com/USAA), USAA lets customers know about tools for managing personal spending, tips for surviving storms, advice on talking to adult children about financial matters, and guidance on how to prepare their children going off to college months before they exit for State U. It also offers an accident checklist iPhone application that guides customers through the process from reporting the accident to securing a rental car.

Deciding how to use social media in customer service and support begins with a plan, just as it does for using the technology in any part of an organization. Managers must determine their target audience, how to meet their needs, and where to invest: what kinds of customer interactions and processes will yield the biggest bang for the buck. Once they craft the plan, they then must do the hard work of empowering employees and power users to handle customers who arrive through social media.

As more and more customers use social media channels to connect to their product and service providers, companies must learn to balance supply and demand. Diving into these channels without being prepared to deal with a crush of traffic could be disastrous, just as is setting up an elaborate operational capability that customers don't need.

But one thing is for sure: Doing nothing with social media in customer service is an even bigger risk. The time has come for companies to exploit social media and better tap the expertise of their employees and customers. Those who do will wonder how they ever relied on their call centers alone to make customers happy.

Microsoft Leads the Way in Using Social Media for Service and Support

Although many companies continue to struggle to determine how best to use social media to assist customers, software giant Microsoft has taken major strides to transform its customer service and support organization using social media.

A conversation with Toby Richards, who heads up Microsoft's communities and online support initiatives, revealed some of the key factors that have enabled Microsoft not only to complement traditional service and support channels with social media but, in some cases, make social media the primary means through which the company addresses customer issues.

"One of the core functions in our support organization is to be the premier listening organization for the company," explained Richards. "We have about 2.3 billion service interactions in a given fiscal year, and the amount of data that can come from those interactions for Microsoft to improve its products, programs, and customer experiences is tremendous. We embrace social media as a way in which we can listen to a set of conversations that we really never had access to before."

(continued)

(*continued*)

Indeed, Richards said that of the 2.3 billion service interactions the company handles each year, only approximately 5 percent are conducted via phone; the rest happen online.

Richards reflected on some of the things Microsoft has done or experienced during its quest to incorporate social media into its customer service and support activities.

The mix of support interactions has changed dramatically by adding social media channels. Microsoft has been on the leading edge of adding online communities to its mix of support interactions to make the support experience more pleasant and effective. "We acknowledge that there's a great amount of [expertise] out there that's not just in our support organization," said Richards. The challenge is collecting and harnessing that expertise. According to Richards, in the past three years, Microsoft's community question-and-answer (Q&A) support has grown approximately 50 percent per year in both volume of use and budget. Importantly, he noted the volume of the community Q&A is 20 times the amount of calls Microsoft receives in a year—or 1 billion customer transactions on the Q&A site versus approximately 50 million inquiries to the call center. "The mix has changed dramatically from just four years ago, where our business was primarily about a big call center type of business," said Richards. "Now we're really looking at a different mix of support resources."

Social media requires different skill sets from support people. Microsoft quickly recognized that social media introduces new challenges in terms of the roles and skills of its employees who provide service and support. "For the past three years, we've differentiated our support roles along two [types of people]," said Richards. "You're either a person on the phone or you're one of our online or social media people. And I would say the skills and roles are very different between the two." The first is what Richards called very "break/fix" oriented. The traditional call center person typically is geared toward trying to solve a customer's problem as quickly as possible and operates under the assumption that by the time a customer has called the company, he or she is fairly upset. In the second instance, support employees typically are dealing with a customer in a different mind-set—a person who is not necessarily in a quandary or looking for an immediate solution to a problem. Instead, people using social media are learning, searching, and educating themselves—and typically respond well to a more conversational interaction. Richards said that Microsoft currently is studying ways to "bridge the divide" between these two groups to enable traditional phone engineers to become effective in providing support via social media. "The area of skills and competencies needed to work in the social media space have been a fairly significant area of learning for us," Richards admitted.

It's critical to identify and manage influencers and subject matter experts effectively. Providing effective service and support at Microsoft requires a high degree of specialized and often technical knowledge. Thus, knowing who has that knowledge—and determining the best way to bring that knowledge to bear on customers' problems—is vital. Microsoft has found that the most knowledgeable people can come from either inside the company or outside it among the customer base at large. The key, Richards said, is recognizing and rewarding those "experts" who are not Microsoft employees so they are motivated and incented to do more. At Microsoft, that takes the form of its Most Valuable Professional program, which today includes 4,000 technical experts in the Microsoft community. "When people who are starting to explore using social media in service have asked me what they should do, one of the things I'd tell them is they have to think about the top people in communities," said Richards. "These are the people customers listen to, whom you deem as expert, and in whom you have a level of trust that they could moderate conversations." Richards said it's critical that a company has a formal way—a platform— for engaging with and managing that subset of influencers and experts. At Microsoft, this platform includes a ratings and recognition system that enables the company to reward those who are participating and increasing their level of engagement. Importantly, Richards noted that such a platform and approach also must work "with the masses so you can identify the up-and-comers as well."

The team handling Twitter responses needs resources and support. The Microsoft Twitter team involves only a dozen or so people. Thus,

(continued)

(*continued*)

they can't be expected to be expert on all aspects of every Microsoft product. "You've got to enable them in such a way that they can either get to the right person based on internal reputation or expertise, or they can get to the knowledge base and search it in such a way that they can get their answer," said Richards. (In fact, Richards said having a robust knowledge management capability is step number one in using social media for service. "If you don't have that, you can't scale.") And how the team communicates their answers also is critical. "We never answer the question in Twitter," Richards explained. "We always point [customers] to a knowledge-based article on the Web or a question-and-answer page in our community forums. Or if that doesn't exist, we actually ask the question on their behalf in the forums, and we include the link to where they would find the answer when somebody actually answers it." His reasoning is that because the nature of social media is one of community, Microsoft would not be doing the community justice by just answering a question one on one. "If you provide answers in such a way that the accurate answer can be searched and found again, making sure that you lead people to the one version of truth, it's a much more effective way of engaging," Richards said.

A company needs to formally designate people to make sure there's one version of the truth. "We're trying to be pretty cautious to ensure that we're pointing people to the one version of truth as much as possible and that that one version of truth is managed by our knowledge management platform," said Richards. Two ways Microsoft does this are providing the ability to correct inaccuracies and enabling people to rate the usefulness of guidance or answers. "If something's wrong, let's correct it," said Richards. "In our Tech Net site for IT professionals, for example, we added wiki functionality to the knowledge-based articles so people could either make corrections or add color commentary, such as how a solution might be applied in a particular market." By enabling users to indicate whether they liked an answer or found it helpful, Microsoft can help build trust and highlight the "right" answers. "The answer from the guy with five stars versus the answer from the guy with one star might actually make a difference," said Richards. "So if you can expose that, it helps point customers to the truth." Of course, managing the truth on external sites the company doesn't control is more difficult, but the principles remain the same: knowing who the influencers and experts are and supporting those people. Richards said that such individuals generally help police answers and conversations to keep things on track and minimize inaccuracies. "It's in everybody's best interest for somebody to chime in and say 'Oh, no, that's not right.' It really normalizes and works itself out as people participate and rate the answers."

10 Social Media: Responding to Customer Complaints

Todd R. Wagner

CHAPTER HIGHLIGHTS

In the world of social media, a company assuredly will encounter negative sentiments about it and its offerings. Thus, it needs to prepare itself for how to respond before it becomes necessary so it is ready to mute the impact of any online flare-ups.

A company must resist the urge to respond to everything. Some negative messages are more important and potentially damaging than others, so it's critical for companies to have a framework for prioritizing which messages to respond to and identifying the type of response each will receive.

In Chapter 9, we discussed the ways in which social media is impacting companies' service and support organizations and how companies can use social media to deliver a more enriching service experience. In this chapter, we explore more deeply the topic of how companies can handle negative sentiments that customers and noncustomers express about them via social media.

Indeed, customer complaints always have been a source of corporate angst. Whether they come through the mail or an e-mail box, the headsets of call center reps, or a salesperson's voice-mail, messages from unhappy customers put companies on the defensive and can pose a threat to an organization's sales and reputation.

However, companies also recognize that complaints are a fact of life. They know they will likely fail to please all the people all the time and that some percentage of their customers will have something negative to say about the organization or its offerings. Thus, to reduce the risk of having unhappy customers spread the word about their bad experiences to workmates, friends, and family, many organizations have established sophisticated processes and systems to answer customer objections. Special e-mail boxes, call center processes and training for handling difficult customers, and escalation routines for dealing with the toughest ones have become commonplace.

Yet customer ire also can be a wellspring of ideas for organizational improvement—*if* a company has the right processes, systems, and skills in place to respond capably. The best companies use their complaint-handling processes actually to improve their products and services as well as the processes by which customers order, obtain, use, and get help with their purchases. Firms such as insurer USAA, department store chain Nordstrom, online broker Charles Schwab, luxury auto brand Lexus, and online shoe seller Zappos are renowned for the ways they deal with difficult customers and how they translate complaints into opportunities for improvement.

But just when companies think they have a handle on customer complaints, along comes social media. Suddenly, many existing problem-resolution procedures are inadequate to deal with a wave of Internet-propelled gripes that can tarnish a brand around the world in a matter of hours. Every day, millions of unhappy customers boot up their computers, click into social networking sites such as Facebook and Twitter, or comment on the proliferating number of product review sites. Some go even further to reach the masses, posting screeds on their own blogs or creating and placing videos on sites like YouTube. Although often entertaining, these rants can be poisonous to a company's reputation.

Customers who complain about companies through social media dramatically raise the stakes. And there's no stopping the trend because consumers' use of social media has exploded. In 2010, nearly half (48 percent) of Americans age 12 and older had a profile on one or more social networking sites, such as Facebook and LinkedIn, double the number in 2008, according to one study.[1] And usage has moved beyond just teenagers. About two-thirds (65 percent) of those between the ages of 25 and 34 belonged to such sites in 2010, and about half (51 percent) of those 35 to 44 took part in social networking sites as well.

According to the Nielsen Co., a global provider of information and measurement of consumer behavior, consumers around the world who used social networking sites spent an average of 5.5 hours on such sites in December 2009, nearly twice the time of a year earlier.[2] And a growing number of these consumers spout off about their bad product and service experiences. Some 20 percent of 1,040 American adults polled in April 2010 said they had used social media to share a negative experience with a product or service.[3] But those same people indicated they were hamstrung in defending the companies they work for against social media attacks: Nearly two-thirds (64 percent) said their firms lacked policies for talking about their organization on social networking sites.

Such statistics are no surprise to companies like Microsoft Corp. By 2009, call centers represented only about 5 percent of the software company's more than 2 billion customer service interactions, with 95 percent coming through social media and other online channels.[4]

This scenario creates a different set of challenges for companies. The first is that the customer interactions spawned by social media are truly out of their control. When they circulate around the world through social media, customer opinions go unfiltered and are made available to all. In this way, social media is the ideal soapbox for an irate customer—a medium that lets him "yell" at the top of his lungs at the top of a mountain and be heard around the world. Whether the beef is true or not, companies cannot control and quarantine it. Real product or service problems that could take months or years before regulators and the public noticed are revealed the moment a customer says "Enough."

The second sea change that social media brings to the world of customer management is speed. Customers who voice their complaints through social media can gain a big audience in little time. Customer complaints travel faster and more virally. With the posting of a blog or YouTube video, the complaint is lodged for the whole world to see. It immediately spreads to others who can pile on, sympathizing with the aggrieved party and perhaps even sharing their own similar experiences with that company. The now-famous incident in which Hollywood director Kevin Smith tweeted to more than 1 million followers about being forced off a Southwest Airlines plane because his heavy body required two seats has become the stuff of social media legend. So has "United Breaks Guitars" song (which, if Web views equaled song sales, already has achieved multiplatinum record status).

The third new challenge that social media brings is elevated customer expectations. Because not just one customer is aggrieved but dozens, thousands, or even millions, it dramatically raises the stakes. Resolution must come much faster, and it better work, lest a company risk sparking another digital firestorm of protest.

How Should Companies Respond?

The three new challenges that social media poses for companies—discussions out of their control, digitally captured negative sentiments that move at light speed, and heightened customer expectations—cannot be ignored. So what can managers do? How can they respond to the growing number of customer complaints coming at them through social media?

First, let's discuss what to avoid. Companies should avoid trying to exercise control over what consumers are saying and how quickly they're spreading their complaints. A restaurant chain can't ignore the customer who takes to YouTube, Facebook, or a review site like Yelp to lampoon her meal, the way a chain could have disregarded or thrown out the meal evaluation card she filled out in the past. (Who knows how many of those cards actually make their way to headquarters given that negative comments can only cast local restaurant managers in a bad light?) An airline no longer can count on missing baggage stories appearing in public only in the form of impersonal government statistics. Companies also should refrain from getting into public "shouting matches" with customers who post negative comments. Appearing to argue with a customer can only make matters worse.

Managers are unable to nip every social media complaint in the bud. It's impossible to monitor and respond to every grievance before it goes viral because there are just too many of them. That makes it infeasible to treat all social media discussion about a company with the same level of attention and response. An organization has to prioritize what it attends to.

Given these limitations, companies that want to effectively manage complaints generated via social media must focus on what to monitor and how to respond quickly and effectively. Doing so requires taking three actions:

1. Establishing criteria to determine which complaints to respond to and guidelines for how to respond.
2. Recognizing the different roles of employees who are willing and able to respond to social media-generated complaints.
3. Designing a measurement system to gauge how well the company is responding to social media complaints and a feedback loop for instituting necessary improvements.

All three actions are important. Taking one or two of them will get one only so far—early successes in cooling down simmering online skirmishes, followed by failures to head off new online attacks. Let's explore each one.

Establishing Criteria and Guidelines for Responding

Because a company is unable to respond to everything, it needs a way to filter out the noise and focus on the most serious social media complaints (e.g., those made by higher-value, loyal customers). A set of criteria such as the one in Figure 10.1 can be useful in that regard.

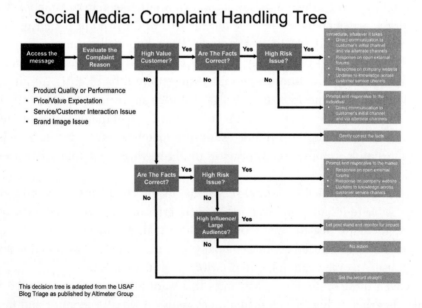

FIGURE 10.1 Complaint-Handling Decision Tree.

The first step in the process is understanding the nature of or reason for the complaint.

Are customers complaining about a product quality or performance issue—that the product fails to work properly or is broken? Or is it a failure to meet a customer's price or value expectation—the product fails to perform as advertised or as written on its box, or according to the salesperson's pitch? A consumer whose new car uses more gas than the miles per gallon advertised, or whose ink-jet cartridge prints 50 percent fewer pages than the box claimed, may feel ripped off. The promise was in black and white, and it was clearly broken.

In some cases, the promises are less explicit; they are consumers' interpretations of the value they would get. For example, how much better organized should a monthly planner make its owner? How does a company measure it? Other customers might have no complaints about the product but are irritated by some aspect of the process of buying it, paying for it, or getting it serviced. A cell phone company that makes it difficult for customers to decipher their billing charges has a problem not with the quality of the service—it might have a very low dropped-call rate—but rather with the way consumers pay their bills.

Brand issues pose a whole different type of problem. What we mean here are actions a company takes about things other than product performance or the way it services them—such as social business practices. One real example: A firm that sources products from low-cost countries whose manufacturers are publicly perceived to pay insufficient wages will have a big brand or image problem if enough customers rail about them on Facebook, YouTube, or Twitter about "exploitation" and attract great attention.

Once it has determined the nature of or reason for the complaint, a company needs to segment and determine which customer complaints to focus on. Three factors are especially important in making this determination. (See Figure 10.2.)

The first factor is the value of the complaining customer. Not all customers are created equal. Some generate far more revenue and profits over their lifetimes. Thus, when customers complain about a firm through social media, a company must determine how much they represent in terms of revenue, profitability, or lifetime value. A customer whose business with the company is large and growing is obviously more valuable that one whose business is small and declining.

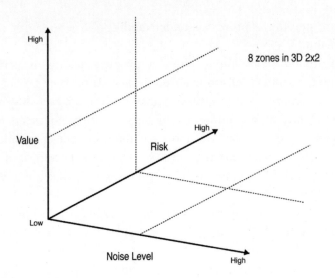

FIGURE 10.2 Prioritization Factors for Resolving Complaints.

The second factor is risk—the potential damage to a firm based on the nature of the problem. The greater the issue—for instance, a dangerous safety problem with a product—the larger the risk.

The "noise level," or how far the complaint could travel via social media and how many people could listen, is the third factor. The extent to which a complaint could spread is a function primarily of how active the complainer is on social media (e.g., the number of accounts the person has on social networking sites, the frequency with which he blogs, and the time he spends on social networks); his following (e.g., how "connected" the person is to others as measured by the number of Twitter followers, blog readers, or Face-book friends), and his credibility (how much the person's words count). Is he viewed as a chronic and idle complainer? Is his opinion highly respected, or is he seen as having an axe to grind?

By considering these three prioritization factors, managers can better assess the potential damage to their business and its reputation from an irate customer who voices his frustrations through social media. Consider eight prioritization scenarios based on different combinations of designating each factor as high or low. (See Figure 10.3.)

Of course, the complaints requiring the most attention involve high-value customers with a high degree of noise and great risk potential. Companies must respond to these complaints most quickly and effectively, doing

Value	Risk	Noise	Response Characteristis
High	High	High	Immediate, whatever it takes • Direct communication to customer via initial channel and via alternate channels • Response on open external forums • Response on company web site • Updates to knowledge across customer service channels
High	High	Low	Immediate, whatever it takes • Direct communication to customer via initial channel and via alternate channels • Response on open external forums • Response on company web site • Updates to knowledge across customer service channels
High	Low	High	Prompt and responsive to the individual • Direct communication to customer via initial channel and via alternate channels
High	Low	Low	Prompt and responsive to the individual • Direct communication to customer via initial channel and via alternate channels
Low	High	High	Prompt and responsive to the masses • Response on open external forums • Response on company web site • Updates to knowledge across customer service channels
Low	High	Low	Prompt action focused on mitgating risk
Low	Low	High	No action – monitor for influence and impact on other customers
Low	Low	Low	No action

FIGURE 10.3 Priority Scenarios.

whatever they can to extinguish the social media fire. The first move should be communicating directly with the customer through the channel the customer used to air her complaint. If she posted her message on her Facebook fan page, posting a comment on that page would be the best way to address her and others who may have seen her post. A company also should respond through other social media channels and open public forum sites (using the same communication it originally sent to the individual and providing proof of resolution, if possible) to ensure that the customer knows she has been heard and to inform others who might encounter the original complaint. Its own web site, call centers, field offices, and salespeople are other customer service channels a company should use to communicate its recognition and resolution of the problem.

To some, this may sound like overkill. But it isn't. Customers with an enormous value to the company, who have a high profile on social media channels, and who are facing a serious issue must be dealt with as quickly and comprehensively as possible.

Complaints of the type in the next level down are of high value, high risk, and low noise. The only difference between these and the most serious complaints is the noise factor: the risk of spreading far and fast is low. It might be a valued customer who has few Facebook fans, or doesn't belong to any LinkedIn groups, or doesn't have a blog and doesn't do YouTube videos.

Perhaps all he did was post a negative review of a serious nature on a product review site. A company certainly wants to keep this customer, but it's unlikely that his comments will travel very far, at least for a while. Still, we believe this kind of complaint needs a rapid response—the same type as the highest level of elevation. The reason: The customer is important, the problem is a serious one, and other customers who might have more influence and followers online may get on their soapbox to spread the word.

Complaints in the third level of priority require responses that are quick and complete because the individual is valuable and influential. But because the nature of the risk of the complaint is low, the response should be directly to the customer through the channel he or she used (as well as appropriate alternative channels). The fact that the complaint isn't about a serious risk to corporate or product reputation means it is less likely to go viral (or less likely to harm the company if it does). Kevin Smith's skirmish with Southwest Airlines would fit this category of complaint. The complaint did go viral, but the airline's business and reputation are largely unscathed. Few passengers require two seats in the first place, and most aren't likely to sympathize because they want *their* spaces all to themselves. Thus, the nature of the film director's complaint was different from a product or service defect.

Complaints in the fourth scenario (high value, low risk, and low noise) demand a prompt response to the individual, just like those in the third zone. However, given the customer's limited audience reach, she is less likely to spread the word, and the response can be a more focused direct response, such as an e-mail.

Complaints in the fifth scenario are actually more serious than those in the fourth. Even though the customer is not a big spender and therefore is not especially valuable to the firm, he has a serious issue and is influential enough to drag many others into the discussion. The noise level is high. The "United Breaks Guitars" incident is a good example of this type of complaint. Compared to large corporate customers that spend millions of travel dollars annually on United, Dave Carroll and his band (Sons of Maxwell) are small change. But Carroll's issue was a serious one for every traveler—the prospect of damaged baggage—and his noise level was elevated because he had a following among country music fans. (That following became much bigger after he posted his YouTube video on the incident.[5]) Other companies have skirmished online with various activists groups, which have used social media to organize for what they perceived to be serious transgressions. In cases such as these, it's easy for a company to be caught off guard and mobilize a response only well after serious damage has been done to their public images.

United was very slow not only to recognize the potential damage Carroll's YouTube video could inflict on its brand but also to respond in an appropriate way. (It took the company a week to acknowledge the video and increase attention on Carroll's needs—all of this after a nearly 9-month runaround leading up to the creation of the video.) In its initial attempts to fully resolve Carroll's complaint, United stumbled badly. At Carroll's request, United agreed to donate money to a music-related charity—but then contributed just $3,000. (The value of the broken guitar and subsequent repairs cost Carroll nearly $5,000.[6]) The company should have responded via the same media— especially given that United has its own YouTube channel ("uniteditstimetofly") and more than 102,000 followers on Twitter. Carroll ultimately released two more related videos, and, apparently, United has learned from the experience. After the release of the second video, Brett Snyder, a writer for BNET's Travel Industry blog, sent the following tweet: "@UnitedAirlines breaks guitars part deux (i think i like this one better)." The airline tweeted back within an hour, directing Snyder to check his e-mail. There he found a lengthy response from a United spokesperson addressing the issue and discussing the overwhelmingly high success rate the airline has in delivering bags safely to their destinations.[7]

Companies with complaints in the fifth scenario must get out in front of these issues before they reach their high-value customers. We recommend posting a response on open external forums and the company web site, along with providing updates on the situation across all customer service channels.

The sixth scenario of complaints deserves close attention because of their serious nature (i.e., they are of high risk). Even though customers have little value to the firm and have a small online following, they need to be heard. The company must take quick action to reduce the risk that the noise increases and high-value customers listen in.

The seventh and eighth scenarios of customer complaints both involve low-value customers complaining about relatively minor problems that are of low risk to product performance and firm image. Thus, they deserve less attention. However, complaints in the seventh scenario come from people with a high noise factor. Those customers can influence others. Thus, the company should monitor how much their rants are spreading through social media. If the negative sentiments are spreading, the firm must take mitigating actions to set the record straight.

Define Social Media Responder Roles

The frameworks just discussed can be very useful to companies in determining how they should respond to customer complaints. However, just as important as the "how" is the "who"—the people responsible for monitoring social media channels and identifying potentially problematic complaints, then mobilizing quickly to address them.

So who is the "who" in the world of social media? At a high level, here are three categories of roles or types of responders:

1. Customer service professionals
2. Employees outside of customer service
3. Customers who care

Customer Service Professionals

Customer service professionals employees must be at the top of their game: highly knowledgeable of the issues customers are complaining about, deft at deflecting anger, and talented at putting thoughts into written words. Importantly, such employees often reside outside a company's customer service department. They may be in marketing, engineering, distribution, or another function. These employees must be identified and permitted to help a company respond (after receiving training on the firm's social media policies). In fact, it can be difficult to retrain call center reps to make them effective dealing with service issues generated via social media. People who are comfortable only with a linear process for resolving customer issues will be uncomfortable when thrown into unstructured problems. The customer "calls" from social media don't arrive in a queue; they appear on one social networking site, then jump to another, then shift to a YouTube video and follow other unexpected turns.

Employees trained to respond to social media complaints have important customer service jobs in an organization, ones that will only grow in importance as more and more customers flock to social media. These employees need to be part of a firm's larger complaint and problem-escalation process instead of a separate group. They need to be in the center of all the people in the firm who deal with and respond to customer complaints so that complaints that come via social media are fed into the traditional customer feedback loop. That will ensure, for example, that a product-quality problem that customers are complaining about on YouTube or Facebook is brought to the immediate attention of the product designers or engineers who can determine what corrective action must be taken.

However, it's important to note that executives will be disappointed if they look to offset the expense of building a social media response unit with a reduction in their call center investments. Microsoft's experience with social media is indicative of this. As mentioned previously, 95 percent of the company's customer interactions today come through social media and only 5 percent through call centers. But that doesn't mean there's been a 95 percent reduction in calls to Microsoft's call centers. In fact, the firm's call center traffic has remained relatively the same. If anything, many calls are taking longer. Customers who can't resolve technical problems using social media spend *more* time with contact center reps because their problems are more complex. Chattering about them on social media didn't work.

But there's good news in all this. Creating a social media response capability allows companies like Microsoft to touch *many* more customers—those it never reached before. That makes for more effective public relations and marketing investments.

Employees Outside of Customer Service

Given the highly public and pervasive nature of social media, it's unrealistic to expect that the formal customer service organization could effectively monitor and address all the negative sentiments being propagated about a company via social media. Hence the importance of the criteria and guidelines for responding we discussed earlier.

But another way companies are addressing the volume issue is by encouraging all of their employees, even those with little or no formal training in customer service, to help defuse situations before they grow into problems. With employees already actively participating in social networking sites and blogs, it makes sense for companies to enlist them as extended "eyes and ears" of the customer service organization. In such roles, employees respond to negative comments about the company as they encounter them (or, at the very least, make sure the situations are brought to the attention of a customer service agent).

Best Buy's Twelpforce is perhaps the best-known example of this approach. The consumer electronics giant encourages its employees from across all operations to help handle customer service issues via Best Buy's Twitter account. Using their company and Twitter ID, employees can register for the service, after which their tweets will be displayed in a single stream on the same page. Once registered, any tweeting Best Buy employee who encounters a customer tweeting about a bad Best Buy experience can respond to the customer by sending a message from the @Twelpforce account. The Twelpforce service enables Best Buy to spot and engage an unhappy customer more quickly, which not only strengthens the bond with that customer but also keeps the issue from spreading.

Customers Who Care

"First responders" to complaints in the social media space can be people other than employees. Some companies have enlisted customers to play this role. Microsoft, for example, recognizes a class of customers it calls "MVPs" (Most Valuable Professionals). MVPs freely share their knowledge, real-world experience, and impartial, objective feedback to help other Microsoft customers use the company's technologies more effectively—thus helping to create more satisfied customers, reducing the incidents of complaints, and relieving some of the burden on the company's contact center. Currently, Microsoft recognizes approximately 4,000 people as MVPs out of the more than 100 million users who participate in the company's technology communities. According to Microsoft, its MVPs answer more than 10 million questions every year. In return, MVPs receive a "small set of services and other benefits" but no monetary compensation.[8]

Financial software maker Intuit also has experienced the benefits of having customers solve other customers' problems. It set up its own online forum—QuickBooks Live Community—to enable customers of its popular QuickBooks product to ask questions and solve problems. In less than a year after the latest version of the software was released, traffic to the community tripled. The company says that at any given time, customers—rather than Intuit employees—are answering approximately 70 percent of questions posed. Besides contributing to the popularity of QuickBooks (thus, boosting sales), QuickBooks Live Community has substantially reduced calls to the company's contact center and generated significant cost savings.[9]

Measuring Performance

Just as they measure how well they deal with customer complaints in traditional channels, companies must gauge their performance in addressing negative sentiments generated via social media.

The social media response unit needs to be measured on, of course, how well it resolves customer problems aired through social media. This will be different from measuring the effectiveness of the call center, which looks at metrics such as types of calls, calls per hour handled, time per call, number of first-call resolutions, and so on. The bottom line of a call center is whether the caller's problem has been solved. That can be measured easily: The customer merely has to answer yes or no to a rep's question.

Social media complaints are much harder to categorize, track, and resolve. A call center can measure how many people are experiencing the same issue. But how does a company ever know if the social media chatter on that issue has gone away altogether—or simply moved to another part of the Internet that the company is unaware of? And while a contact center rep can get closure by asking a customer if the problem is solved, it is less easy to declare victory in social media. The complaint may have been solved by another customer without the company knowing it.

Despite those hurdles, companies do need to measure how well they're responding to the social media chatter about them. Three metrics—different from those used in a traditional call center setting—are especially important:

1. The "mood" of the people who talk about the company via social media channels
2. The level of advocacy among customers: How many customers post supportive comments about the company's products or services and help other customers resolve issues they are having
3. "Handoff," or how well a company can identify complaints that stump the social media crowd and bring those issues in-house for effective handling

Furthermore, with tools such as Web crawlers, text mining, and sentiment analysis, companies *can* collect, categorize, and measure the number of complaints aired every day with sufficient accuracy. And, to be sure, they can measure how well their own people responded to a social media customer crisis—how fast customer service took to the Internet and how quickly key areas of the company made their experts available to troubleshoot the problem of the day.

All measures should be accompanied by rewards and recognition systems—internal acknowledgment of all those who helped head off a brewing social media crisis. Often those are the most effective incentives companies can provide to rally employees to the defense of public attacks—attacks that we should expect will come more frequently and passionately as more customers embrace social media.

Conclusion

The adage "Perception is reality" really applies to customer complaints generated via social media. A customer who takes to social media channels to air her dissatisfaction with a product, service, or company may be authentic and her complaint may be genuine, or she may be issuing falsehoods in an attempt to punish a company or retaliate for some perceived slight. Unfortunately, whether a customer's complaint is legitimate is no longer the point. The fact that it's "out there" and has the chance to gain a life of its own means companies need to act.

How they should act depends on a variety of factors. In most cases, a swift response to address the situation—whether its involves correcting inaccuracies, telling their own side of the story, or admitting culpability and offering a customer appropriate redress—is called for. The efficacy of this response will depend largely on how quickly a company can identify an issue, assess its severity and risk, determine the appropriate actions, and mobilize the right people.

11

Staying Out of Trouble: Complying with FTC Disclosures

Chris Boudreaux

CHAPTER HIGHLIGHTS

The Federal Trade Commission, which is charged with ensuring truth in advertising, for years has published a set of guidelines to help advertisers and marketers comply with existing laws. Recently the organization announced revisions to the guidelines that address the growing presence of endorsements and testimonials in social media.

Companies using or planning to use social media as a marketing or advertising channel should read these revisions carefully and, where appropriate, seek legal advice on how to interpret and implement them.

Consumer-generated content has radically increased the sources and volume of information, opinions, endorsements, and testimonials available on almost every imaginable topic. As of July 2009, the majority (approximately 66 percent) of the information that we receive about products, services, and organizations now comes to us through social media. As a result, many marketers now invest significant effort to distribute their marketing messages through influential publishers of social media.

Unfortunately for consumers, advertisements in social media are not always easy to recognize. For example, when a blogger says that she loves her car, or someone professes his love for a new book on Twitter, we, as readers, may not know whether that person was paid or rewarded by the manufacturer of those products.

In order to help consumers judge the information they receive through social media, many governments are taking steps to ensure that advertisers make it clear when an endorsement or testimonial was rewarded by the advertiser. As one example of such developments occurring in various jurisdictions around the world, this chapter focuses on changes that occurred in the United States in December 2009 and their impacts on four audiences: advertisers, consumers, employers, and employees.

What Is the Federal Trade Commission?

In the United States, the Federal Trade Commission (FTC) tries to ensure truth in advertising, so that if consumers see an ad on television or online, for example, they are aware that it is an ad and that the information contained within the ad is reasonably truthful and reliable. On October 5, 2009, the FTC addressed the growing presence of endorsements and testimonials in social media by announcing revisions to the guidance that it gives to advertisers on how to ensure that their endorsements and testimonials comply with the Federal Trade Commission Act of 1914.[1] On December 1, 2009, those Guides took effect.

The FTC has published the Guides since 1980, and it has always required endorsers to disclose their relationships with advertisers. As Mary Engle of the FTC said in a video on the FTC web site, "What's new is we're applying this principle in today's world, in the world of social media, where you can't always recognize an advertisement just by looking at it."[2]

For example, the FTC states on its web site: "Under the revised Guides, advertisements that feature a consumer and convey his or her experience with a product or service as typical when that is not the case will be required to clearly disclose the results that consumers can generally expect."[3]

What the Guides Say

The document published by the FTC and containing the guidelines covered in this chapter is entitled Federal Trade Commission (16 Code of Federal Regulations (CFR) Part 255), *Guides Concerning the Use of Endorsements and Testimonials in Advertising*. As the FTC states:

The Guides are administrative interpretations of the law intended to help advertisers comply with the Federal Trade Commission Act; they are not binding law themselves. In any law enforcement action challenging the allegedly deceptive use of testimonials or endorsements, the Commission would have the burden of proving that the challenged conduct violates the FTC Act.[4]

The changes published to the Guides in October 2009 included these five:

1. **Consumer endorsers were added.** Advertisements that feature a consumer and convey his or her experience with a product or service as typical when that is not the case will be required to clearly disclose the results that consumers generally can expect.
2. **Safe harbor was removed.** The 1980 version of the Guides allowed advertisers to describe unusual results in a testimonial, as long as the advertiser included a disclaimer such as "Results not typical." The revised Guides no longer contain that safe harbor.
3. **Examples were added.** The FTC added new examples to help consumers and advertisers understand what constitutes an endorsement by bloggers or other "word-of-mouth" marketers. Specifically, the FTC sought to clarify what is meant by "material connections" between advertisers and endorsers. This may include payments or free products that must be clearly disclosed.
4. **Celebrities were included.** Celebrity endorsers were added to the guidelines. Specifically, both advertisers and endorsers may be liable for false or unsubstantiated claims made in an endorsement or for failure to disclose material connections between the advertiser and an endorser.
5. **Nontraditional advertisements were included.** The FTC provides that celebrities have a duty to disclose their relationships with advertisers when making endorsements outside of the context of traditional advertisements, such as appearing on a talk show or within social media.

The FTC Guides define endorsements as:

any advertising message (including verbal statements, demonstrations, or depictions of the name, signature, likeness or other identifying personal characteristics of an individual or the name or seal of an organization) that consumers are likely to believe reflects the opinions, beliefs, findings or experiences of a party other than a sponsoring advertiser.

Endorsements "must reflect honest opinions, findings, beliefs or experience of the endorser," and they "cannot convey any express or implied representations that would be deceptive if made directly by the advertiser."

A "product" includes any product, service, company, or industry.

The FTC does not specify how one should disclose, simply stating that the disclosure must be "clear and conspicuous."

Common Mistakes in Interpreting the Guides

The Guides created no new laws. Deceptive advertising was already illegal, and the U.S. government has long treated commercial speech differently from noncommercial speech. What changed is that endorsements in social media are now considered commercial speech. At some point in the future, when the FTC brings a case to court, the FTC's interpretation will be tested in the court. In the meantime, the Guides are the clearest direction we have.

The FTC stated that it intends to apply the endorsement guides to producers of social media and advertisers but not to mainstream media journalists. Some critics have labeled this an unconstitutional assault on free speech. Others simply are concerned about different rules applying to bloggers than to journalists, when the differences between the two types of writers are not so clear. Not all bloggers are journalists, but some certainly are.

However, the FTC is not limiting or restricting speech. Instead, it is saying that it will treat commercial endorsements on blogs exactly the same way it treats commercial endorsements in other media. Journalists who endorse a product are required to disclose any connection they have to the product, and so must anyone else producing such content. Under the new Guides, neither new media nor old media are allowed to deceive consumers, and that seems pretty fair.

Because the FTC did not specify a minimum value to qualify for coverage under the Guides, many people have tried to infer minimum values of compensation that the FTC will enforce. However, there is no such minimum requirement. Any value can get a company into trouble.

Some have complained that bloggers always will have to remember where or how they obtained an item before they write about it. That is simply not true, for two reasons:

1. The Guides are not retroactive.
2. No one expects a blogger to remember something that happened many years ago. Instead, the FTC uses the same test it has used for years: Would a reasonable person be deceived without more clear disclosure? If someone received a free box of chocolate five years ago, he probably doesn't need to disclose.

When the Guides were published, a few journalists speculated that the FTC would impose fines of $11,000 per violation; however, the Guides do not provide for any particular penalties. Fines or penalties can be assessed only by a court as the result of a legal enforcement process, during which the FTC would have to make its case for deceptive advertising.

Impacts of the Changes

Four groups of people should understand the changes: employers, employees, advertisers, and consumers. First, we discuss the impacts for employers and employees, and then we cover specific considerations for advertisers and the consumers who play a role in advertisers' social media campaigns.

Employers may be liable for certain social media publishing activities of their employees. Specifically, an employer may be liable under certain circumstances (1) if an employee makes statements about the employer's products or services in blogs or social utilities without disclosing the connection between the employer and the employee, or (2) if the employee makes false or unsubstantiated statements regarding the employer's products or services. In order to help employers interpret the Guides, the FTC provided this example:

An online message board designated for discussions of new music download technology is frequented by MP3 player enthusiasts. They exchange information about new products, utilities, and the functionality of numerous playback devices. Unbeknownst to the message board community, an employee of a leading playback device manufacturer has been posting messages on the discussion board promoting the manufacturer's product. Knowledge of this poster's employment likely would affect the weight or credibility of her endorsement. Therefore, the poster should clearly and conspicuously disclose her relationship to the manufacturer to members and readers of the message board.

In its comments to the revised Guides, the FTC stated that it would consider an employer's establishment of appropriate procedures in determining whether to seek legal enforcement against the employer because of inappropriate endorsements or testimonials made by its employees. However, the FTC provides no definition of "appropriate procedures."

The Guides allow employees to publish anonymously. Their identity is not important. Rather, their employment is the fact that must be disclosed. If they publish anonymously, and they write about their employer's products or services, then they must disclose their employment relationship, but they need not disclose their identity.

The same requirement applies to agencies acting on a company's behalf. For instance, if an individual works for a public relations or advertising firm and leaves a comment on a review site, the individual needs to identify his or her relationship to the client.

Regarding advertiser compliance, advertisers are liable for any false claims that consumers make if the advertisers gave the consumers payment or a free service in exchange for trying the product or service and writing or speaking about it. The size of the payment, the value of the product, and the size of the endorser's audience are not relevant.

Finally, advertisers must document their disclosure policy, make the policy clear to their affiliates, and ensure adequate monitoring and auditing of their disclosure compliance programs.

In its enforcement of advertiser compliance, the FTC has stated that its enforcement efforts will focus on advertisers rather than the consumers they enlist in their social media campaigns. In fact, the only FTC investigation conducted to date focused on the advertiser, not the bloggers, involved. (See sidebar "Ann Taylor Investigated for Blogger Gifts.")

Ann Taylor Investigated for Blogger Gifts

In 2010, the Loft division of fashion company Ann Taylor invited bloggers to preview its summer 2010 collection, offering a "special gift" and promising that those posting coverage from the event would be entered into a "mystery gift-card drawing," where they could win between $50 and $500. The invitation explained that bloggers must submit posts to the company within 24 hours to find out the value of their gift card.

The unusual request for posts to be submitted for a prize received media scrutiny and caught the eye of the FTC. "We were concerned that bloggers who attended a preview on January 26, 2010 failed to disclose that they received gifts for posting blog content about that event," Mary Engle, the FTC's associate director-advertising practices, wrote in a letter dated April 20 to Ann Taylor's legal representation.

In April 2010, the FTC informed Ann Taylor that it intended to take no action against the company because, according to the company, the January preview was the first and, to date, only such event. Also, only a small number of bloggers posted content about the preview and several of those disclosed the gifts. Finally, Ann Taylor's Loft division adopted a written policy regarding its interaction with bloggers.

Source: "Ann Taylor Investigation Shows FTC Keeping Close Eye on Blogging," *AdAge*, April 28, 2010.

How to Comply with the Guides

Technology is rushing to catch up to the needs of employers, advertisers, and individuals challenged to comply with these FTC requirements, so here are a few suggestions.

Employers

We suggest that employers take these seven actions to ensure their compliance and that of their employees:

1. Update social media policies to reflect the FTC Guide revisions in order to proactively inform employees of their obligations.
2. Educate employees. All of them.
3. Monitor to ensure compliance with disclosure requirements and accuracy of information. Ensure that social media listening and monitoring capabilities filter for relevant employee statements.
4. Correct inaccurate or misleading information.
5. Define and implement a process for handling employee statements that create liability for the company, once they are identified through listening and monitoring capabilities.
6. Consider implementing one of the emerging technology solutions that aspire to provide scalable, auditable, and compliant disclaimers for companies.
7. Document the company's policies and the communication of those policies to employees. (A company can't just say it did it. It has to be able to prove it.)

Advertisers

We suggest that advertisers take these 14 actions to ensure their compliance and that of their affiliates:

1. Determine the appropriate disclaimers that affiliates should implement and when they should use them.
2. Define appropriate policies for affiliates and publish them to affiliates, as required by FTC Guides.
3. Monitor to ensure compliance with disclosure requirements and accuracy of information.
4. Do not use an endorsement from an expert or celebrity unless there is confidence that the person still subscribes to the views presented. If the person's opinion has changed, do not use the endorsement.[5]
5. If the advertisement states or implies that the endorser uses the product, and the endorser ever stops using the product, then the advertiser must stop using the endorsement.
6. Correct inaccurate or misleading information.

7. Consider implementing a technology solution that will automate disclosure standardization, audit trails, and analytics. CMP.ly is a new software firm that aims to deliver a scalable compliance management solution that will automate FTC-required audit trails with supporting analytics.

8. If the advertiser conducts outreach to bloggers, it must inform the bloggers about their obligation to disclose. We suggest providing guidance that is specific to the campaign at hand rather than providing the same generic guidance to bloggers across different campaigns.

9. Provide guidance and training to employed and affiliate bloggers concerning their need to ensure that their statements are truthful and substantiated. Substantiation must include, when appropriate, competent and reliable scientific evidence. Consumer endorsements are not considered competent and reliable scientific evidence.

10. If the results that an endorser's experience with the advertiser's product are not what consumers generally will achieve, then the advertisement must clearly and conspicuously disclose the generally expected performance in the depicted circumstances. One cannot simply state "These results are not typical." One must state the typical results that consumers can expect.

11. If the advertiser operates an online customer community, update community policies or terms of use to inform community members of their obligations, to the extent that any incentive is provided for endorsing the products.

12. Keep blogger outreach programs simple and easy to understand. Provide guidance and training to word-of-mouth agents and employees, especially the ones charged with developing and executing social media programs.

13. Document policies, the communication of those policies to affiliates, and monitoring of affiliates' disclosures.

14. If an advertiser portrays an endorser as an expert, then the endorsement must be supported by an actual exercise of that expertise in evaluating product features or characteristics that fall within the domain of his or her true expertise. For example, a chemical engineer cannot be introduced simply as "an engineer" within an endorsement of a sports car's performance. The advertiser must clarify the nature and limits of the endorser's expertise.

Employees and Consumers Publishing Social Media

We suggest that individual social media publishers (such as bloggers, consumers, and employees) take these seven actions to ensure their compliance:

1. Say nothing about a product or service unless there is evidence to support that the statements are truthful and substantiated. The individual is liable for unsubstantiated claims if the statements fall within the definition of an endorsement according to the FTC.
2. Think twice about working with companies that do not provide disclosure information.
3. Push back if companies are not providing the information or support needed to comply with FTC Guides.
4. Read agreements carefully.
5. Correct inaccurate or misleading information.
6. A quote from someone or description of what someone said should fairly reflect the substance of what the person said; quotes and descriptions should not deliberately or inadvertently distort the original meaning.
7. Always tell the truth, and tell it with confidence.

Disclosure Approaches

The FTC does not specify how to disclose. Although the Guides include examples to illustrate when disclosure is required, they do not provide a checklist or examples of disclosures. Instead, the Guides simply require "clear and conspicuous" disclosure of material relationships between sellers and endorsers, when those relationships would not otherwise be clear to the consumer.

There are many ways to be clear and conspicuous. For example, put the disclosure at the top of a blog post, at the top of the blog sidebar, or within the text of the post while writing the endorsement.

In general, the reader must have an opportunity to see the disclosure without searching for it. If writing a very long blog post, place the disclosure at the top and bottom of the post. When there is a question, simply ask yourself, if you were reading someone else's blog, where would you want to be informed about the endorsement or their connection to the product?

Rather than expressing affiliations in a shy or timid way, tell the truth about advertiser or employer connections candidly, casually, clearly, and confidently. Consumers are bombarded by so many people trying to take advantage of them that candor will be attractive. Rather than obscuring or hiding the connection or compensation, let the language presume that the connection is totally aboveboard and acceptable. Visitors will trust the recommendations more when they see a clear, candid, and confident disclosure.

For all types of social media, the Word of Mouth Marketing Association (WOMMA) strongly recommends prominently posting a "Disclosure and Relationships Statement" on blogs or web sites. Such a statement fully discloses how the writer works with companies in accepting and reviewing products and lists any conflicts of interest that may affect the credibility of the content. For a great example, see Walt Mossberg's Ethics Statement on AllThingsD.com.[6] Walt has been reviewing products and services for years, and consumers around the world trust his opinions.

The FTC does not require that bloggers publish a standing disclosure policy like Walt's. In fact, policies like his Ethic Policy do not satisfy FTC disclosure requirements in any way. However, we strongly recommend that bloggers include such a statement in their blogs in order to help build trust and confidence among their readers.

To be clear, disclosures must appear within each post, tweet, or status update that contains an endorsement or testimonial governed by the FTC Guides. In addition, if an employee blogs about his or her company's products, citing the identity of the employer in the profile may not be a sufficient disclosure. Bloggers' disclosures should appear close to each endorsement or testimonial that they post.

Moving Forward

As the FTC has begun to investigate potential violations of its Guides, it has consistently focused on organizations rather than individuals. As a result, the burden of compliance rests on employers and advertisers, which must maintain and communicate sufficient policies, processes and audit trails of both. For this reason, organizations of all types and sizes should define, document, and communicate compliance policies, whether they use social media marketing or not.

Resources

Blog With Integrity pledge and badge: www.blogwithintegrity.com/

Bureau of Consumer Protection web site: www.ftc.gov/bcp/index.shtml

Federal Trade Commission, 16 CFR Part 255, Guides Concerning the Use of Endorsements and Testimonials in Advertising: www.ftc.gov/os/2009/10/091005endorse mentguidesfnnotice.pdf

Federal Trade Commission Act, incorporating U.S. SAFE WEB Act amendments of 2006: www.ftc.gov/ogc/FTC_Act_IncorporatingUS_SAFE_WEB_Act.pdf

Federal Trade Commission Act, by sections, Cornell Legal Information Institute: www.law.cornell.edu/uscode/html/uscode15/usc_sec_15_00000041----000-.html

Living Ethics Blog, by the Word of Mouth Marketing Association (WOMMA): http://womma.org/ethicsreview/

To file a complaint in English or Spanish, visit the FTC's online Complaint Assistant at: www.ftccomplaintassistant.gov or call 1-877-FTC-HELP (1-877-382-4357).

Video answers to FAQs by Mary Engle, Associate Director, Bureau of Consumer Protection, Federal Trade Commission: www.ftc.gov/multimedia/video/business/ endorsement-guides/endorse_mary-q1.shtm

IV

Beyond the "Pilot" Phase: The Core Components of the Agile Digital Enterprise

12 Creating and Implementing a Social Media Technology Platform

Anatoly Roytman and Joseph Hughes

CHAPTER HIGHLIGHTS

Social media introduces substantial impacts across a wide range of tools, business processes, and data interfaces. In fact, technology arguably is the biggest barrier companies encounter in embracing social media effectively.

To smooth the adoption of social media, organizations need an integrated social media platform that supports all the key social media–related activities. Such a platform is not available out of the box but, rather, must be built using a combination of new and existing software solutions.

Throughout this book, we've explored various aspects of social media, some of which are more difficult to master than others. This chapter focuses on the technology piece of the puzzle, arguably one of the biggest challenges companies will encounter in embracing social media.

To date, companies have instituted social media technology in two phases: experimental and business transformation. The experimental phase was all about the tools. Companies deployed components of social media, such as blogs, product ratings, discussion forums, and customer comments as one-offs—isolated and often uncoordinated initiatives that paid little attention to the existing technical infrastructure. These tools usually were tied to a specific campaign that was meant to have a short-term impact—for example, to give the chief executive officer a voice to comment on a pressing public issue or customers the chance to weigh in on a new product concept.

But we are past the experimental stage. Social media must be seen in a larger, more strategic context—in the way companies manage their entire customer relationships. Creating great Web experiences for customers is a key goal of customer relationship management (CRM) technologies today, and social media has become a key part of those Web experiences. In fact, we agree wholeheartedly with customer experience experts Seth Godin and Paul Greenberg, who point to companies such as Disney that are using the Web and social media to *empower* customers rather than to *manage* them, to put customers in the driver's seat rather than the back-seat. They and managers at Disney's travel and vacation business (Disney Destinations) talk of moving from CRM to CMR, or customer-managed relationships.[1]

This is the business transformation phase of social media, and it requires much more planning, resources, and experience than the experimental phase that preceded it. The business transformation phase moves past stand-alone, outside-the-firewall skunkworks initiatives. It focuses on linking social media technology with a company's core information systems. The connections, however, are "loosely coupled" with a company's traditional infrastructure, including its active directory, content management systems (CMS), data warehouse, web site analytics, logistics management (in some cases), e-mail manager, CRM software, and others.

To make social media technologies a key way of interacting with customers, managers must take a much more thoughtful approach to selecting the right technologies and building a sustainable and scalable infrastructure in the constantly changing world of social media.

Value of Integration

As they move from the experimental phase to the business transformation phase of social media, most companies will realize their previous social media efforts were fragmented and out of sync. They also will realize that they have barely capitalized on the great power of social media.

If its marketing, sales, service, and other functions interact with customers through social media in a disjointed way, a company will be asking for trouble—big trouble. Imagine this scenario: A customer has trouble with a product ("It doesn't work as advertised" or "It's too hard to use," etc.) and lets his Twitter followers know about it by tweeting his complaint. The marketing department gets the tweet (because it is responsible for "listening to the voice of the customer") and responds by saying "Sorry you are having trouble. I will get you some help." Someone in marketing sends an e-mail to customer service, which in turn asks the product team for advice. Customer service tries to enter the customer complaint into the firm's CRM system. But the system doesn't recognize the customer ("@NJMom") in the database. In fact, a Twitter address isn't permitted to be entered. The product team gets back to service with some ideas, but the service rep is out to lunch. Even when she returns, it becomes the 100th item on her priority list, and so the complaint sits unanswered for a week. Meanwhile, the customer who had expected he could tweet and get instant service gets very angry. He embarks on a mission to denounce the company.

An unlikely scenario? Not at all. Remember what Jeff Jarvis said about Dell in August 2005 in his "Dell Hell" blog posts on BuzzMachine? Jarvis, who commanded a large audience, complained about the computer company's refusal to replace or fix his broken machine. Dell already was in the process of making substantial changes to its customer service approaches to make them more responsive and effective, but the Jarvis incident added a sense of urgency to Dell's initiative. If a company is known for its good or great service and can't react quickly to the Jeff Jarvises of the world, it stands to be derailed—even if one person's bad social media experience with the firm is highly unusual.

In such cases, a company's social media technology approach will slowly or quickly kill the firm's reputation. What accounts for such disjointed responses to customers? It's the experimental approach that most companies took to social media. Their data from online customer interactions resides in multiple silos. They installed social media applications as point solutions to point problems—for example, a blogging tool, or customer discussion forum site, or a product review Web page. Each one has its own rules. Each one focuses on its part of the CRM process. A customer who tweets a complaint may be the same customer who sounds off on the company's product review site. But because the applications were implemented separately, the company doesn't know that. Another customer may post gripes on the company's new online customer forum. But that system isn't linked to the CRM system, so the company can't positively identify the source of the gripes.

Why does this happen? For one thing, few companies have a single person responsible for the entire digital customer experience. Joe in public relations is responsible for the corporate blog. Marge in product development handles the product review site. Bill in customer service manages the customer discussion forum. And Ann in marketing is in charge of monitoring Twitter. They all have different bosses. As a result, no one is in charge of making sure that Joe, Marge, Bill, and Ann work closely together every hour of every day to deal with customers who appear in their channels. This is typical. In some companies, some of the responsibilities are handed to external parties, such as marketing agencies, which can result in one more fumbled handoff.

Even when all parties report to the same person, they still can be out of sync with one another because they lack the data to understand what's happening at the level of individual customers. They're working with aggregate-level statistics—for example, "Tweets about us have risen 200 percent this week," or "The number of comments to our blog posts has grown 400 percent." But that doesn't help Joe, Marge, Bill, or Ann determine what to do about the newest version of Jeff Jarvis or Dave Carroll (United Breaks Guitars).

CRM Déjà Vu

The fragmentation of social media responsibilities will feel very familiar to many managers. Ten to 15 years ago, their companies are likely to have responded to customers through non-Web channels in a similar uncoordinated fashion. Salespeople had little idea what customer service told their customers, and the marketing function typically was out of the loop as well. This is what ushered in CRM software in the first place: the allure of marketing, sales, customer service and other functions all working off the same customer database, and having access to the same, up-to-date information on customers so that the left hand of the company knew what the right hand had done. By coordinating the actions of sales, customer service and marketing, companies were able to orchestrate the customer experience. "Creating compelling customer experiences" became the mantra.

Just when companies thought their CRM systems were sufficient, along comes social media. Suddenly companies must take the coordination of sales, marketing, customer service, and other customer-related functions to an entirely new level. They must incorporate social media into their marketing, sales, and service operations and synchronize the actions of in-house personnel who post blogs, monitor Twitter, manage Facebook and other pages on social networking sites, and police their firm's product review and discussion web sites.

The Social Media Platform

Key to integrating social media into key corporate functions and processes is what we call a social media platform. A social media platform is technology that enables a company to identify and aggregate in one place all of its interactions with customers as well as the social media chatter of those customers about the firm (in addition to noncustomers who take to blogs, discussion boards, etc.). The role of this platform is clear (although not easy): Find out who is talking about the company and its products, policies, and so on through social media and get that information to the people in the company who can take appropriate action.

We discussed the social media platform in Chapter 5 on the "voice of the customer." We mentioned the platform's crucial role in allowing a company to listen to both "onboard" communities (web sites owned by a company) and "offboard" communities (those not owned by the firm). The platform plays another important role: filtering information that is important and thus requires a response.

In light of these roles, the social media platform has become an essential new element of a company's technology infrastructure. It is a new engine that enables a company to provide the next-generation customer experience. Exactly how does the platform work? It receives social media content from many channels: blog posts, Twitter tweets, social networking sites, discussion boards, product review sites, and many more. It uses analytics software to monitor trends and help managers decide what to do about them. And this new social media platform is tightly integrated with a company's existing CRM system. The social media platform combines and connects all this software seamlessly, which lets managers focus on how they should respond to customers who use social media, not on troubleshooting the platform.

Currently the social media platform cannot be bought from one software vendor; some software companies provide key pieces of the platform, but

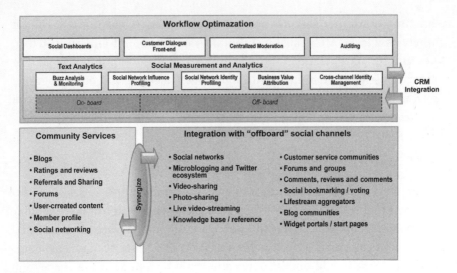

FIGURE 12.1 The Social Media Technology Platform.

none sells the entire suite. As a result, companies must build the platform more or less from scratch, although they can and should take advantage of the commercially available software pieces of the puzzle.

The platform has six core components (see Figure 12.1):

1. Community services (i.e., onboard social media channels)
2. Integration with external social media channels
3. Work flow optimization
4. Text analytics
5. Measurement and analysis
6. Integration with the existing CRM system

In the next sections, we explain each component in greater detail. We discuss some of the key technology components available today as well as companies that are using such components to improve the experience their customers have by interacting through social media.

Community Services: Technology for Building the Social Media Channels a Firm Can Control

Perhaps the most basic components of the social media platform are the ones that let companies build and maintain onboard communities. These technologies provide such social media services as:

- **Blogs.** The technology should enable firms with multiple product brands and multiple internal bloggers to contribute to a corporate blog.
- **Ratings and reviews.** These web sites (or "plug-ins" to an existing web site) allow Web viewers to rate products and services (i.e., vote on them), provide product reviews/critiques, and comment on the quality of those reviews (a feature called *review ratings* and often seen on web sites as "Was this review helpful?"). Review ratings also can cover product pages, blog posts, and user-created media. Such capabilities are provided by several vendors (e.g., Telligent).
- **Referrals and sharing.** These usually come as plug-in capabilities that give users display badges for sharing content through traditional and social media.
- **Forums.** Forums are multibrand, multitopic bulletin boards that let customers participate in discussion groups organized by topic.
- **User-created content management.** (including wikis). These technologies provide a multibrand, multiuser media-sharing platform for video, images, audio, and text.
- **Member profile management.** These provide tools that let customers decide what information they want to provide on a web site: for example, photos, information preferences, linked channels, and privacy settings.
- **Social networking.** These are integrated multibrand networking platforms that allow for friend/follow, organic groups, calendars/events, direct messaging, tagging, and activity feed.
- **Cross-channel synchronization.** This synchronization provides seamless integration of user experience across all in-house social media channels (single sign-on, preferences propagation, contextual coherence).
- **Ideation or idea management.** Ideation takes input from internal or external sources in the form of ideas that could include text, images, videos, or documentation.

No single technology company has products covering all of these Web services, although a few (such as Telligent and Lithium) provide most of them. Companies must decide how they will fill the gaps.

Integration with External Social Media

This component of the social media platform links a company's social media capabilities to the social media channels that are outside of its control—for example, Facebook, Twitter, and external blogs. It enables a company to "fish where the fish are"—comb the Web's many places where customers and noncustomers hang out and provide content as short as a comment on a blog and as long as a one-hour video on YouTube.

Why "fish where the fish are"? Why shouldn't a company simply monitor the customer remarks on its own web site? It's because there are much greater numbers of customers in the external social media. Facebook, for example, has more than 400 million users, and its sights are set on 1 billion in the near future. Twitter has 85 million users who tweet messages and nearly 200 million who either tweet or read tweets.[2] YouTube's users number in the hundreds of millions. In all likelihood, many more customers will be commenting on a firm in these external social media channels than the ones the company owns. Thus, a company must monitor such chatter, and that's what external social media integration tools are all about.

There are several key elements of this technology component:

- **A social application framework.** This is a reusable application framework for social platform apps (e.g., Facebook apps, Google Gadgets). It reduces development costs and lets a company rapidly build new applications as well as plug into the relevant platform services.
- **API backbone.** This is abstraction layer that is platform-agnostic. It lets a company minimize the impact of changes made in the underlying social APIs (application programming interfaces).
- **Spiders.** These advanced algorithms parse the Web looking for structured and unstructured data in search of comments about a company, its products, people, policies, and the like.
- **Connectors and wrappers.** These constitute a common library of utilities that connect a company to external social media services (Facebook, Digg, and other social networking sites) and wrap them. They also provide common web site features that let viewers print and translate documents and download PDFs. The directory of destination sites continues to grow organically. A key challenge, however, is keeping the sharing tools up to date.
- **Referrals.** Referral services such as ShareThis can be used to share branded web site content using e-mail addresses.

These and other technology tools are becoming essential to keeping a window on the social media world. A company should not set off for the vast sea of social media content on the Web without them.

Social Media Work Flow Tools

The social media work flow component enables companies to define which social media events require attention, the kind of attention they require, and who in the organization must act. The work flow component also features a tracking mechanism that monitors whether the person responsible for handling the issue did in fact handle it. If that person doesn't, the tracking mechanism escalates the issue, bringing it to the attention of someone else.

Social media work flow solutions must be tightly integrated with a company's established work flows—for example, the routines that its customer service organization follows in its CRM system. (We talk more about this later in the chapter on component number six, integrating social media tools with CRM.)

Text Analytics

We explored this technology in Chapter 5 and Chapter 6. Here we discuss the elements of text analytics software and their business utility.

But before we do, let's define what the term "text analytics" means. For this, we'll rely on Seth Grimes, who chairs the annual Text Analytics Conference:

[Text analytics] solutions mine documents and other forms of 'unstructured' data. They analyze linguistic structure and apply statistical and machine-learning techniques to discern entities (names, dates, places, terms) and their attributes as well as relationships, concepts, and even sentiments. They extract these 'features' to databases for further analysis and automate classification and processing of source documents. They exploit visualization for exploratory analysis of discovered information.[3]

One of the key words Grimes uses is "sentiments." Sentiments are the way people feel about a company, its products, policies, people, and other issues. One of the most important jobs of text analysis software is helping an organization analyze how people feel about it—with those feelings, of course, expressed through social media. In helping a company listen to what's being said about it in social media channels, text analysis is technology that:

- **Analyzes the content of these conversations to determine the tenor or "sentiment" of the chatter (positive, negative or neutral).** It then must filter which chatter is important to respond to. The technology has the ability to infer from unstructured text a person's emotion and attitude toward an issue, an emotion that typically is expressed as either 0 (negative) or 1 (positive). The technology must recognize sentiments that may be language, syntax, or context dependent. For instance, "I hate this product" is obviously a negative sentiment. However, a remark such as "I like your plentiful automated teller machine (ATM) locations, but your ATM fees are too high" is more complex. It has both a positive and negative sentiment in the same sentence. In Appendix 1 we show how one CRM vendor, RightNow, has integrated sentiment analysis into its case management platform.

- **Is able to perform "Entity Extraction."** What does this mean? It refers to the software's ability to discern people, places, or things in the text— that is, to determine the true meaning of a word that may have multiple meanings. A classic example is the word "progressive." In one context, progressive is a verb; in another, it is the name of an insurance company. In search technology and social text analysis, companies must be able to understand people, places, and things quickly and automatically (i.e., with as little human intervention as possible). Who is the author of this rant on Facebook? Are they a customer or influencer? Should we care about it? Where is the story being told? Is this about my product or someone else's?

- **Is able to "Classify" the data.** Another ability of text analytics is classification (also known as faceting and clustering). Text analysis gurus call classification the ability to categorize data into related groups. After a company extracts social media data and analyzes whether people are being positive or negative about the company, it must classify those comments. If a company analyzed 1,000 Amazon.com reviews of its products and its competitors' products, it might classify the entities and sentiments that were expressed by manufacturer, by product, and by positive or negative feedback. Search companies call such buckets facets. Companies in this space also may refer to supervised versus unsupervised clustering. Unsupervised clustering means the system is smart enough to do most of the classification automatically—without human help.

A final key feature of text analytics software is natural language processing (NLP). This is the Holy Grail of text analysis, in our view. NLP is technology that can divine the true intent of a writer (or speaker). It is used most often in the world of search engines. It allows people to type in plain language (and thus not have to know arcane syntax) to answer a question. Search engines use NLP to generate the most relevant search results; as a person types more words "the best way to fly from Fort Lauderdale, Fla., to Boulder, Colo.," the search result should narrow, not expand.

Measurement and Analysis

The fifth component of a social media platform, measurement and analysis, enables a firm to gauge the impact of social media conversations on its business as well as how well it has responded to those discussions. A social media platform must be created with metrics that keep managers informed on their firm's online reputation.

And the metrics must be meaningful because it's very easy to generate metrics that have little value. For example, it is not important for a company to know how many people are talking about a particular subject. What *is* important for that firm is understanding customer sentiment toward its brand, especially if those feelings are changing. In addition, it's crucial that managers know how customers' present sentiments are affecting sales, market share, and margins. This is especially true for companies using social media in their marketing campaigns. They must be able to make a connection between customer sentiments (as expressed through social media) and the campaign's performance—for example, new customers converted, sales generated, and so on.

The measurement and analysis component of the social media platform must be tuned to the right metrics. There are five key elements of this component:

1. **Buzz analysis and monitoring.** This feature is about analyzing trendy topics and customer sentiment in each social media channel and customer segment. It is also about discovering new topics that consumers are chattering about as well as monitoring the competition. Social media enables a company to inform its buzz analysis to the customer. It could display trend topics of interest to buyers on its web site. Some technologies provide the ability to set alerts based on reaching a certain threshold—for example, when 50 customers complain about the same issue, it's time to take action.

2. **Social network influence profiling.** This feature lets companies capitalize on the positive influence of customers. Influence profiling identifies influencers and whom they're influencing. Companies that reach out to such influencers can quickly change the minds of many, many people.

3. **Social network identity profiling.** This is a different type of profiling from the influence type. Identity profiling is about enriching a company's insights about customers with additional attributes derived from profile and activity stream data. Identity must be processed and fed to those in charge of the customer experience and marketing campaigns.

4. **Business value attribution.** This ability allows a company to map between social metrics/events and business metrics to be fed into business analytics capabilities (e.g., use in Marketing Mix Models (MMM), return on investment analysis).

5. **Cross-channel identity management.** The same customer may make remarks through many social media channels. The challenge for many companies is recognizing that the "JoeyBoy" from Facebook is the same person as "JoeyB" from Twitter and "JBoy" from its discussion forums. To understand everything "JoeyBoy" is saying about a company requires consolidating his multiple identities into one-leveraging text analytics of the profile data publicly available, supplemented by clues in the company data.

As customer service departments become more proficient with social media, they must enhance their traditional measures of performance. Just as "average handle time" is a crucial measure in the contact center, so is measuring response time to customers who raise their voice in social media. We refer to these measures as SMART—social *media average response time*.

Measuring SMART is more difficult than tracking average handle times. Companies must measure their response time to onboard and offboard social media. And if a company uses its online community to help customers, it needs to measure its community's response time as well. To be sure, getting a community to answer customer questions (such as the ones that technology vendors like Microsoft run) is a big benefit to a company. With the community helping, it has that many more able customer support agents. But companies can't abdicate customer support to the community. They need to know how quickly and how well the community is responding to customer questions. Tracking those metrics gives a firm some real insights into the "vibrancy" of its community. (One example is Lithium's Community Health Index (CHI), which tracks a combination of members, content, traffic, interaction, liveliness, and responsiveness factors.[4]) If the community isn't responding, the firm must respond. No onboard communities should be ghost towns. So an example SMART calculation could be that as long as the CHI is good, we can wait for an hour before jumping in ourselves—because community may answer for us. But if the hour expires and no one has replied, we need to reply.

Even companies with offboard communities—communities they can't control—often monitor what's going on in them. DirectTV, for example, is rumored to monitor DBSTalk, a prominent offboard community.

Companies answer and track every phone call that comes into their contact centers. They need to do the same with social media if the author of a comment is a customer—which is where the social identity profiling comes in to play. If the social media author is influential, then a response is warranted even if the person is not a customer. A Tweeter who has thousands of followers must be treated like a VIP customer—even if she doesn't buy very much. It is important also not to forget the customer identification step. Many companies jumped straight to influence measurement as the only alert mechanism. They should use this new medium to proactively improve the customer experience and the customer relationship, not just act in self-defense. Thus, identity is key. Even if you can't immediately tell the full customer's name, you can tell from text analytics that they are a customer. If a tweet says "I had trouble with my XBrand Router" you can be sure that they are a customer of XBrand—and then ask for the true name in your offer to help.

Cable operator Comcast knows this well. It monitors any social media mention of "#Comcast." But it asks customers who have issues to Tweet them at the "@comcastcares" address with their customer information. Comcast is better able to monitor its response time to complaints or inquiries that come into the address. To our knowledge, it doesn't monitor its response times to general tweets about the firm.

Another way to handle this is to require sign-ups on onboard forums—the online places a company owns where customers can weigh in and share their experiences and knowledge with other companies. That provides an easy way to monitor who is saying what. Based on the sign-up information provided, a company can tell who is a customer and who isn't. That customer ID should be linked immediately to the CRM system of record. The forum can be in Jive, Liferay, Telligent, InQuira—it doesn't much matter. What does matter is that the company needs to link what's happening on its forums to what's in its CRM systems.

CRM Integration

Social media is a critical channel for companies to use to listen and react to customers. The platform must give companies a deep understanding of their customers' preferences—and based on the actual behavior they display (what they're complaining about in Facebook, etc.). But it's not the only channel. The contact center, e-mail, traditional marketing and sales campaigns, and the conventional sales forces will not go away soon, if ever.

Thus companies need to link their social media platform to their enterprise CRM systems. Social CRM systems that collect data and facilitate relationships with customers and influencers must be connected to the corporate CRM system. The pieces of the platform that must connect to the CRM application differ, based on what function they link to: marketing, sales, or service.

For marketing, the social media platform must feed the data and interactions from all the social media chatter into the traditional "marketing funnel" through which people move from prospects to customers. Take, for example, a firm that uses social media in a marketing campaign to increase the number of people who register for its online forum. It must make sure its CRM system can manage those people properly so that it can develop stronger relationships with them.

The key elements of a social media platform that link to marketing include:

- **Customer dialogue front end.** This is an enterprise application front end for public relations professionals, marketers, and customer service agents. It lets them interact with customers in social channels across brands and organizations. The application includes capabilities to measure and manage the impact of viral campaigns.
- **Social dashboard.** This is a monitoring and reporting capability for measuring how well a company addresses customers' problems.
- **Centralized moderation.** This enables a company to centralize the moderation of content on its social media channels. It includes automatic spam detection, smart filters for moderation prioritization, and conflict management tools.
- **Auditing.** This provides historical tracking of conversations and interactions, letting a company monitor its performance and compile documents for regulatory purposes.

Social media not only gives marketing a new tool for communicating to (and with) its target audience; it provides the sales force with a new way to get closer to customers. The technology of a firm called InsideView is instructive here. Technologies have been around for a while that give salespeople newsfeeds on a particular topic. But, as illustrated in Figure 12.2, Inside-View's SalesView system goes one step further: It takes data from social media channels such as LinkedIn, Twitter, Facebook, and Jigsaw and integrates it with traditional news sources.

Technologies such as this are making that long-desired dream of sales and marketing professionals—getting a 360-degree view of the customer—a reality. Gaining that view requires companies to collect offboard social media data on their customers, whether consumers or businesses. Those in charge of selling products and services must get access to this data quickly. That means much of it can't be stored in arcane databases that require technical assistance to extract. It must be easily accessible to all employees on the front lines—especially the sales force. And this social media will change: Companies now have a constantly changing trail of social data they can track and leverage. Virtual- or registry-based Master Data Management (MDM) becomes key—tracking core customer data and links—as opposed to classical MDM which strives for one universal data model. Virtual MDM is more suited to the social media views of customers.

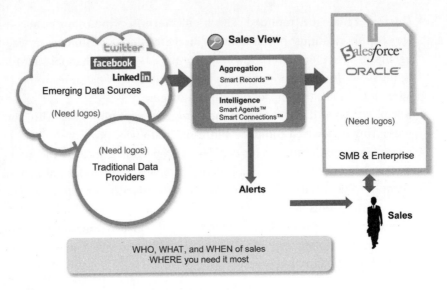

FIGURE 12.2 InsideView's SalesView System Integrates Social Media and Traditional Data into a Company's Existing CRM System.

Customer service is the third function to which a social media platform must connect. As we discussed in Chapter 9, social media has major implications for customer service and support. The biggest need for companies here is to tell quickly if an issue that is voiced through social media is a new or already-known problem, whether the complainer is a customer, and who will respond (for example, the call center or the onboard community).

Most companies today have a much larger staff manning the call center than they have addressing social media channels. Let's say a company has 20 people assigned to social media and 10,000 in its call centers. Should the company give all 10,000 agents access to social media? Probably not. But the 20-person social media staff must get bigger. And that staff needs a summary of the issues that are being heard in the call centers—and in real time. The team also must be able to tell the call center when issues are raised through social media—that is, to create cases/issues).

This will require deciding on a decision support system (DSS), which integrates social media data, or extends a company's CRM case tools to social media channels. It also will require what we call a *virtuous loop knowledge management* capability. This capability can help a company track what people are asking it through social media so that common questions (and answers to them) can become featured prominently on the company's web site (or on its call center agents' screens). Similarly, the solutions that best solve those problems must be tracked so the advice given to customers (or the advice knowledgeable customers in a company's online community give customers) gets better and better.

The way a firm collects and creates knowledge about how to solve a certain problem must help it get better at identifying and solving the problem. A virtuous loop knowledge management capability can help a company not only grade the information its customers give other customers about how to solve a problem but also move the best advice to call center personnel in real time.

An overlooked need in the social media market is the ability to track queries and the usefulness of responses to them. InQuira and Endeca can tell the most common queries in a period of time and the search engine results that people clicked on. A spike in a certain type of query—for example, "Product overheating"— should trigger an automatic alarm in a company's support center.

If search engines are spewing out results that customers are ignoring, that suggests a company isn't prepared to solve the problem (at least online). That is a big warning sign.

Barriers to Developing the Social Media Platform

As companies increasingly realize that a social media platform is a critical piece of their information technology (IT) infrastructure, they will spend a significant time and effort to build it. But even those with the greatest of internal technical resources will not find the goings easy. They will face several stiff challenges. Based on our experience with major companies around the world, we next review the most common barriers and offer insights on how to overcome them.

The first barrier is managing accelerating innovation in social media technology. A large and rapidly increasing number of technology companies provide pieces of the social media platform. For example, according to http://wiki.kenburbary.com, nearly 150 vendors sell social listening software, and more than 20 peddle community services technologies. And remember, these are only two of the six core social media platform components.

Keep in mind that many of these companies most likely won't exist in five years. That's just the nature of venture capital–funded start-up space in the IT industry. For every Google, Yahoo! or EMC in Silicon Valley, Boston's Route 128, or some other hot spot for technology start-ups, many more firms fail. But even among the surviving technology vendors, the technology they sell is evolving rapidly. The companies that evaluate which technologies to buy will be firing at a fast-moving target.

That makes it critical for companies to place the right bets. To minimize risk, companies should use a limited number of vendors and clearly define their relationships with them. In some cases, a firm should work with a company that can integrate the many technologies into a single platform, even if that company doesn't sell social media software. It may even make sense for a company to let a third party manage the social media technology infrastructure so the company can focus on using social media to market, sell, and service customers better rather than spend time keeping its technology running.

The pace of innovation in Web technology is moving at an incredible speed, especially in the social media space. That makes it difficult for companies to keep up. We've seen this for 15 years. Many companies continue to struggle with building and updating their web sites. As more and more customers access those sites using social media applications on their mobile devices, companies have even more bewildering technology choices to make.

We've had firsthand views of this. One pharmaceutical company has approximately 400 projects using new social media technologies in progress across multiple brands and regions. That is far too many. What's worse, many of those projects that started as cross-departmental or cross-functional initiatives are reverting back to "siloed" efforts. That, of course, will foster a fragmented response to customers who interact with the company through social media. We predict that the drug company will implement perhaps 10 percent of its 400 experiments. Still, that would mean the company likely will end up with 40 or so social media tools that don't work with one another and are likely to be unsupervised.

How does a company prevent such social media technology chaos? To manage social media innovation effectively, it must be centralized, under the direction of one person charged with helping the organization leverage the technology.

Centralizing the identification and acquisition of social media technology enables a company to avoid an ad hoc approach to innovation and to adopt one with structure and discipline. It lets a firm continually track social media technologies and their relevance to the organization. It also enables the firm to rapidly build and test new applications and integrate them with its existing social media platform. The result: a rigorous process through which a steady stream of new ideas are identified, tested, studied, and ultimately accepted or rejected.

The second big barrier to building a superior social media platform is combining two types of data in real time: the unstructured data of social media and the structured data of traditional CRM systems. Structured data is organized in a predictable pattern. Relational databases put information into tables, columns, and rows. Object-oriented databases organize information as classes and members. Hierarchical databases (which still can be found on many old mainframe computers) organize data in a hierarchy. CRM applications store data in SQL databases. All of this data is rigidly structured according to the rules of the software that houses it.

In contrast, unstructured data coming from social media outposts—blog posts, product reviews, news articles, Twitter tweets, and so on—arrives in its original form, more or less as plain-text documents. The SQL databases of CRM systems struggle mightily to organize and store such unstructured data.

Further complicating this picture, companies need to understand what the torrent of unstructured data and structured data means very quickly. If a product reviewer is blasting an offering, the company must know right away whether the blaster is a customer and exactly what he or she is complaining about. The company's knowledge about the customer is most likely in its CRM database, while knowledge about the product may be in the product catalog (or, more subtly, in the summation of case history) as well as in the knowledge management system. Finally, to understand what the customer is saying, the company might have to discern her gripes across many channels. (Many of the most irate people take their complaints near and far so that all can hear.)

Unfortunately, there is no widely recognized CRM package on the market today that can help deal with such a customer. It takes a combination of technologies, which we describe in Appendix 2.

Here, we show an example combination of technologies—specifically, how Attivio Search and Salesforce.com can work together to address this structured and unstructured data combination issue.

Overcoming technology vendors' sins of the past is the third big barrier to implementing social media platforms. Technology companies selling text analysis and search software are known in IT circles as issuing loads of unfulfilled promises. Often it was because the technology didn't work as claimed. Sometimes the technology wasn't at fault; the customer botched its implementation.

But we'll put the brunt of this challenge on the technology vendors: They need to demonstrate that the world has changed, that their technology has made major strides in analyzing raw text and searching for critical information. As we stated earlier in the book, social media technology vendors don't have to promise that their products are 100 percent accurate. But they do have to show they are better than previous text analysis and search technologies.

Moving Fast in the Social Media Ecosystem

The technology behind social media is moving at warp speed. It is difficult to understand and keep track of all the innovations and the firms behind them. It is even more difficult to determine whether those with great products today will be around tomorrow.

Nonetheless, companies need to understand what social media technology is all about, how it can further their goals, and which horses to bet on. Those that navigate through the complex and ever-evolving social media digital ecosystem will have a big leg up on those that can't keep pace.

13

Social CRM on the Move: Mobility Implications for Social Media Programs

Greg Jenko , Lars Kamp, and Saj Usman

CHAPTER HIGHLIGHTS

A new crop of social media software is being built just for mobile devices are redefining the way people trade experiences with others they are connected to online. These applications enable consumers to use mobile devices to get trusted information on businesses when they're literally in the marketplace.

Two vectors can help companies determine the impact of social media mobile applications: location and immediacy. Via mobile social media, customers can influence other customers in a particular vicinity to do, or not to do, business with a firm. And mobile social media enables customers to broadcast instantly good and bad experiences with companies, with no cooling-off period. With mobile social media advancing quickly, companies need a coherent strategy that maps out how they can capitalize on such applications.

Over months or years, word of mouth can propel a product to stratospheric heights. Just ask the founders of the Hula Hoop (demonstrated on the playgrounds in Los Angeles in the late 1950s), Tamagotchi virtual pets (embraced by Japanese youngers in the mid-1990s), or even Google (unveiled to Web users in 1998).[1] Happy customers tell their friends and acquaintances about a product, which over time spawns to legions of fanatics. Conversely, word of mouth about a bad product or bad customer experience can wreck a company's reputation.

Now social media lets people share their views with thousands or even millions of others around the world in minutes. That creates a whole new world for word-of-mouth marketing. In fact, social media puts word of mouth on steroids. And that forces companies to deal with it effectively, as our other chapters have explained.

But the story doesn't end there. The rapid growth of mobile computing devices means people can be "digitally social" outside the home or office. A rapidly growing number of consumers with mobile phones are using social media such as Facebook, Twitter, and Foursquare, and the number is expected to continue to increase with the prevalence of smart phones. The result: Companies need to pay close attention to what they're doing in the field. Customers are letting others know about good and bad experiences at the very moment they're having them—in the restaurant ("rude waiter"), on vacation ("great hotel") and in-flight ("I'll never fly this airline again!"). And the people they're reaching often are using their own mobile devices to read these comments—many times at the moment of purchase. All in all, mobile devices loaded with social media software are beginning to give companies great opportunities as well as great fits.

And it's just beginning. A new crop of social media software is being built just for mobile devices. The technology lets consumers find other consumers and tap their brains when they're out and about, arming them with recommendations that they trust to make purchases large and small. Using software from such companies as Foursquare and Gowalla, people are asking others on the fly whether to patronize the businesses right in front of them—the Italian restaurant on the left side of the street, the Irish pub a block down, or the apparel shop on the right—or whether they should keep moving.

These mobile applications are redefining the way people trade experiences with others they are connected to online. For example, search engine juggernaut Google has introduced a technology called Google Goggles that lets a person hold an object in front of his or her mobile phone (initially, ones with Google's Android operating system), scan it, and identify it. If a person holds up a book in a bookstore, the technology will recognize and do a Web search on it, so the person can read reviews on Amazon and gather other feedback on it. In other words, the consumer doesn't have to type the name of the book into a search engine. (Typing text into mobile phones frustrates many consumers.) When a customer points a mobile phone at a store, Google Goggles can retrieve information on the store (including its name, reviews of the store, etc.) Now imagine using the technology with Twitter. A person could hold up a smart phone in front of a bunch of wine bottles and ask people to recommend which ones are best. How's that for real-time feedback at the point of purchase!

Or consider Shopkick. This start-up aims to turn brick-and-mortar stores into virtual worlds that enhance the shopping experience. The company is developing a product called CauseWorld that lets people check into a business and donate money online to those that they feel are behind a worthy cause—for example, a restaurant in San Francisco that will donate a dollar for clean water in a village in India. Consumers collect "Karma Points" every time they check in.

Such mobile innovations are not coming just from the world of technology companies or start-ups funded by venture capital (VC). Long-established companies of many types are jumping into the social media mobility fray. One company has found a way not so much to convince consumers to shop its local establishments but rather to ratchet up the average "ticket." The $5 billion restaurant operator Dunkin' Donuts launched a social media tool in June 2009 called Dunkin' Run that lets customers collect orders from their friends with a mobile device and submit them to the nearest Dunkin' shop. That saves time for the person who is saddled with the morning coffee run. And, of course, it makes the local Dunkin' store cash register ring.

Other companies like paint manufacturer Benjamin Moore are giving consumers mobile applications that let them find the product that they need. The company enables consumers with iPhone 3GS cameras to snap photos of their wall to find the Benjamin Moore paint color that matches it. The application then tells the customer where to find the closest store that sells its paints.[2]

Who Should Pay the Most Attention? Thinking about Location and Immediacy

To be sure, social media applications gone mobile won't have the same impact on every industry and on every business in an industry. The ability of consumers to use mobile devices and get trusted information when they're literally in the marketplace won't affect all businesses equally. Which ones will the technology impact the most?

We see two vectors that can help managers determine the impact of social media mobile applications on their company: location and immediacy. Social media enables customers to influence other customers in a particular vicinity to do, or not to do, business with a firm. Companies with products purchased in many locations (e.g., a retailer with hundreds of stores) rather than from one or just a few locations have more at stake—or more opportunities to pursue, depending on how one looks at it. That's the location vector.

The immediacy vector relates to the ability of mobile social media to let customers respond instantly to good and bad experiences with companies—and to let other potential customers know about them. The immediacy quality of mobile social media means there's no cooling-off period. Social media comments that spread through mobile devices are often nasty. That greatly increases the chances for very negative sentiments to spread. The impact—on customers making local purchasing decisions with very little time to make them—can be severe.

What kinds of companies need to take notice the most? We believe it's those with many locations around the world—retailers of all types, restaurant chains, and retail banks, to name a few—whose customers make impulse decisions. Consumers armed with their Facebook, Google Goggles, Twitter, and other social media applications in their pockets or pocketbooks stand to be influenced the most on purchasing decisions they make in the field, with little time to make them. Go to this particular Indian restaurant on East 53rd Street? I'll check the people who follow me on Twitter or Facebook. What's the best power drill to buy while I'm in Home Depot? I'll look at product reviews on my iPhone while I'm in the store. Purchases that are more considered—that is, larger-ticket items that consumers spend more time to research—and that can be bought from many locations are far less likely to be impacted. A new hot water tank, automobile, or roofing contractor purchase is more immune to the impacts of mobile social media applications.

To be sure, social media is critical. People are asking their friends on Facebook, LinkedIn, Twitter, and other places about phones, cars, contractors, recreational vehicle rentals, and the like. It's just that they're less likely to need an answer on such purchases at a moment's notice when they're shopping in the marketplace.

Companies whose products and services are highly influenced by location and immediacy need to pay special attention to mobile social media technology. Technology's ability to deliver the right information at the right time in the right location to their customers is rising inexorably. These businesses need to move quickly to exploit mobile social media technology—*and* to understand how to defend against the downside.

Why must companies act fast? First, remember Moore's law about the increasing power and falling cost of computing power. Named after Intel cofounder Gordon Moore, the trend is that computing power doubles and prices have dropped in half about every two years since the 1960s. This shows no signs of abating. Combine that with rising telecommunications bandwidth—the ability to transmit much more data over the Internet and wireless infrastructure—and the result is social media applications that can do increasingly greater things at lower prices (and thus attract a wider consumer audience). The computer and telecommunications industries are putting into the hands of millions of people the power of accessing huge amounts of data, anywhere at any time. People are hungry for information at the moment of need—information to make much better purchasing decisions. The data that a mobile device can deliver (in text, video, audio, etc.) is no longer largely constrained by computing power or telecom bandwidth. In fact, a much bigger constraint is how much people can read and what their fingers can type on the small screen of a mobile device.

The second reason for getting real with mobile social media is the outbreak of innovation in this sector. Mobile application start-up companies are proliferating. The funding is there; VC firms are projected to spend a total of $4 billion on social media and mobile software companies in 2010 and 2011.

But even firms that lack start-up funding aren't severely hampered; the barriers to entry for software companies in this sector are nonexistent. In the 1990s, when the Web was commercialized, Web start-ups had to purchase expensive computer technology—servers, software, and data centers to launch their businesses. Today, cloud computing has largely done away with mobile software companies' need for capital equipment. Rather than buying servers, they can rent from firms that provide computing services over the Internet (the "cloud," as they say). Furthermore, companies can distribute their social media applications over the Internet. That allows them to bypass costly retail distribution networks. Telecommunication carriers such as Verizon and AT&T, as well as mobile device makers like Apple, are becoming the distributors of mobile social media applications.

All of this explains why companies such as Foursquare have emerged so quickly. The company got off the ground with just over a $1 million in seed capital. With more than 500,000 users by March 2010, the company received a $20 million VC investment in June 2010.[3]

These companies are empowering a whole new breed of consumer: highly informed, very bold, and extremely picky. They come armed to the local marketplace with information from their peers about the pluses and minuses of local establishments.

Navigating through Rough and Uncharted Seas

Companies trying to figure out what to do in the mobile social media space are operating in a foreign land. It is very difficult to predict what technologies to pay attention to because of fickle technologies and even more fickle consumers. The field, ruled today by garage-based start-ups with no clear business model, is in its infancy. But rest assured that the situation won't stay that way for long. Mobile social media will rapidly evolve from a marketing and brand-building tool for companies to a fully functioning interaction channel, one in which customers can find other customers easily to learn about businesses and their offerings. The implications are enormous for all— businesses that sell to consumers (B2C), businesses that sell to other businesses (B2B), and businesses that sell to intermediaries such as dealers and distributors (B2I).

The technology challenges alone are daunting. If all a company is doing with mobile technology is pushing out its brand messages, the world is a lot simpler. The marketing function can handle that. But as customers start demanding the ability to transact business with a company through mobile devices anytime and anywhere, the company's web site mobile software (and all the technology behind it) better be ready. Remember all the early problems companies had optimizing their web sites for different PC-based Web browsers (of which today there are three main players)? The problems in accommodating different mobile devices dwarf those.

So which devices should a company focus on? Apple's introduction of its highly portable iPad—consider it between a smart phone and a small laptop computer—heated up one of the first real discussions of technology standards. Apple chief executive Steve Jobs faced down the developer of Flash technology (which sets Web images into motion), Adobe, by preventing iPads from using Flash. The decision for companies on whether to use HTML5 or Flash in their social media mobile applications is just one of many tough technology choices on how to manage the brand across a myriad of devices, each of which can use quite different technology.

But that isn't the only technology challenge. Another is around managing online content. The requirements of content management will explode as companies try to optimize the way customers use everything from text-only devices, to smart phones, to tablet computers such as the iPad. The mobile technology ecosystem is evolving quickly. A company's internal information technology people are shooting at a fast-moving set of technology vendors and technologies. Companies like Foursquare could be big businesses—or be gone in two years. Large mobile players such as Google, Apple, Nokia, and Research In Motion all started acquiring mobile companies in 2005, mainly at the top layer of the stack—that is, software. A sign that these companies expect the biggest value creation to take place in software and services, rather than networks and network access, the industry's traditional value pools: Google's acquisition of a $500 million stake in WiMAX (high-speed internet access technology) operator Clearwire got written down to $0 in a matter of two years. As of 2010, both Google and Apple are acquiring start-ups almost on a monthly basis, with prices ranging from $30 million (e.g., Vark) to $750 million (e.g., AdMob).

The challenge this presents for companies is this: Who should they partner with? Which companies will be here tomorrow, and which technologies are consumers likely to embrace? Even on the mobile advertising front—one of the few sources of revenue that most industry analysts agree is here to stay with the mobile Web—there remain many big questions. Will there be an über marketing service that can handle different mobile advertisements?

Last, how does a company reliably predict how consumers will react? How will people want to use their mobile devices? Will they accept advertising on their devices, or shut them off? Will they want advertisements with video on their iPhones and Androids? And what about people who drive, one of the key users of mobile devices? How do companies plan to interact with people who shouldn't be texting or typing while they're at the wheel? Will they want (and use) speech-enabled applications—software that bends to their oral commands? All this is about anticipating consumer preferences. It is about how people want to interact with companies that sell products and services: before, during, and after the sale. Trying to figure out which technology vendors, applications, and other technologies are the right ones to work with—all while the business models of social media mobile applications are still in high flux—is tricky. The risk of wasting big investments looms large.

Even if customers like the social media applications they're using on Facebook, the iPhone and iPad, and other mobile services, that is no guarantee they'll love them forever. Customer usage of mobile applications declines rapidly (with certain Twitter and Facebook apps as exceptions). In fact, the average customer retention rate is less than 30 days. The challenge for companies like Dunkin' Donuts and Benjamin Moore paints is how to keep their mobile apps relevant in the face of a finicky crowd.

Creating a Mobile Social Media Strategy

Despite all the uncertainty that we've painted in this chapter, managers face even greater risks if they wait for the dust to settle. Putting planning on hold for two years surely will leave a company far behind competitors that are in the market with social media applications for mobile devices today—even if they've stubbed their toes.

So how does a company create an effective strategy? How does it navigate through these uncharted waters and get to its destination when the destination itself isn't clear? The next steps will bring that destination into view—even if every detail doesn't emerge.

The first step is assessing how much business stands to be impacted by social media brought to mobile devices. The factors of location and immediacy provide a good starting point for determining this. But keep in mind that a company is not at the mercy of consumers in the field or the morale of its field operations people. Mobile social media is a double-edged sword: an intelligence-gathering weapon for the consumer (to weed out bad operators) as well as for a company. Indeed, customer complaints can spread rapidly over mobile devices and scare away other customers from shopping with certain companies. However, the technology also allows these companies to pinpoint their operational problems in the field and fix them fast.

Companies must monitor the local chatter on mobile devices. They need to know by the hour what people are complaining about—whether a chain retailer's rude cashier in its Hoboken, New Jersey store, a hair in the soup at a restaurant chain's Santa Barbara, California, location, or the poor hotel service at the unit in downtown Chicago. Listening to the social media chatter gives companies a new window on their worlds, a way to see in nearly real time what's going on inside their operations around the world.

The second step in creating a strategy for mobile social media is realizing things will be different depending on whether a business is selling to consumers, businesses, or channel intermediaries (wholesalers, distributors, etc.). Each business needs to define the appropriate call to action that is tailored to the specific needs and situations of its customers and determine the types of mobile transactions it needs to focus on. Should a company center on brand image marketing? Generating sales through transactions (as the Dunkin' Run application did)? On helping the customer in the research she may do before making a purchasing decision (but not the purchase itself)? (The Benjamin Moore paint application is a good example of that.) Or should a company's mobile strategy make life for the customer easier after he buys a product or service? To some extent, this will depend on whether the organization's business is B2C, B2B, or B2I. We see B2C companies focusing greatly on marketing and branding. Coca-Cola's "My Coke" rewards points program is a good example. Customers get points for future purchasers by entering text into a mobile device off a bottle cap. B2C companies might also focus on sales transactions (à la Dunkin' Donuts). This is unlike a company that sells through intermediaries, such as Procter & Gamble. We can't see P&G creating a direct sales channel through mobile devices.

B2B companies face different issues with mobile social media. Because they usually don't have thousands of locations for their customers to purchase their offerings and because their purchases are typically more considered, they aren't likely to have the opportunities that B2C companies have in creating applications to boost sales transactions at the point of purchase. B2B companies should look to focus on developing relationships with their customers through the mobile Web.

After deciding whether it wants to market, sell, or provide postsale customer service over the social Web, a company will need to determine its interaction channels: How do customers want to interact with the company? What technologies and applications are they using? And can the company influence what they use? Despite today's proliferation of disparate devices and software, the good news is that standards are on the way. Device makers, software companies, and the firms that build social applications for the mobile Web are all driving standards. More and more, companies are seeing a foundation on which to build their applications.

Yet even after a company makes what appear to be sound technology choices, it must monitor the performance of its vendors daily and how its customers are using the technology. Why? When customers no longer value an application, they stop using it or stop spending money on it. In the mobile ecosystem, these changes happen daily and weekly. A company doesn't have a year—or sometimes even a month—to get it right.

After it has decided on the technology, the types of users, and the types of interactions it will have with them, a company must develop models for information security and analytics. Social media compounds the security problems that companies face with their technology. Mobile devices are stolen, viruses can run rampant on social applications, and breaches can have disruptive consequences to customers and a company's own operations. Even if data is secure, it is challenging to determine how to gather, process, and analyze mobile social Web data. Social media data complicates the world of business analytics. The data that flows from mobile devices complicates it even further. There are plenty of opportunities for hackers to intercept the interaction between a user's device, the network, and the cloud and simply hijack a user's social media profile—as Silicon Valley venture capitalist Guy Kawasaki discovered. Kawasaki's Twitter account was hijacked in June 2009 and used to push malware to his more than 140,000 followers. The malware would then reroute certain Web requests in order to phish a user's passwords for other applications, such as a user's accounts with online retailers, service providers, and banks. And it doesn't stop there. Other examples for hacked Twitter accounts are Britney Spears and even President Barack Obama.

Companies whose businesses have the most to gain or lose from mobile social media must place the most attention on how they manage all the social media chatter generated from mobile devices. This is about striking the right governance model. Companies should appoint someone to focus on the mobile space, as we said earlier in the book to be the case with social customer relationship management. Mobile computing is too dynamic and important to be a part-time job today. Some companies may need several people to focus on social media in mobile channels—one on what customers are doing, another on the technologies, a third on the vendors, and a fourth on the competition. Macy's and Walmart have posted director-level positions for heads of mobile strategy—entirely new jobs. They're important because they're about how those retailers can use mobile technology to better engage with customers so they buy more merchandise in the store.

Next Step: Get Serious

Many companies are dipping their toes in the water in the mobile space. Some are publishing random tweets on behalf of their chief executive, hoping they will impress customers. Others are pushing advertisements on mobile devices. But nothing replaces a coherent strategy, one that maps out how a company will go on the offense and defense as customers share their glee and ire on mobile devices.

14

New Rules for Tools: IT Infrastructure Implications and Options for Supporting Enterprise Social Media

Robert Wollan and Kelly Dempski

CHAPTER HIGHLIGHTS

Chief information officers (CIOs) are in an important position to help their companies become "more social"—that is, actively monitor and manage the soaring number of conversations customers, employees, and partners are having about them on the Web. But for CIOs and other managers of the information technology (IT) function, it's a role that won't be easy to play because social media technology is far different from previous generations of IT.

To help their companies fully leverage the power of social media, CIOs must add to, revise, or even unlearn a number of long-held beliefs about how they buy, develop, and implement information technology. These new learnings, or new rules for the new tools, substantially alter the way CIOs must work with their counterparts in marketing and other functions as they develop and maintain social media applications.

The job of the chief information officer (CIO) has changed dramatically during the past two decades. Once inwardly focused as management information system (MIS) directors, CIOs in most large organizations today play a much larger role over a much broader landscape: every activity that a company's information technology tentacles can reach, especially through the Web.

Social media expands the CIO's role even further. It ups the ante for CIOs, making their jobs more consequential. The reason is that social media connects the company directly to customers, creating an unprecedented opportunity to market better, service customers more effectively, improve product development, and accomplish other competitive mandates. In this way, social media is one of the best things to happen to CIOs and their information technology (IT) departments, as they now will play a more direct and strategic role in the success of the business.

But social media also makes the CIO's role much more complex. In fact, many CIOs will have to adapt the beliefs they've built over decades about the way to run a first-class IT operation. These beliefs include the need to make technology efficient through scale and the value of disciplined and lengthy technology purchase processes. CIOs also will need to rethink their innate desire to decrease the complexity of the technology footprint—that is, of having many fewer software applications to maintain—as well as the need for stable technology platforms that can be integrated easily with a company's present and future systems.

Let's explore the new seven rules for tools that CIOs and the IT organization must adopt to help their companies fully capitalize on social media technology.

New Rule #1: The CIO Must Embrace These Dynamic Technologies

Social media channels are new and rapidly changing. Services such as Twitter, which didn't exist a couple of years ago, are making constant changes to their systems to deal with massive growth and evolving business plans. They are changing constantly to define themselves, address technical challenges and privacy concerns, and meet the demands of a large and highly opinionated user base. Therefore, while they represent new opportunities for CIOs, they also create new challenges in that they will have a far shorter shelf life and no singular selection or solution will satisfy the functional need. CIOs need to resist the urge to ignore these opportunities until they reach maturity or to dismiss them as groups of "disposable" technology.

These dynamic technologies contrast sharply with traditional IT solutions. CIOs historically have closely scrutinized technologies such as Enterprise Resource Planning (ERP), customer relationship management (CRM), financial systems, and marketing applications for their prebuilt capability, stability, and longevity. CIOs purchased enterprise applications because they offer a well-architected software foundation on which to build future technology enhancements. The components of a technology solution were expected to be stable, with long and well-published update cycles. New features were added to serve the interests of the enterprise, not the public. In other words, IT managers have sought the technology equivalent of the bricks in their built-to-last castle.

Today, CIOs must understand that the social media landscape is constantly changing at a pace that is far more rapid than any tool they've used before. They need, therefore, to rethink every aspect of the procurement and development cycle. They must have processes in place to identify emerging channels quickly and need to place the appropriate bets on the channels that succeed (while accepting the risk that some channels might not). They also have to procure and build systems very quickly, with a focus on experimentation and iteration rather than tightly scheduled and lengthy release cycles. Finally, they must build systems that can be quickly adapted to new features, new application programming interfaces (APIs), or entirely new services. Today's social media services can literally change overnight, and the CIO must be nimble enough to change with them.

New Rule #2: The CIO Must Manage Social Media Data

Rule #1 addresses the things a CIO must do to manage social media systems. But there also are new rules for how the CIO must handle the data flowing to and from those systems. The data coming from social media can be incredibly rich, plentiful, and delivered in real time. Through social listening, CIOs can see what people are saying about a product or brand within seconds of their saying it. They can mine deep demographic information about their Facebook followers, or influence patterns within a social network. This rich data can be the basis for valuable insight, especially when it is coupled with the other data within the CIO's sphere of influence.

The problem with social media data, like the systems themselves, is that it is constantly changing, poorly formatted, and difficult to control. Business users can gain a significant amount of insight from integrating social data, such as buzz metrics or influence scoring, with sales patterns and traditional marketing data. But to do so, they need data that is cleaner and formatted to support such integration.

This type of data cleansing, reformatting, and integration falls within the traditional IT domain. Therefore, the users of this data will be dependent on the CIO and IT organization to provide the services needed to best leverage social media data. CIOs will need to provide the data management services, along with the appropriate linkages among the social media systems and the other internal systems. Importantly, they will need to be aware of some of the privacy concerns that come with using such data, especially in countries with tighter privacy laws. And they will need to do all of this quickly to keep pace with changes in social media channels. As in Rule #1, CIOs must be very nimble in how they deal with the data, especially as business users become more dependent on the rich insight it provides.

New Rule #3: The CIO Must Become a Social Media Power User to Influence Change

In traditional IT systems, the CIO is in control of gathering the requirements that drive changes to the IT software suite. The CIO will work with the specific group of *internal* users—and a homogenous group at that—to understand their needs and pain points, consolidate the information into requirements that mesh with the priorities and schedule of the IT organization, and pass those requirements to the software vendor or development team. The vendor, which sells to the CIO, will make the changes that are most requested by their customers. In short, the CIO is in control, and rarely is caught off guard by changes.

In social media, the situation is completely reversed. Services such as Facebook and Twitter are highly focused on acquiring new users. CIOs, and in some cases even advertisers, are barely an afterthought. In this world, rather than being in control, CIOs can find themselves in a position of constantly playing catch-up as current services change and new ones emerge from an expansive, largely *external,* group of users.

Therefore, today's CIOs must pay close attention to the social media ecosystem so they can predict changes before they occur and quickly understand how these changes could impact their organizations. For instance, CIOs shouldn't be surprised at 800 percent growth in Twitter users or scramble to respond as services such as Foursquare become more popular. Rather, they should be watching the trends and, in some cases, doing their part to accelerate the trends.

Because the social media ecosystem is driven by social media users, CIOs should become active social media users, or at least pay close attention to those who are. A CIO who is willing to take risks and use social media in innovative ways will be in a better position to lead and influence the evolution of these technologies. Although CIOs are no longer in the driver's seat, it is possible for them to be a part of the change instead of simply following and responding to it.

New Rule #4: The CIO and the CMO Must Be Equal Partners from the Outset

The preceding rules focused on the role of the CIO in building and managing social media systems, dealing with social media data, and even innovating in the social media world. However, the current reality is that in many organizations, the chief marketing officer (CMO) is the owner of social media activities. So how should a company develop social media applications: Should marketing lead IT, or should IT lead marketing? The answer is neither.

A social media program that is owned by the IT organization is unlikely to realize the full marketing potential of social media. Likewise, a program owned entirely by the marketing organization will not be fully optimized with respect to the operation of the technology and the integration of social data into the company's many IT systems.

Therefore, using social media effectively requires both marketing and IT professionals to work far more collaboratively than they have on previous marketing technology initiatives. In traditional models, such projects force a lead role by IT, with business liaisons and sponsors leading from arm's length. One of the new rules of social media is that marketing and IT must be equal and active partners in making social media come to life. (See Figure 14.1.) The marketing function can't be "IT's customer." Furthermore, the jointly developed team must report to the CMO *and* CIO, not to one or the other.

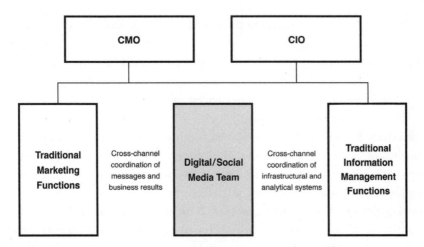

FIGURE 14.1 The New Project Team Organization Structure for Developing Social Media Applications.

As teams expand to include external partners, one of the biggest gaps CIOs will have to close in their IT skill sets will be to understand the complex world of marketing agencies. For many years, marketing agencies (such as the large advertising firms) brought little technology to the table; their expertise was in creating marketing content—print, broadcast, and other ads—and placing them in the right media. But many new marketing agencies, especially those in the social media marketing space, are blurring the lines among the work of marketing agencies, data providers, and technology vendors. The IT/marketing team must know how to work with these agencies as well as with marketing research and other organizations that can be important pieces of the solution.

New Rule #5: The CIO and CMO Must Rethink the Structure of the Social Media Team

Many of today's top CIOs began their working life in a world without the Internet or even e-mail. Traditionally, a skilled CIO and IT team were a group of individuals who grew up in the IT world. They lived through slow evolutions in IT systems and data centers, and therefore were experienced enough to manage those systems and to recognize the value of the next stage of evolution.

Similarly, the people entering the workforce today have grown up with an awareness of social media and have likely written more e-mails than letters. Their worlds at school and at home have been defined by tools such as Facebook, YouTube, and Wikipedia. As some would say, they are digital natives. They are arguably much more experienced in understanding the new systems and keeping pace with the changes.

As we noted in Chapter 4, we consistently see a generational divide in organizations, with younger people often more social media fluent than older ones. As a result, companies will have to take a risk on social media–savvy employees who may lack deep knowledge of traditional IT systems and project management skills to lead their social media initiatives. At the same time, however, companies also must look for opportunities to infuse the social media development team with strong project management skills that will enable it to implement large programs with consistent quality.

Like many start-ups, where a seasoned chief executive is paired with tech-savvy young founders, the CIO should couple social media gurus with team members who provide operational discipline. These experienced team members are also in the position to act as liaisons to the other parts of the business and to provide reality checks on timelines, budgets, and internal politics. However, both sides of the generational divide must understand the skills they bring to the table and know when to get out of the other's way and when to learn from the other.

Rule #4 explains the need to create a multidisciplinary group. This rule requires the group be multigenerational. Therefore, it is critical that the CIO and the CMO work together to assign a team leader who can work in both worlds and across the business. That team leader also must understand the various roles and differing levels of expertise and carefully manage the team to ensure the highest performance.

Furthermore, the social media team likely will expand past the boundaries of the internal organization to include players such as agencies, social media tool vendors, and other suppliers. Like the tools they provide, some vendors will be immature and unsophisticated. Therefore, the internal team will have to rethink how it purchases from and relates to vendors. This is where both sides of the generational divide must work together to provide both the technical and business due diligence to ensure the team makes the right decisions.

Finally, CIOs must remember that social media is social; it has a strong personal component. Therefore, team members should understand the social dynamics of these tools as much as the technical dynamics. Team members will have to make reasonable decisions about how a Facebook app works or how a particular field of personal data is shared among internal systems. Choosing team members carefully based on this skill will help ensure against embarrassing or ineffective social media tools.

New Rule #6: The Social Media Team Must "Fish Where the Fish Are"

There also are new rules about where CIOs' sights must be set to participate in social media. In the past, it was fine for CIOs to keep their focus solely on their firms' systems. With social media, this is no longer the case.

The first web sites gave companies a way to monitor how many people were interested in their organization's online presence and which pages they liked. The rise of social media forces companies to measure what customers are doing and how they're acting far outside the walled gardens of their web sites or online company stores. Most likely, customers and other parties are commenting on a firm regularly in Facebook, LinkedIn, Twitter, and numerous other social communities. Those aren't sites the company owns, controls, or manages.

Whether a company's web site becomes its focal point for understanding its customers is now up for debate. At the very least, CIOs must take the lead (if their marketing counterparts aren't) in getting the organization to change *where* they go to understand what customers are saying—that is, from their own web sites to the social networks their customers belong to.

But even those social networks are changing. Facebook, Twitter, YouTube, and other highly popular social sites are increasingly becoming the place where customers search for information, purchase applications for their computers, and, of course, network with others. Facebook's and YouTube's search engines are among the most heavily used today. If a company is not working with such firms to understand the terms people are using to find it and its products and services (as well as its competitors and their offerings), an organization's marketing messages will have a much harder time connecting with them.

The need for a company to market its own social media applications in places such as Facebook, LinkedIn, and Twitter will place further challenges on the IT department. Those applications must be easy to use and "cool"—that is, catch the fancy of customers, especially younger ones.

New Rule #7: The Team Leaders Must Define New Metrics

Finally, CIOs also must help their organizations understand what the real value of social media systems can be and develop appropriate metrics for different business goals. For years, organizations experimented on social media sites because it seemed like the thing to do. Today's tools and users are much more mature, and everyone is working to understand how to justify and measure the true value of social media.

"Social media" is a broad area, with a wide range of tools that can be used for a wide range of goals, each with its own metrics and success criteria. One group might want to use online forums to reduce service costs and lower response times. Another might want to run a viral video campaign to increase sales and brand awareness. Yet another might be interested in harvesting ideas from customers to improve products more effectively. Each of these goals falls under the heading of "social media," but each uses very different technologies and metrics.

Therefore, it is up to the social media team and the CIO to play a more active role early in the game to clarify the social media landscape with the business, evangelize the opportunities, define the overall systems (with integration points), and finally define success criteria that are business relevant, technically feasible, and appropriate to a given social media channel. Social media is an exciting area for CIOs. It's an area where they can lead the way for the business into an entirely new set of opportunities. However, doing this will require the team to be even more aware of the needs of the business and to express the value of social media not in technical terms, such as uptime and number of transactions, but in business terms that demonstrate the power of these new technologies.

Conclusion

CIOs have been rewarded for many years for creating a stable technology infrastructure that continually improves the way a company's key processes operate. Risk reduction, technology efficiency, and reliability all have been implanted on every CIO's head. But social media represents a quite different type of technology—one with new risks that come with the new rewards.

The IT function will need to reshape the way it budgets to accommodate the more dynamic technology cycles of social media. Yearly purchasing plans won't cut it. Money must be there to acquire new technologies that were not around last quarter. IT also will have to live with far less clarity around vendors' future technology directions (i.e., beyond the next two to three quarters). The three-year IT road map—of both a company and its technology vendors—will have far less value.

CIOs also must pay greater attention to the significant impact social media will have on the people aspect of their operations. Gone are the days when systems projects are staffed and led largely by IT professionals who serve their internal customers—the rest of the business. As social media technologies become an increasingly larger portion of a company's applications portfolio, business users—in particular, those from the marketing organization—must play an equal role in the development team. And CIOs must recognize the value that social media–fluent individuals can bring to the development team, even if they lack the skills and training in traditional project management disciplines.

IT executives who can make this work—who can combine the new technology of social media work with the old technology they have mastered for years—will be highly valuable commodities in the years ahead.

V

Empowering Employees for Social Media Success

15 Culture Traits, Employee Incentives, and Training

Christine Eberle

CHAPTER HIGHLIGHTS

The use of social media affects the culture of organizations from multiple dimensions: from how the enterprise adopts social media internally, to how it recruits and retains employees, to how it supports a customer-centric and collaborative operating model that fully leverages social media channels.

A human capital strategy for social media—organized around defining talent needs, discovering sources of talent, developing talent for ongoing high performance, and deploying talent to the most appropriate areas of the business—is critical to a company's ability to effectively embrace and benefit from social media.

Social media is affecting corporations from multiple dimensions. It's increasingly becoming a way of life for employees, customers, partners, and competitors. Employees want to work differently, and customers want to buy and be served differently. As a result, companies need cultures that can adapt to social media as integral to the organization.

In many enterprises, such cultural change could mean significant transformation. Developing a culture that embraces social media requires changes to a company's human capital strategy from role definition to recruiting, development, and rewards and incentives. However, benefits come naturally when cultural change is addressed and social media is well implemented.

As People Change, So Must Corporate Culture

People of all ages and demographics have adopted social media technologies. For many, it's becoming a way of life. Technology-savvy consumers increasingly are using social media to conduct research on companies, products, and services as well as make purchases and troubleshoot service issues. They collaborate via social media to influence the actions and purchases of others and to jointly innovate. And as these consumers represent an increasing share of the workforce and customer base for many organizations, their impact on corporations—and particularly corporate culture—is significant.

In fact, because the millennial generation (those born between 1977 and 1995) has been immersed in technology throughout their lives, it's completely transparent to them. "Technology doesn't exist. It's like the air," said Coco Conn, cofounder of the Web-based Cityspace project. "As technology relentlessly advances each month, Net Geners just breathe it in, like improvements in the atmosphere."[1] Recent Accenture global research confirmed the extensive use of social media among millennials. According to that study, 55 percent use instant messaging, 45 percent use social networking sites, and 31 percent use online collaborative tools for work purposes.[2] (See Figure 15.1.)

Already numerous individuals around the globe (particularly the younger generation) view social media as a fundamental aspect of life. They thrive on freedom, collaboration, flexibility, social connectivity, and trust-based relationships. They have a different norm about the way they communicate and the things they value. They are collaborators in every part of their lives and blend their careers with their entertainment and thus expect work to be fun. Cultural fit is as important as salary when hunting for employment. They leverage technology to create flexibility in when and where they work and to customize their jobs.

This social media–savvy group communicates digitally by instant message, chatting, and texting. In fact, "for Net Geners, e-mail is so yesterday. It's what you use when you write a polite thank-you letter to a friend's parents."[3]

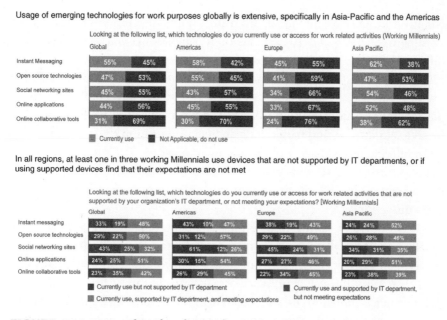

FIGURE 15.1 Use of Technologies by Various Groups of People.

Source: "Jumping the Boundaries of Corporate IT: Accenture Global Research on Millennials' Use of Technology," Accenture, 2010.

Although older millennials (ages 23 to 27) globally still spend an average of 6.8 hours a week writing or receiving work-related e-mails, mid-millennials already in the workforce spend just 4.2 hours a week on e-mail. Among that group, real-time alternatives are gaining ground, such as text messaging via mobile phone (3 hours) or instant messaging (3.2 hours). The trend is even more pronounced among high school and young college students.[4]

With the first wave of the 80-million-member millennial generation reaching adulthood, four generations are now employees and customers working and shopping together simultaneously. This year, millennials are expected to comprise 40 percent of the workforce. The 46-million-member Generation X (those born between 1965 and 1976) is beginning to move into senior leadership positions. Baby Boomers (those born between 1946 and 1964 and the second-most populous generation) have ruled the workplace for years, and while the average retirement age in the United States is 61,[5] recent studies suggest that Boomers may delay retirement up to nine years due to the recent recession.[6] With because workers are delaying retirement, corporations still employ a number of individuals from the "Silent Generation" as well (those born between 1925 and 1945). This multigenerational workforce has vastly different skills, needs, motivations, and work styles.

In Accenture's recently released book *Workforce of One*, authors Susan Cantrell and David Smith emphasize that for corporations employing multiple generations, understanding learning styles, personality, wellness profiles, behavioral patterns, and networking and communication styles is fundamental to offering a broad array of choices to employees.[7] For companies pursuing mass customization of talent management, social networking can be a critical part of this differentiated approach to boosting employee productivity and satisfaction.

Every company selling to or employing social media–savvy individuals must recognize that its entire human capital strategy must reflect this new reality. Company practices must encourage collaboration, both internally and with customers and partners. Workforce approaches must be tailored to the different generational needs and preferences. Plans must be in place to bridge generational gaps and effect change. Social media strategy must be aligned with business goals to realize strategic outcomes. Companies that incorporate these potentially dramatic shifts into their talent management strategy will be better able to attract and retain talent and achieve high performance.

The Cultural Challenges Social Media Presents

The use of social media affects the culture of organizations in multiple dimensions: from how the enterprise adopts social media internally, to how it recruits and retains employees, to how it supports a customer-centric and collaborative operating model that fully leverages social media channels. As a result, there are several differences required in the talent strategy of organizations embracing social media versus the traditional ways that talent management has been done. Enterprises need considerable change in focus in how they hire, train, reward, and retain employees. Consequently, as companies embark on social media and increased collaboration, they face many common culture and talent-related challenges. Organizations should consider both their collaborative reach and their alignment with business goals as they build their social media strategy.

Leaders Underestimate Benefits and Fear Risks

Many organizations initially struggle with the concept of introducing social media in general. The legal aspects of enterprise social media solutions are a primary concern. Executives assume the use of social media will require significant overhead to audit and police employee contributions. One common executive concern is that social networking tools that are not mediator moderated would enable employees to complain or make negative comments about the company and expose the business to legal risk. They also worry about degradations to employee productivity. For instance, comments such as "We don't think it's going to be a good use of people's time" or "We think we're going to see people chatting about their personal lives and not getting their work done" are common objections.

These objections were reiterated in a recent survey conducted by the Society for Marketing Professional Services. The study showed that the predominant barriers preventing companies from using social media were "not understanding how to use it," "just another thing to keep abreast of," "not convinced of appropriateness," and "not convinced of effectiveness."[8] Executive resistance to social media is very similar to executive resistance to employees using personal computers or e-mail in years gone by. And in these cases, history has come to two major conclusions: It's largely impossible to stop adoption of technology as it evolves, and the fears are typically unfounded. The same conclusions are true with social media. Many organizations report that social media positively impacts employee satisfaction, particularly in service organizations.

Enterprise Culture Change

Company culture and policies also can hinder social media adoption and collaboration among employees. (See Chapter 17 further insights on this issue.) The process of collaboration must be built into the fabric of the corporate culture. Yet, from Accenture experience, culture transformation is one of the most difficult endeavors executives can face. Often internal leadership teams compete with one another instead of collaborating. And these competitive attitudes filter down to employees and staff.

Transforming a culture for collaboration through social media is especially challenging with today's multigenerational workforce. Some employees are reluctant to adopt enterprise social media solutions such as expert forums, networking, and collaboration tools. Many, especially older, employees are not comfortable communicating via social media channels and are resistant to joining in on the use of new capabilities. This results in communication gaps in the workforce as nonadopting employees are cut off from their coworkers' ideas and vice versa if they don't openly communicate via the same communications channels.

Silos and Organizational Change

There is no one "right way" to organize, but typically organizational design change is required for social media adoption. For example, in one large telecommunications company, a regional human resources (HR) organization model prevailed, meaning every location had a resident HR person. The company decided to centralize its HR organization structure and create a shared services group. It enabled the organizational change with social media tools. Instead of going down the hall to speak with the local resource, employees were asked to make a phone call or "chat" via social networking with a representative from the shared HR group. Such a change required a shift in the way people worked and a cultural shift to become comfortable with collaborating via means other than face-to-face communications.

Organizations often unintentionally inhibit the collaboration enabled by social media due to the silo syndrome. In an organization suffering from silo syndrome, each department or function interacts primarily within that silo rather than with other groups across the organization. This manifestation of silo syndrome breeds insular thinking, redundancy, and suboptimal decision making. Silos also commonly extend to systems and data. Instead of reaching across the organization, people move information and decisions vertically, thus decreasing speed and limiting information flow.

Rewards and Incentives

Homo sapiens are creatures of habit and unconsciously but routinely ask themselves the same questions when doing something they are not willing to do: "What's in it for me? What's the benefit for the employee, for the team? Do I get something for this?" Historically this also has proven to be the case for the many employees who are willing to collaborate only when the question of what is in it for them is answered and communicated throughout the organization.

Traditional rewards and incentive models are no longer appropriate for employees interacting in social media channels. Rewards and incentive structures must change to encourage collaboration. Yet a recent study showed that only five percent of companies offered collaboration incentives.[9] Incentives needn't be simply monetary in nature. Mentoring, coaching, and recognition are highly motivating to some individuals.

For example, employees who work in social networking service queues often target the most difficult, most vocal customers with complex problems and significant word-of-mouth impact. Customer service agents are monitoring social networking sites, looking for complaining customers and trying to solve their problems. These agents manage the absolute hardest service cases that have the most impact on the image of the company. For these employees, typical incentives and metrics such as how many calls are handled, call length, efficiency, sales, up-sales, and first-call resolution just don't work. In addition, traditional bonuses (sometimes up to 20 percent of agent salary) are based on how well agents serve in a call center environment. None of those operational metrics applies to the employees who are dealing with social networks. Organizations must develop a better rewards and incentive structure to ensure that social media agents are being rewarded based on their capabilities and contributions.

Scaling of Talent Needs

Given the relatively short existence and rapid acceleration of social media, there is a relative scarcity of resources with specific social media capabilities, from customer service, to data management and analytics. That is a key reason why organizations are finding that customer-facing social medial channels are easy to pilot but difficult to manage at scale. Typically these roles require a higher degree of specialization and training than traditional customer service roles. Consequently, it is difficult for service organizations to staff social media channels from existing customer service staff. Unless an enterprise has a good talent management strategy that reflects these shifts—including new job definitions, hiring profiles, and revamped training, rewards, and incentives—it will struggle to grow the capability successfully due to resource constraints.

Tools and Knowledge Management Capabilities

Knowledge management content tools must be updated with external sources of content as social media and networking channels grow. This is a significant consideration in a talent management strategy. After all, to do their jobs, employees need a repository of information on which they can rely.

Take, for example, the dialogue that occurs in an online forum. A telecommunications customer is having issues with a bundled modem. He has television, Internet, and phone service through the company and, for some reason, his wireless Internet connection isn't working. He calls the company, and it is unable to help. He complains on an online forum. Another technically savvy customer on the forum is able to provide an answer that solves the problem. That is just one example of the wealth of content on forums and other social media that needs to be integrated into knowledge management tools. However, capturing such content is fraught with challenges: One can't verify the accuracy of the content, the sources are always changing, and the data is typically unstructured. Companies must create policies and methods for workers to access and use such content, and employees must be comfortable with ambiguity and using personal judgment regarding the quality and appropriateness of the information they find.

Keeping Up with the Pace of Change

The definition of social media and the channels that customers use shift constantly. Consequently, the customer-facing employees who support these channels must adapt. For example, a company develops a social media strategy for handling customer inquiries, and it has a group of trained agents who scour Facebook and Twitter for comments on the company. It has developed rules and policies and training for these employees that are very specific to those social media channels. However, while today customers are really active on Twitter, there's always a competitive channel, such as mahalo.com, emerging. Slowly, people migrate from one channel to another channel. Social media workers must stay on top of the always-changing environment and adapt their job requirements and the work they do to reflect what consumers are using to communicate about companies externally.

Creating a Strategy for Social Media Success

Many, if not all, of the challenges just discussed can be mitigated through a comprehensive human capital strategy that proactively addresses the changes required for collaboration and social media adoption. Organizations must

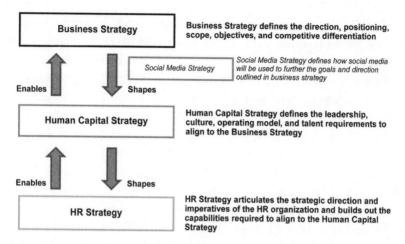

FIGURE 15.2 Just as an Organization's Social Media Strategy Must Align to an Overall Business Strategy, So Must an Organization's Human Capital and HR Strategies Align.

recognize that leadership commitment, new roles, and changes to recruiting, organization design, learning, technology, and rewards and incentives all must be made to effectively embrace social media. The majority of the remainder of this chapter will focus on an organization's human capital strategy as it pertains to social media.

The model in Figure 15.2 offers a framework to consider the comprehensive changes required at all levels of the organization, including HR Strategy, Human Capital Strategy and Business Strategy; taken as a whole, these changes encourage adoption of social media and the associated benefits to the organization.

Human Capital Strategy

Any organization's social media strategy should be developed with consideration to cultural differences in the larger environment in which the company operates. Role definition, recruiting, training, and rewards and measures are all influenced by the broader culture in which employees and customers live. For instance, social media adoption in the United States is very different from social media use in China or India or even some European countries.

Millennials in the Chinese workforce spend an average of almost 34 working hours a week on communication tools versus almost 11 hours for the rest of the world.[10] In addition, between 2005 and 2050, the working-age population of emerging economies will increase by 1.7 billion, compared with a decline of 9 million in developed economies.[11] And the U.S. Bureau of Labor Statistics reported that more temporary jobs were created in December 2009 than in any comparable period in the past 20 years.[12] As all of these trends affect workforce strategy, it is clear that human capital strategies for social media cultural adoption also should consider the culture and trends in the markets within which the company is doing business.

As part of the human capital strategy, there must be visible commitment from leadership to drive a culture of collaboration. To demonstrate such commitment, executives, starting at the very top, should communicate often using social media channels. Executives must use collaboration tools and social media as a standard part of executive communications. For instance, one company has a blog written by the chief operating officer to update company information, with the intent to demonstrate that he is open to all employees through the Internet. The messages provide insight about his work activities and are also of a personal nature.[13] Companies should make the tools pervasive by embedding them in the desktop interface, and executives should make social media a standard part of doing business.

In addition, companies should explicitly consider the diversity of their workforce along multiple dimensions (including social media savvy) as part of talent strategy development. The emerging practice highlighted in *Workforce of One* is about bridging the needs of the collective team and the individual and aligning people practices with strategy and with individual needs.[14] The idea of capitalizing on difference becomes so embedded into an organization and its everyday operations that the very structure of its people practices and policies changes to flexibly capitalize on individual differences.

Just as consumers today can define and create their own content using YouTube or Wikipedia, employees now can define and create their own people practices without any centrally defined limits, choices, or policies designed to serve particular employee segments. With employee-defined personalization, for example, individuals can define the learning they need through wikis, blogs, YouTube or Facebook–like applications, and on-the-job experience. The U.S. Navy has taken this concept to heart. Employees—not HR—set compensation levels in hard-to-fill jobs through an online job auction web site.

Define Needs

Collaboration approaches enabled by social media are best implemented when they explicitly further specific enterprise goals. Hence, the talent needs of an organization for social media adoption should reflect what is required to accomplish the business goals and to enable social media to further the goals effectively. To this end, organizations should undertake a role-specific analysis of desired business outcomes. These role-specific outcomes can be anything from "decrease customer churn by connecting with customers on public forums," to "develop more efficient products that better meet customer needs," to "foster better collaboration amongst corporate teams."

Once the role-specific business outcomes are defined, the organization can articulate the necessary business capabilities employees must possess to be effective in their roles. Examples include "ability to troubleshoot customer problems and manage sales leads effectively using social media," "ability to define and differentiate social media products and offerings," and "experience using corporate collaboration technologies to improve employee productivity." Finally, these business capabilities directly lead to the basic competencies employees must possess or develop in order for the organization to be successful, such as "value selling," or "product development," or "collaborative leadership."

These business outcomes, business capabilities, and competencies can be used to define job profiles, develop new learning strategies, guide business performance scorecards and rewards and incentives programs, and identify skill gaps in the existing employee population. Only through a careful evaluation of role-specific business outcomes, business capabilities, and competencies can an organization anticipate the roles that social media must play in its human capital strategy as it seeks to recruit, develop, and retain a high-performing workforce.

Discover: Attract and Source Talent

Creating a culture that embraces collaboration and social media also requires changes to recruiting strategy. Companies must understand differences within the diverse talent pool, segment prospective employee groups, and develop creative new channels to reach each segment. For instance, when recruiting social media users as potential employees, companies should use employees' channels of preference and communicate with them in ways they value (for example, posting company profiles and job opportunities on Facebook, Twitter, and LinkedIn). Accenture has adopted such an approach. We now routinely host "open houses" in our virtual office in Second Life, inviting interested candidates to come in and learn about the company. In addition, it is important to follow up with candidates using text messages or other social media channels both informally and formally. Accenture's experience has been that more candidates accept our employment offers when we've connected via social media than when we've simply sent a standard "thank you" e-mail.

Develop Talent Potential

To encourage employees to learn new attitudes, behaviors, and skills, companies must review talent development programs and incorporate advanced learning methods. Ironically, social media provides a superior platform for training that transforms culture, even if the nature of the culture transformation is social media adoption. Companies are experiencing significantly greater return on investment from interactive and collaborative learning compared with traditional instructor-led classroom training.

"Learning 2.0," as Accenture calls it, combines innovative approaches and technologies in Web 2.0 learning, knowledge management, and real-time performance support. These capabilities and technologies help companies deliver learning at the point of need and in formats that can adapt to the requirements, working environment, and learning styles of individual learners. As a result, employees report they are more competent and confident in doing their jobs. And confidence is a proven predictor of success. Components of a Learning 2.0 approach that drive higher performance in corporate learning include:

- **Accessible across multiple channels**, allowing for learner-centric distribution modes including instructor-led training, e-learning, podcasts, wikis, and blogs.
- **Flexible**, to allow for content reuse, allowing for multipurpose learning assets available online, in the classroom and in audio/video format.
- **Modular**, to enable learners to find and consume just the portion of the content that is relevant to them and to the task at hand.

- **Dynamic**, allowing learning objects to be updated by subject matter experts in the field as key content changes.
- **Collaborative**, so learners can easily contribute content, share lessons learned, and add to both their personal and the organizational knowledge base.
- **Engaging**, such that learners want to participate in consuming and creating content because it holds their attention and interest and they are recognized for their participation.
- **Personalized**, meaning learning experiences are relevant to an employee's role and work context and are delivered at the point of need.
- **Measured**, so the impact of learning on job performance is tracked, and learners can be more accountable for contributing and consuming knowledge related to their jobs and their organization.
- **User-generated**, meaning more content will be provided by users, increasing the relevance of learning to actual performance needs and driving down overall training costs.

One example of a more nimble learning organization that brings together a number of Learning 2.0 principles is Microsoft's Academy Mobile, which helps the company's salespeople learn a particular product or solution so they can capitalize more quickly on customer opportunities. The academy provides information that is always fresh, such as what other salespeople are doing in the field that is producing successful results. Content comes from product experts and salespeople, and also can be harvested from conference calls, presentations, and third-party vendors. It is then turned into short deliverables, such as podcasts and video podcasts, or vodcasts, and shared across the network. Microsoft has an internal user base of 22,000 for the academy, which it also has opened up to 5,000 partners in its distribution network. The academy user base generates more than 500 podcasts per month, and these have significantly increased the sales force's knowledge about products, competitors, and sales best practices. The academy also gives the field a communication channel for immediate feedback to sales, product, and learning leadership.

Deploy Talent: Right Place, Right Time

As companies bring in new social media–savvy employees who possess a different work style and value set than current employees, the culture must transform to embrace everyone. Therefore, companies need an integration plan that addresses social media advocates and resisters and tools that bridge the gap between the two groups. Several proven transformation techniques are highly relevant to such social media culture transformations. Some of these include:

- **Use a rapid knowledge transition tool kit built on social media to help share knowledge across the organization.** Knowledge sharing is critical, especially between long-tenured staff and new recruits. Often companies bring in younger employees, and they have no means by which to learn the context of the company. The integration fails, the new employees become disengaged, and the company never receives the benefit from all the skills and energy these recruits were bringing to the organization.

- **Set standards and requirements for use of collaboration technologies to overcome resistance to change and to encourage use.** For instance, the annual review process in which all employees participate might leverage social media for supervisors and employees to collaboratively set goals. This ensures social media is built into tasks that every employee performs.

- **Focus on middle management.** In most change initiatives, leaders have experienced significant change. They understand that change is part of doing business, and they're more comfortable with the ambiguity often present during a transition. New employees are typically eager and willing to take on whatever change, tool, or new role that is required. Consequently, the employees most in need of incentives and attention during change are middle management. About two in five middle managers feel there are differences between generations in communication styles (43 percent), technical savvy (42 percent), values (41 percent), and respect for authority of supervisors (39 percent). In addition, middle managers age 45 or older are most likely to find it very difficult to work with or manage multiple generations, especially millennials.[15] Consequently, although middle managers have the most impact on long-term sustainable culture change, they often have the hardest time dealing with transition. Employing buddy systems, change agents, and change networks can help to make sure the company is driving the adoption of collaboration and change within social media–enabled functions. Employees who are highly motivated to use social media channels are often the best champions within change agent networks, regardless of their ranking within the organization.

To further support employees in social media adoption, companies should pick a desktop technology and implementation plan that make social media and enterprise knowledge exchange a standard job function. Such technology should embed collaboration and knowledge management into work flows. Without appropriate technology in place, it is much harder to address cultural change. Employees are forced to focus on the mechanics of getting work done and can't take full advantage of the collaboration and benefits enabled by social media channels.

For instance, a company has a process that allows customers to reach a company agent through a tweet or a text message. The agent then contacts the customer via a return phone call. Technology must enable all of the information to be captured so there is continuity between the tweet channel and subsequent phone call. Without the right technology in place, an agent is not going to be able to do a good job supporting the customer.

Measurement and Alignment

Successful cultural adoption of social media requires restructuring rewards and incentives around social media success metrics where appropriate. For instance, a social media customer service team may have three measures as components of its reward structure: word-of- mouth scores, resolution scores, and some measure of productivity. Of critical importance is building feedback loops. When implementing a new capability that involves social networking, an organization should establish a two-way dialogue and constantly request and monitor feedback.

All of these step-by-step considerations are important components of successful social media adoption within an organization. After all, enterprises no longer can ignore social media. Currently, leading organizations may be differentiated by social media use, but soon it will no longer be a choice but rather table stakes for long-term viability. Organizations must make the investment to develop an end-to-end social media strategy, especially the often hardest, most frequently overlooked aspect of culture shift and change management. When social media enables an organization's employees to develop formal and informal networks, and collaboration capabilities transcend the physical walls of an organization, typical benefits include retention of top talent, greater productivity, happier customers, and a more agile organization overall.

Social Media Adoption at HOK

Several companies are aggressively moving down the path of integrating social media into their talent management strategy. One example is HOK, a global architecture firm that has aggressively adopted social networking applications since its corporate communications team began trying them out in the spring of 2008.* The corporate communications team manages various social media applications that serve internal and external audiences and serve as an indirect marketing, recruitment, and retention tool. Internally, HOK's employees have been extremely receptive to these applications, and many have become highly engaged, especially with the Life at HOK blog.

Life at HOK, www.hoklife.com, was established to help change the external perception from "HOK the big company" to "HOK the creative people" helping with recruitment and retention, appealing to future business partners and clients, connecting with traditional and new media members, and even strengthening the firm's internal design culture. The blog has received dozens of inquiries from people looking for jobs. Online friendships and conversations are better connecting HOK's people around the firm and, as people get to know each other, fostering true collaboration.

The HOK Network YouTube channel, www.youtube.com/hoknetwork, houses several formal and informal videos of HOK professionals talking about projects, ideas, and events. The HOKLife YouTube channel, www.youtube.com/hoklife, features videos by the Life at HOK bloggers. This application allows an external audience to see the intimate culture of HOK's global offices and disproves the notion that HOK is a large, inaccessible company.

HOK's primary Flickr account, www.flickr.com/hoknetwork, is used to promote both formal and informal photos of HOK's people and projects. Posting this imagery allows HOK to become more accessible to a broader audience. HOK has two Twitter accounts. The HOKNetwork account was designed for firm-wide updates and news information about the firm. The SomeChum account, with more than 730 followers, is run by the HOK media relations manager and is used to disseminate news related to HOK and the architecture profession and to connect with an audience who ordinarily wouldn't follow HOK.

The HOK Careers page on Facebook was designed to give potential recruits an opportunity to be a part of HOK's Facebook community and to ask questions about what it's like to work at the firm. Fans of the page have posted numerous comments and inquiries. HOK uses LinkedIn as a secondary tool to the HOK Careers page on Facebook. The company profile page on LinkedIn simply offers a quick snapshot of the firm and indicates HOK employees who are on the network. VisualCV is a supplementary recruiting tool to the firm's traditional careers homepage at www.HOK.com/careers. Although recruits must officially apply for positions at hok.com/careers, VisualCV allows them to submit interactive, multimedia resumes and view HOK's own VisualCV, which contains videos and office information and directs them to other social media applications. This tool allows HOK to reach a new audience that otherwise might not have applied for a position at HOK and shows that HOK is on the leading edge of technology and new recruitment methods.

*Social Networking for Competitive Advantage," Society for Marketing Professional Services (July 2009).

16

New Roles and Responsibilities

Chris Zinner and Vanessa Godshalk

CHAPTER HIGHLIGHTS

To capitalize on social media, a company must create new roles within its organization. These roles likely will evolve as an organization increases its social media investments and determines the most effective roles and skills required to support those investments.

Many existing roles—including those in the C-suite, brand and product managers, sales and service representatives, human resources and learning professionals, and legal teams—also must change in response to the opportunities and challenges social media presents.

Effective communication, stakeholder involvement, and change management are key elements to successfully creating new social media roles or teams.

Allone has to do is scan for "jobs in social media" and a plethora of opportunities arise. With social media becoming a major player in how people communicate and interact with each other, it is only natural that the advent of social media jobs would follow. Entire web sites are dedicated to social media jobs, such as www.jobsinsocialmedia.com and www.socialmediajobs.com, while other recruiting and job posting web sites, like www.simplyhired.com, have large selections of social media opportunities for interested individuals (more than 22,000 job postings at the time). With job titles of "social community manager," to "social media strategist," to "social lead generator," to "social media evangelist," companies everywhere are trying to bring in talent who can help harness the power of social media to attract new customers or potential employees, collaborate on new products/services, or create engaged customer communities. Does this mean that any organization pursuing social media strategies must create a host of brand-new positions and create entirely new teams? Most organizations do not have the luxury of budget or time to build new divisions within their company focused solely on a topic like social media. It also isn't realistic for companies to swap out individuals they already have in marketing roles or to have to hire 100 percent from the outside to develop a new capability.

It is true that organizations engaged in social media activities require new and different skill sets due to the way that social media introduces new technologies and new ways of interacting with internal and external audiences.

To tap in to social media, employees need new skills including the ability to:

- Manage a customer community.
- Design products that can be marketed through viral techniques.
- Integrate data from social media outposts, such as Twitter, Facebook, and YouTube with data that lives behind the corporate firewall.
- Manage business processes across teams that need to collaborate much more than they did in the past.

The good news for companies is that the ability to align its people to its social media goals is within reach, and many of the foundational practices that companies have employed for years to design and develop high-performance teams still will work in this new era of social media.

This chapter identifies how companies can build high-performance social media teams. Building upon Chapter 15, which describes the importance of aligning a company's human capital strategy with its business and social media strategies, this chapter takes a closer look at the specific organizational impacts of social media; in particular, what are the *new* skills, roles, and responsibilities organizations will need to capitalize on social media, and what are the impacts to *existing* roles and responsibilities? After describing the various new and evolved roles in social media, the chapter ends with a description of how to plan for and execute the organizational changes required to design and implement new or evolved social media roles.

Building a High-Performance Social Media Team

The first step in building a high-performance social media team is to anchor all human capital decisions in the context of the business strategy. Just as it is important to align an organization's social media strategy with the business strategy (as discussed in Chapter 2), a company's human capital plans must align to the business (and social media) strategies employed by the organization.

Far too often, we see business leaders who understand the importance of building a new organizational capability, such as a social media team, and are willing to invest significant resources to ensure success, only to fail to address critical organizational and human capital issues. These leaders are willing to invest in strategy and operational planning; they are willing to buy or build enabling technology; and they are willing to reengineer their processes. However, when it comes to designing and developing high-performance teams, the efforts undertaken by business leaders are often underwhelming. Many companies, when designing a new organizational structure, still tend to lock a group of senior executives in a conference room one night after work, order in dinner, and draw the new organization on a whiteboard (as opposed to taking a more concerted and disciplined approach to avoid common pitfalls of designing an organization around individual people, or creating jobs that combine contradictory tasks). Or when it comes to hiring or developing employees with critical new skills (such as those required in social media), business leaders absolve their responsibilities and assume that all talent acquisition or talent development activities belong to human resources (HR). Or when implementing organizational changes to address strategic opportunities (such as harnessing the power of social media), companies neglect to manage change in such a way that promotes excitement and adoption and combats resistance or apathy. In these instances, organizations that do not pay appropriate attention to organizational or change management factors often suffer one or many of these consequences:

- Lack of buy-in from key stakeholders, which can lead to stiff resistance.
- Organizational structures with overlap, unclear roles, and conflicting responsibilities, which produces turf wars, bureaucracy, and organizational stagnation.

- Inadequate internal communications to explain new capabilities, why they are important to a firm, and how they will work.
- Insufficient resourcing and/or unqualified pipeline of talent, resulting in a mismatch between business demands and suitable supply. This can be particularly damaging if a company has started down the path of investing in social media (for example, setting up community pages) but lacks sufficient talent to keep up with customer traffic, which can quickly erode customer relationships.
- Inadequate skills due to insufficient or misaligned training, lack of knowledge management systems, or poor collaboration. This situation ultimately creates widespread perceptions that the effort is a poorly designed reaction to the latest fad in the market.

If organizations spent the same amount of time and energy on the organizational, human capital, and change management elements (of creating social media capabilities) as they did on strategy, technology, or process reengineering, we believe they would find far more success in harnessing the collective power of social media.

In the end, a company's competitors are likely to be quickly organizing for success in social media, to engage their customers, business partners, and employees. Organizations that want to compete in a world where social media is revolutionizing the way business is conducted are at risk if they leave employees to, in effect, make up the organization's response to social media as they go along.

New Roles of Social Media

Once an organization has made the commitment to pursue a social media strategy, it will need to determine which roles (new or evolved) are required to support this strategy.

A recent article in *Bloomberg Business Week* ("Twitter, Twitter, Little Stars," July 15, 2010), commented on the surge of new corporate roles focused on social media. "Opportunities in corporate social media are popping up faster than cat videos on YouTube (GOOG). In addition to Petco, in the past few months, Sears Holdings (SHLD), Panasonic (PC), the Fifth Third Bank (FITB), the National Association of Homebuilders, Citigroup (C), Electronic Arts (ERTS), AT&T (T), Fiji Water, Godaddy.com, and the Ultimate Fighting Championship have all sought or hired social media experts. In Las Vegas,

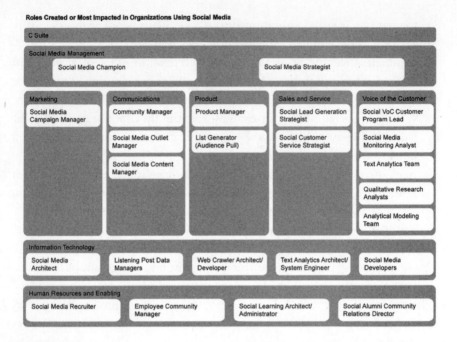

Roles Created or Most Impacted in Organizations Using Social Media

C Suite				
Social Media Management				
Social Media Champion		Social Media Strategist		

Marketing	Communications	Product	Sales and Service	Voice of the Customer
Social Media Campaign Manager	Community Manager	Product Manager	Social Lead Generation Strategist	Social VoC Customer Program Lead
	Social Media Outlet Manager	List Generator (Audience Pull)	Social Customer Service Strategist	Social Media Monitoring Analyst
	Social Media Content Manager			Text Analytics Team
				Qualitative Research Analysts
				Analytical Modeling Team

Information Technology				
Social Media Architect	Listening Post Data Managers	Web Crawler Architect/ Developer	Text Analytics Architect/ System Engineer	Social Media Developers

Human Resources and Enabling			
Social Media Recruiter	Employee Community Manager	Social Learning Architect/ Administrator	Social Alumni Community Relations Director

FIGURE 16.1 Roles Created or Most Affected in Organizations Using Social Media.

Harrah's Entertainment recently circulated a job listing for a "corporate social media rock star." In Chicago, Buick went looking for a handful of "social media ambassadors" to help manage Tweet to Drive, which allows customers to schedule test drives from home via Twitter. At the same time, traditional public relations and marketing powerhouses such as Ogilvy & Mather are bulking up their expertise to fend off social-media-focused startups."

To help organizations understand the various types of roles required to succeed in social media, we have compiled a list of the most common ones. (See Figure 16.1.)

No organization can create all of these roles at once, and the number and diversity of roles that an organization needs will vary based on the type of social media activity it is pursuing. The more likely path is that roles will evolve as the organization increases its social media investments and determines the most effective roles and skills required to support those investments. Also, each role may not be a full-time occupation, consuming the full working hours of one person. For example, social media architects may design and build other types of software applications in addition to social media interfaces and applications.

The next sections describe the most significant new roles we see for companies to embrace and adopt social media.

Social Media Management

Social Media Champion

Whenever an organization approaches a significant change, someone at or near the top must lead—someone who understands the organization and can influence the leaders who control its resources.

Change can start at the very top, with the chief executive officer (CEO), although sometimes it begins below the CEO. In all cases, someone with real power must take personal interest in the success of social media to achieve significant business outcomes. This is the role of the *social media champion*. An example of a social media champion at work is within Zappos, where CEO Tony Hsieh led the charge with his active participation and leadership by example. As with any major change effort, the social media champion knows how to influence junior and senior people across the organization. This person creates excitement and executive sponsorship. He or she gets the right people in the organization behind the initiative.

Social media champions may not create the vision for social media, but they buy in to it and support it as if it were their own idea.

Social Media Strategist

The *social media strategist* creates the organization's vision for social media— how the company will exploit it across business functions. Sometimes this person is senior and experienced enough to also serve as the social media champion, but not always. This person may take his or her vision to a higher-level executive, who then serves as the champion.

In any case, the social media strategist is the rare person who can seamlessly discuss Web application technologies with the chief information officer, lead-generation concepts with the chief marketing officer, business case development with the chief financial officer, and organizational design with the CEO and chief human resources officer. This person understands the far-reaching impacts of social media throughout the organization and can envision the path forward for the organization. Social media strategists are pioneers among their peers, and they consistently look for opportunities to expand the organization's social media capabilities.

The social media strategist's scope of work is an operating strategy, not a marketing campaign strategy. If an organization has a social media road map, it is the strategist who brought it to life, and he or she refreshes it regularly. In addition, the strategist guides the business cases required to secure funding for the road map and can easily explain how social media creates value for the organization and its customers.

Voice of the Customer

Social Voice of the Customer Program Lead

An organization may need to create a new role for a *social voice of the customer lead*, or it could fill this role with the person who leads an existing voice-of-the-customer program. Whatever the case, this person is responsible for identifying new opportunities for mining customer insights from sources including social media, surveys, focus groups, web site feedback mechanisms, and call center documentation. Then the person must work across the organization to implement processes and technologies that continually mine the data from those sources, integrate it, and develop insights that can be used to improve marketing, sales, customer service, recruiting, and more.

Social Media Monitoring Analyst

The *social media analyst* operates and monitors social media listening tools. Analysts see the conversations occurring in social media in real time. They identify issues, classify them, and then route them to the right internal team (marketing, product development, customer service, etc.), which determines what to do about them.

For example, the analyst might identify an emerging issue with a recently released product. She routes the issue to product development for root-cause analysis and to customer service, which must formulate a response when customers phone the call center.

Given the ubiquity of social media today, every organization must develop an ability to rapidly identify and respond to emerging issues in social media—either internally or through the services of a social media agency.

Text Analytics Team

The people who make up the *text analytics team* are business analysts who maintain the categories and sentiment tuning of the voice of the customer text-mining platform. They work with functional heads to understand the topics and categories of interest to the business. Then they teach the text-mining system how to recognize customer online dialogue that relates to these categories. Essentially, these individuals ensure that the tools the company uses to monitor social media become more accurate over time.

They also work (sometimes in conjunction with the information technology (IT) department) to tune sentiment analysis technologies to reflect industry-specific and company-specific language. A common example is the word "sick." In the medical industry, "sick" is generally negative. Among skateboard enthusiasts, "sick" is generally positive. In many organizations, the same words can have very different connotations.

Finally, these *voice-of-the-customer text analysts* work with *text analytics architects* in the IT department to identify the right text-mining techniques and platforms for mining the customer insights a company desires.

Qualitative Research Analysts

Traditional *qualitative customer research analysts* plan and run customer focus groups, phone surveys, and interviews. Now they must learn the processes and technology required to harvest the same types of qualitative insights through social media, and at scales never before possible. This shift from traditional research and survey methods to a blended model that incorporates social media is discussed in a recent *Harvard Business Review* article by Andrew O'Connell.[1] "Stuck between traditional polling, which is getting more difficult and expensive, and cheaper surveying of unrepresentative panels, the field is due for a radical rethink. At least one thing is clear: In their quest to probe the public mind, survey firms will make greater use of the vast amounts of digital data that people wittingly or unwittingly provide about themselves."

Analytical Modeling Team

Analytical modeling teams are responsible for analyzing customer data and building high-end analytical models for solving high-value business problems. These teams must evolve to move beyond traditional structured data analytics and propensity modeling, to a model which takes advantage of the data available in social media outlets. This new data includes both the transactional social media data (when available through published application programming interfaces [APIs]) and unstructured customer verbatims (the postings that customers submit in various social media outlets). Such new data has the potential to increase the accuracy of existing models, but in order to integrate social media data from text-mining platforms with existing voice-of-the-customer data, companies must develop new skills.

As organizations expand their social media capabilities and gather more data from this new set of customer interactions channels, they will need more sophisticated skills, such as the ability to create more robust propensity models based on customer verbatims in their native, unstructured formats—as opposed to applying text mining first and then moving the output into traditional models. Companies will need to invest in new skills and expertise to support the various algorithms required for such sophisticated analytics, such as Latent Semantic Indexing (LSI), a popular clustering algorithm.

Marketing

Social Media Campaign Manager

Social media campaigns are significantly different from traditional marketing campaigns. Although social media marketing is not a focus of this book, it is important to at least mention that the viral and real-time qualities of social media require marketers to possess new skills to manage social media campaigns. Social media marketing is about content, not commercials, and can be targeted and personalized in very powerful ways through technologies such as Facebook Connect. Experience and knowledge of this new paradigm is critical for the emerging group of *social media campaign managers*.

Communications

Community Manager

Many companies are creating their own online communities for customers and prospects to share their views on a firm and its offerings, trade tips on how to use its products and services, and provide feedback that a firm needs to hear. Developing and maintaining a successful online community requires a lot of nurturing, care, and hard work. At the heart of every successful online community is at least one supportive and social personality who interacts with community members to resolve conflicts, answer questions, and maintain an engaging and constructive environment.

This is the role of the *community manager*. Community managers are required for all types of communities, including external customer communities and internal employee communities. All *community managers* must appreciate the perspectives of community members. They also must understand and have access to the right people in their own organization so they know where to go when they need help or to resolve an issue for the community. As described by David Armano, Senior Vice President at Edelman Digital, "A *community manager* acts as an ambassador for your organization, whether that person is an employee or contracted to manage your social Web presence. A good *community manager* gives a human form to the faceless corporation. On Facebook Whole Foods, for example, community managers have created a forum that impels customers to respond to its posts. They also often informally engage their customers in the process."[2]

Social Media Outlet Manager

As companies ramp up their social media initiatives, they may dedicate resources to manage each social utility (Facebook, Twitter, YouTube and so on). This is similar to the company that has people focused on creating and executing strategies for specific marketing channels such as direct marketing, public relations, and print advertising; or interaction channels, such as mobile, retail, or e-commerce. *Social media outlet managers* work closely with content managers corporate communications, and marketing to develop a strategy to make sure they are delivering the right messages to each target audience in their respective media outlet.

Social Media Content Manager

As part of a company's marketing efforts, the *social media content manager* leads the creation, sourcing, and publication of content that helps to drive increased traffic and activity on the company's web site and other social media outlets. Such content can include blog articles or Facebook fan page content. *Content managers* should coordinate viral propagation of content through additional social media, such as microblogs (for example, Twitter) and traditional media, such as press releases to journalists.

The *content manager* collaborates with marketing strategists to define or refine profiles for target audiences and identify topics relevant to the target audience and the organization. The *content manager* then uses those profiles to guide content development, and ensures timely measurement of content performance against business objectives. Is the content attracting the external audience? Do they return? Finally, the *content manager* is in charge of continually improving content development, publishing, and syndication.

Sales and Service

Social Lead Generation Strategist

One of the most common questions we hear is: "How can I use social media to generate new sales leads?" Instead of investing in a consistent strategy that is appropriate to generate such leads without risking the corporate brand, many companies often leave it to their sales representatives to figure it on their own. By doing so they run the risk of creating the perception of inappropriate selling and alienating their customers and prospects from participation in their Facebook pages or following the company on Twitter.

Generating leads through social media requires understanding viral marketing mechanisms and comfort with real-time customer interactions. That makes social media very different from all other lead-generation tools. As a result, some organizations have created a new role focused on lead generation through social media. This *social lead generation strategist* understands the techniques that are most effective in generating new leads through social media.

One of the most important jobs for this person is getting the sales staff to agree clearly on how to define what constitutes a qualified lead. Is it a person who says "I like this company" on Twitter? Someone who joins the company's Facebook fan page? The *social lead generation strategist* then must continually collaborate with sales managers to improve the quality of leads, with the goal of jointly improving conversion rates over time.

Social Customer Service Strategist

For years, investments in customer service have focused on reducing the overall cost to serve—whether it was a focus on optimizing contact center agent average handle time, early investments in interactive voice response (IVR) technology, or emergence of self-service solutions (online, mobile, kiosk). What has happened over time is that those companies that really focused on providing a superior customer service experience—Ritz-Carlton, Amazon, Lexus, and USAA, for example—found a key differentiator in developing loyal and engaged customers. The options for providing customer service have expanded with the advent of social media, and many companies today are realizing that there is real value in integrating more social elements into their customer service model. The *social customer service strategist* understands how to employ social media for customer service purposes and determines the best uses of social media to understand customer service concerns and provide answers back to customers via social media outlets.

Consider the recent move by AT&T to focus more energy on social media for customer care purposes:

> In the face of the launch of iPhone 4 and unrelenting customer dissatisfaction AT&T has set aside resources to focus more on its customers on social media. This discontent is registered by an average of at least 10,000 mentions of AT&T on social sites each day, the company told *AdAge* this week— if not more—so the company is responding by ramping up its social media customer service resources.
>
> AT&T is now set to advertise its "social media customer care" on monthly bills and web sites to get more customers to take their service problems to social media outlets.[3]

Information Technology

Social Media Architect

The *social media architect* is the IT counterpart to the social media strategist described earlier. The architect turns the technology components of the strategist's vision into reality. The architect is deeply familiar with social media technologies as well as with the organization's technologies and technical capabilities. The architect knows what the organization is capable of building or when it should call a specialist technology consultant.

The *social media architect* is a leader who is highly respected by technologists in the organization. Because IT evolves so quickly, these architects actively write software code to maintain a deep understanding of the latest relevant technologies, which is one source of the respect they hold through the IT organization.

Listening Post Data Managers

Listening post data managers are technical professionals who manage the collection, integration, and publishing of data consumed and analyzed by the voice-of-the-customer text analyst. They work with the voice-of-the-customer team to understand the needs of the business and the organization's "listening strategy." They also prioritize efforts across "listening posts" (for example, specific social utilities or segments within selected online communities). Finally, they design the technical process for merging customer data from all voice of the customer data sources (for example, social media, call center systems, customer surveys).

Web Crawler Architect or Developer

The *Web crawler architect* or *developer* is responsible for developing and deploying Web crawler technologies to automatically extract online content from web sites and social media outlets that are not supported by the company's social media monitoring tool or in the case where public APIs do not exist. For example, if a niche, but important, online community contains comments on a company's product, but the web site provides no official method for gathering that data over the Web, a crawler can access the relevant pages on the community web site, then process the content of those pages and organize it for inclusion in social voice-of-the-customer programs.

Text Analytics Architect or System Engineer

Text analytics architects and *systems engineers* maintain the systems used by the text-mining analysts. They understand text-mining technologies including natural language processing (NLP), lexicons, linguistic rules, clustering, and machine learning. In addition, they know how to apply these technologies to categorize content and analyze sentiments.

Although most companies do not develop the software applications that use these technologies, all organizations benefit from access to these experts when selecting and managing a vendor solution to support social media listening and analysis.

Social Media Developers

Social media developers implement, integrate, and maintain onboard social applications and related middleware, such as Lithium, BazaarVoice, Clarabridge, Kapow, and many more.

Human Resources and Enabling

Social Media Recruiter

The opportunities for improving the yield of recruiting activities have intensified in the world of social media. If leveraged appropriately, companies can use social media to generate a strong recruitment marketing campaign, attract potential sources of talent, and even engage with potential recruits in a discussion about what a career within a particular company is all about. A *social media recruiter* understands how to employ various forms of social media to create an employment brand, communicate an employee value proposition, create buzz about potential opportunities, source new pools of talent, and engage in dialogue with potential recruits.

Employee Community Manager

Similar to the community manager within communications (who is focused on external customer community development), an *employee community manager* is responsible for establishing and nurturing internal employee communities, whether they are organized around particular communities of interest (for example, a particular capability within a company) or are broad communities within a company focused on driving employee engagement.

Social Learning Architect/Administrator

As described in Chapter 15, exciting advances in the field of social learning (Learning 2.0) are starting to enable organizations to marry technology with performance support needs, to provide employees with learning at the point of need in formats that are more engaging and authentic than traditional modes of learning. As described in David Smith and Susan Cantrell's *Workforce of One*, leading organizations are moving away from defining a one-size-fits-all linear learning curriculum from on high, and instead, are encouraging and allowing employees themselves to create learning content and dynamically pull and push it to one another on an as-needed, highly customized, collaborative basis. Instead of turning to a book or a course if there's a tech problem, for example, an employee may look up friends on a corporate version of Facebook, locate a friend of a friend who has knowledge or experience in that area, and instant message him or her with a question. Or the employee may post it on an online threaded discussion group of like-minded people in a community of practice, post it on a blog or wiki, or initiate a chat group. Alternatively, the employee may search for a video online that captured a person working to solve that particular technology problem or troll for knowledge that has been codified and posted by another employee and ranked in terms of usefulness by others in an online knowledge marketplace. The *social learning architect* is the individual who keeps abreast of these types of emerging social learning trends and opportunities and provides the organization with a blueprint and vision for enabling social learning capabilities.

Once an organization pursues social learning as an option for providing employees with point-of-need training, a *social learning administrator* helps establish and monitor the efficacy and use of the social learning channel. This includes: educating the enterprise on how to contribute content and expand the company knowledge base; monitoring learner reviews and feedback; providing guidance and/or incentives for user-generated learning content; and collaborating across the enterprise to solicit new and relevant training content.

Social Alumni Community Relations Director

Many companies have found through the years that maintaining strong relationships with its former employees, or "alums," make good business sense. Whether it is to protect a company reputation from disgruntled employee tweets or to use former employees as potential business leads or partners, social media presents new and cost-effective means of remaining connected with former employees. Universities have long been active in alumni relations, which is why it is no surprise that they have been tapping in to social media for everything from helping graduates find job opportunities, to supporting fundraising efforts, to collaborating on particular topics of interest. Companies that recognize the value of keeping in touch with alumni will find it helpful to establish a *social alumni community relations director*, whose responsibility it is to develop and maintain strong employee alumni relations via social media forums, complemented by in-person and other media options as appropriate.

Existing Roles that Must Evolve

In addition to the preceding new roles companies need to create, many existing roles will have to undergo considerable change to be able to accommodate social media.

The C Suite

The most effective social media strategies are supported and well understood at the top of the organization—the C-suite (for example, chief executive, operating, marketing, and information officers). Because social media impacts nearly every department in an organization, the success of a comprehensive social media strategy depends on engagement and support from everyone in the C-suite. Therefore, each C-level executive must learn the relevance of social media to the company's industry and their function.

Simply reading research reports will not do the trick. Senior leaders must engage in social media to fully understand it. This means creating an account on LinkedIn, Facebook, and Twitter—at the very least—then logging in periodically and experiencing social media firsthand.

Leaders should treat social media like Jack Welch treated the Internet when he was CEO of General Electric. When Welch realized how critical the Internet would be to GE's businesses, he mandated that every senior executive find a GE employee under the age of 25 to serve as an Internet mentor. Welch realized that the Internet would dramatically alter GE's businesses, and the most efficient way for his leaders to learn the Internet was through the younger GE employees who already "got it." As a side benefit, those younger employees developed relationships with senior executives. Most organizations could benefit from the same approach to social media today.

Brand Manager

Brand managers must define how to leverage this new medium to enhance the brand of their product. Whereas social media monitoring/problem management is taking a reactive, defensive approach to protecting the company brand from erosion in social media channels, the *brand manager* must take a proactive, offensive approach to pushing out messages through social media in the attempt to create viral messages and increase demand for the brand. Compelling examples of using social media for proactive brand management and viral marketing is Toyota's Sienna YouTube video series called "Swagger Wagon," or Old Spice's recent viral campaign in which the celebrity character in the viral commercial video responds to questions posted on Facebook and Twitter with video responses.

Brand managers must be able to identify the key influencers in social media outlets and co-opt them (directly or indirectly) in an attempt to amplify the positive buzz (or cease negative buzz) around their products. Doing this requires highly creative people who can harness this game-changing medium to market and brand in ways never before possible.

Inbound Marketing Specialists

Although a fairly new role in most organizations within the past several years, *inbound marketing specialists* are masters of digital marketing who focus on driving traffic to a company's web site; now they must expand their skills to harness the power of social media outlets. Understanding the capabilities and limitations of search engine optimization (SEO) on popular social outlets helps an organization focus on those that will maximize the return on investment. *Inbound marketing specialists* must keep abreast of emerging technologies, such as Arkayne–a social platform for online marketing–to use engaging content in social media outlets to drive traffic back to a company's web site or leverage trust networks to refer customers to the best and most authoritative content, regardless of ownership of that content. Customers care about content, not commercials or company web sites. Companies that can best capitalize on this attitude set themselves up for driving traffic and business to their web sites.

Product Manager

If there is one position where social media is truly a game changer, it is the role of *product manager*—those tasked with developing products that meet the needs and wants of profitable customer segments.

Prior to social media, *product managers* were some of the biggest consumers of primary customer research (surveys, focus groups, etc.) and secondary market research (to identify changing needs of the marketplace and competitive trends). However, social media gives *product managers* real-time and collaborative feedback opportunities—that is, to interact directly with customers and prospective customers.

However, *product managers* must be retrained on how to capitalize on this new paradigm. How do they listen inductively to the social voice of the customer? How do they leverage social media to create and engage communities of customers and prospects, to obtain feedback along the way at various milestones of the product development life cycle? How can they assess sentiment toward their product in customer comments? How can they distinguish between the squeaky wheel that may be the minority from the large, silent majority that will drive most of the profits from their purchase of the product?

Social media research is fundamentally different from traditional customer and market research. *Product managers* must transform their approach and skills to seize this enormous opportunity.

Communications Manager

Prior to social media, *communications managers* coordinated the company's customer communications strategy across traditional communication vehicles such as e-mail, web sites, newsletters, and other electronic and hard-copy correspondence. Social media outlets and customer communities have added a new dimension to this strategy—one that harnesses the power of continuous, peer-to-peer, transparent dialog as opposed to simple "one-way" communications. Today *communications managers* must evolve their skills to succeed in this new paradigm.

Contact Center Sales Agents and Customer Service Representatives

Contact center sales agents and *customer service representatives* both have the ability to leverage social media to improve their understanding of customer sentiment prior to engaging in customer interactions. Within contact centers, the *telesales agent* has the challenging job of handling perturbed prospects who answer outbound sales calls or answering inbound calls from those interested in purchasing a new product. Social media now offers the opportunity for these agents to be aware of and use customer sentiment on various topics to adapt sales messages accordingly—if they are adequately skilled to do so and enabled by propensity models that suggest product offers based on information mined from social media behavior.

The second role is the *contact center agent* or *customer service representative*. Already skilled at assessing a customer's sentiment based on the conversation and adapting their style accordingly, these individuals must be retrained to be able to reference new customer information derived from social media to enhance the way customer service is provided. This includes interaction history on social media during the context of providing customer service. However, this interaction history is different from previous calls, e-mails, and chat. The way it can and should be referenced must be determined by organizational policy, and representatives must be trained accordingly. It also could include the averaged "customer sentiment" for the customer being serviced at that time. Representatives must be trained on how to access this asserted sentiment as well as how to adjust their language and their style accordingly. Last, in the cases of companies that have opened up social media as a bona fide customer service channel, they may choose to route issues, complaints, and request submitted via social media through the system in the same way e-mails are routed today. The policy likely will dictate a different procedure for social media versus e-mail, and reps will need to be trained accordingly.

Field Sales

Often, the heart of a company's revenue generation engine, *field sales representatives* salivate at the possibility of mining new leads from social media outlets. However, as discussed earlier, a company must develop a strategy for mining and developing leads from social media in a way that creates value for both the company and the customer—and does not alienate the community by behaving in a way that is equivalent to trying to sell to those sitting next to you at a dinner party. Field sales reps must be trained that social media is a place to do what they do best: build relationships. It is an opportunity to allow customers and prospects to get to know, like, and trust a company— and then, in the right situation, to build a business relationship with the organization. Social media has not changed the "offline" fact that if someone is too aggressive or selling in an inappropriate environment, prospects not only can be turned off, but the company's brand can be negatively affected.

Legal Advisor for Social Media

Legal issues related to privacy, intellectual property, trademark infringement, and trade secrets are not new; however, social media presents new challenges to these traditional legal issues. A company's *legal advisor for social media* must be able to set the policy toward employee participation as company representatives in social media outlets. Theoretically, any employee could respond to a customer or prospect comment on a Facebook fan page. But what is the policy? Who can respond? And under what circumstances? What are employees allowed to say, and what topics and language do they need to avoid? And how can the legal experts create a system that balances managing the risk to the organization with the need for speed and agility in response to social media postings?

Other Partners

Internal company roles are not the only roles a company must consider in light of its social media strategy. Relationships with *other partners* such as ad agencies or web site hosting providers may need to be rethought in light of the company's social media goals. For example, an ad agency that continues to focus on "push marketing" with little to no attention to integrating marketing efforts with digital and social media options might not be the right partner if a company's plans include aggressive use of social media outlets for marketing and customer engagement.

Putting the Pieces Together

In creating a social media strategy, an organization must decide when to develop skills internally, when to hire new employees, and how to ensure the skills of those people grow over time—in ways that support the evolution of the organization.

In some cases, an organization will decide to use the services of an experienced social media agency rather than trying to build and sustain the capabilities in-house. For example, many organizations hire an agency for their social media listening, analytics, and campaign strategy efforts. Without doubt, significant analytical skills are required to make sense of the river of data from social media listening tools. As a result, many organizations can benefit from agencies specializing in such analyses.

Whether it uses such agencies or not, a company will quickly find that social media will force change throughout the organization. Managers must equip the workforce with the right tools, training, and skills to use and respond to the torrent of customer and other market information ushered in by social media. Unfortunately, no single, perfect answer exists to reskilling a workforce. Although it is helpful to learn lessons from companies that are mastering social media, how an organization staffs up to respond to the social media revolution will vary from company to company. Chapter 15 provides actionable examples and advice for organizing around defining talent needs, discovering sources of talent, developing talent for ongoing high performance, and deploying talent. The next section provides insight into the practice of designing or redesigning an organization to include some or many of the social media roles described above.

Designing the Organization

A recent study by the *Economist* asserts that leaders interested in the design of their organization have an edge. They believe that "an organization behaves in the way it is designed to behave. If it is not designed correctly—an analogy is a poorly designed racing car—it will not be successful."[4] The importance of carefully designing an organization is bolstered by Accenture's high-performance-business research which provides an understanding of the characteristics that enable elite organizations to consistently surpass their competition. Upon review of thousands of companies over several years, it became clear that high-performance businesses consistently designed (and redesigned) their organizations to be adaptive. This allowed them to respond quickly to market opportunities and changes, excel at innovation and be able to flex and adapt their organization, people and infrastructures rapidly, whilst maintaining high performance. The most pioneering organizations exhibited several, if not all, of the following:

- Organization structures and processes that readily adapt in response to shifts in business strategies and external demands.
- An organization design driven by clear governance principles intended to minimize bureaucracy.
- People who excel at working across boundaries and an organization that excels in the creation of networks and alliances (inside and outside) to achieve flexibility.

- An organization structure aligned with strategy that may vary depending on business function or geography.
- Highly-innovative products and services are developed on a regular basis.
- Diversity encouraged at all levels of the organization, including points of view and ways of doing business, reflected in the ready adoption of new and innovative ways of doing business.

What is fascinating about the characteristics of high-performance businesses over the past decade, is that many of the key organizational traits (being adaptive; collaborating, working across boundaries and so on), are many of the same traits that are required for an organization to be successful in its social media activities. While the roles of social media may be new to many companies, the practices that leading companies employ to effectively design an adaptive organization still hold true today.

We believe that organization design is more than just the structure of the organization. It includes defining an organization blueprint that aligns with the organization's context and strategic intent; developing the organizational processes such as performance management and talent management to support the organization's social media goals; and defining the jobs and teams to deliver on the organization's strategic objectives.

Failure to adopt a comprehensive solution will result in an inability to implement a new strategy, including a social media strategy.

When done right, organizations can reap many benefits, including:

- Increased likelihood of achieving strategic objectives via alignment of strategy with the structure, resources, and processes.
- An organization that is adaptable and responsive to a change in strategy.
- Improved process and governance efficiency and effectiveness.
- Appropriately allocated intelligence, resources, and purpose across an organization.
- Enhanced employee engagement and productivity.
- A structure that supports effective succession planning and talent sustainability.
- Economies of skill and scale to deliver bottom-line savings.

Remember that it is not possible to design a structure "once and for all." Organizations must remain adaptive and in sync with evolving strategy and external trends—especially in the case of social media, which continues to be a highly dynamic and evolving field.

To design and implement new roles and organizational structures that support a company's social media goals, a time commitment will be required from the organization's leaders. It is critical that leaders invest time in the process of aligning their organization design with the strategic intent of their organization. This is necessary to gain clarity and ensure the organization is in line with its strategic objectives, specifically those identified in its social media strategy. Adequate time also must be built in to develop the supporting management processes that enable the behaviors in the new organization. This is the "secret sauce." And finally, the leadership team must "own" the new or evolved organization as well as understand what their roles are and how their behaviors have to change to fit with new management processes.

Key Lessons Learned

When redesigning organizations to capture new capabilities, such as those required to embrace social media effectively, a company should keep in mind a number of key success factors.

For starters, it's not advisable to create a structure in isolation. Instead, key stakeholders need to be involved throughout. Furthermore, a company should expect that the organization design effort will take 30 percent longer than anticipated due to the need to align so many stakeholders.

A company also should never expect the structure to be the panacea—it is not the answer to everything—and should ensure that its structure has a solid foundation in the organization's strategy and organization blueprint.

As tempting as it may be, a company should not design an organization for specific individuals or groups. Rather, the design should be people-agnostic. Also, it's critical to design the organization for tomorrow, because today's organization will be redundant by the time it is designed.

When designing jobs and teams, a company should consider the competencies required for each job and the available talent pool. Doing this will help prevent creating a job that a company can't find resources for and will allow the organization to consider career paths and succession planning. A company also should consider its talent strategy and resource pool: Is it creating jobs that fit with its employee value proposition? If there isn't a value proposition, the company should validate its assumptions with leadership.

Similarly, it's important to consider whether the new structure works with the existing culture and, if not, which specific interventions are required to embed new behaviors and lead to a changed culture.

Designing a new organization can be emotionally wrenching for various members of a company. It's important to help these individuals work through their own change perspective, as this likely will impact their network, source of power, and motivation. Often internal change resistance dilutes an organization design during implementation or prevents it entirely.

Finally, HR must also be involved throughout—even if it isn't a formal participant in the process. As a new organization is implemented, HR will need to realign its processes (recruitment, performance evaluation and so on) and will maintain the newly designed structure and jobs going forward. Adequate time also should be built into the initiative to develop the supporting management processes that enable the behaviors in the new organization.

Like any major influential development, social media makes "business as usual" obsolete. Companies that have been most successful in leveraging the power of social recognized this early and took the steps necessary to develop the strategies and the related skills and organization structures required to make social media an integral part of their everyday operations.

17

Social Media Policies

Chris Boudreaux

CHAPTER HIGHLIGHTS

Because of social media, every company employee now has the opportunity to be a spokesperson for his or her employer, whether intentionally or inadvertently. Thus, a strong social media policy is critical to helping employees understand the boundaries of their social media activities relating to their employer.

Every organization likely will need multiple social media policy documents for different purposes and audiences. Importantly, these documents should avoid focusing solely on protecting the company from risk—in other words, only spelling out what's forbidden—and, instead, strike a balance between empowerment and accountability so that employees are encouraged to use social media in the right way to promote and differentiate the company in the marketplace.

In most countries, social media lets employees easily interact with customers, suppliers, job candidates, and shareholders any time, from anywhere. Although some countries restrict access to social media and the Internet in general, in most countries, many companies permit employees to write a blog post about their firm, tweet about their job, or otherwise share their feelings about their employer at any time.

The result: Every employee is a potential touch point to the marketplace—a spokesperson who can significantly harm and also greatly enhance the organization's reputation. Social media gives such employees a mouthpiece when they are at the office or even when they are home.

In addition to putting their reputations at risk, companies that allow employees to sound off through social media can expose themselves to malware (software that can invade a firm's computer systems) and brand hijacking. They also can lose control of their web site content as well as violate country disclosure laws, rules, and record-keeping requirements. (In the United States, the Federal Trade Commission provides disclosure guides to companies), and breaking the law on record-keeping requirements. Even if a company does not use social media for its own purposes, employees who use it privately can do great harm. That's why every organization must implement effective social media policies for employees.

However, protecting a company from risk is only one of three important reasons to implement social media policies. In fact, companies need social media policies to help employees protect themselves. In addition, the most advanced organizations use social media policies to differentiate themselves in the market. By educating and empowering employees to use social media in very specific ways—ways that other companies have ignored—these organizations have built competitive advantages.

This chapter describes the current state of social media policies in organizations and provides tips for creating policies that go beyond risk mitigation to differentiate a company in the market.

Organizations Need Multiple Policies for Different Purposes

Every organization will likely need multiple social media policy documents for different purposes and audiences. Such documents could include the following:

Social Media Policy for Employees

The social media policy for employees, the primary focus of this chapter, is what most people mean when they say "social media policy." The document requires input from marketing, legal, human resources (HR), and business operations, and it provides guidance to all employees in the organization. Typically, the document links to existing, relevant documents, such as privacy policy, sexual harassment policy, and ethics policy.

Guidelines for Employees Working in Social Media

Organizations should separate broad guidelines for the entire employee base (the social media policy for employees) from more operational guidelines for workers who use social media as part of their job. For example, if the company asks product managers to create Twitter accounts to interact with customer communities, the organization should establish a standard format for Twitter IDs to ensure consistent branding. That is not the kind of guidance an organization needs to issue to everyone in the company.

This document might also describe the expected response times for different audiences in social media.

This document is likely to be owned and maintained by different people from the ones who write the social media policy for employees, so separating the documents will simplify how they are updated. In addition, this policy is different from the crisis plan, which is less of a policy document and more of an operating procedure document.

Community Policy

Organizations that operate an online community typically publish guidelines for the users of the community, explaining acceptable and unacceptable uses of the community. This document is frequently called the Terms of Use. The document usually explains how the site is moderated, its policies on privacy, how it uses cookies (software code planted on users' computers to track their usage of the community), and advertising-related disclosures.

Manager Training

Consider a separate document for managers, and include it in training for new managers, just like sexual harassment training. For more information on why organizations should educate their managers about social media, see the section titled "What a Social Media Policy Should Be."

Banishment Is Not a Policy

Although organizations around the world are rapidly adopting social media, many are still waiting until they understand it better. For those enterprises, banishment is their social media policy: Employees who use social media at work or at home (if they mention the company) will be terminated. According to a March 2010 survey of 257 security and information technology professionals by nCircle, 39 percent of organizations ban the use of social media in the workplace.[1]

For organizations that are not yet ready to jump on social media, this may seem like an effective policy. But there are two significant issues with it:

1. **Such policies are impossible to enforce.** Most employees can access social media at work through their own mobile phones, which employers cannot control. In fact, most people access social media throughout the day, or when they have a break. In the nCircle survey just mentioned, half the information technology respondents had no idea whether employees at their company complied with their ban on social media. Further, in March 2010, Web security firm F-Secure found that one quarter of Facebook users that it surveyed use the social networking site "all the time" at work and "friended" their manager. Another 35 percent said they access Facebook occasionally at work.[2]

2. **Employees can easily use social media outside of work.** Even in the highly regulated financial services industry, more than half of financial services professionals use LinkedIn or Facebook for work or personal pleasure.[3] Companies simply cannot control what employees say about them in social media.

As Robert Straud, international vice president of the Information Systems Audit and Control Association, stated in June 2010, "Historically, organizations tried to control risk by denying access to cyberspace, but that won't work with social media. Companies should embrace it, not block it. But they also need to empower their employees with knowledge to implement sound social media governance."[4]

To be clear, banishment is not a policy; it's a pipe dream.

State of Social Media Policies

Today, most social media policies focus on protecting the company from risk with boilerplate language, such as "respect copyright," "respect others," or "link to sources." Very few organizations have truly thoughtful policies that balance empowerment and accountability. In fact, a December 2009 study of publicly available social media policies on SocialMediaGovernance.com found that only one-third had language that was unique to the organization and helped employees use social media to support its unique goals.[5] (See Figure 17.1.)

The study also found that most organizations are not setting clear boundaries on how employees should use social media. For example, 82 percent said nothing about employee use of company trademarks in their personal social media. Only 7 percent prohibited use of company trademarks, and only 11 percent told employees to seek permission before using company trademarks.

If companies are concerned about losing control of their brand in a world of social media, they must define and communicate the boundaries employees must honor with respect to the brand. Yet most companies do not.

Many people tasked with writing their organization's social media policy wonder how long such a policy should be. The study on SocialMedia Governance.com found a wide range of document lengths. (See Figure 17.2.)

Most of the social media policies were 500 to 2,000 words long. Only a handful of policies were fewer than 300 words or more than 5,000 words. Even so, we typically do not advise any particular length for a social media policy.

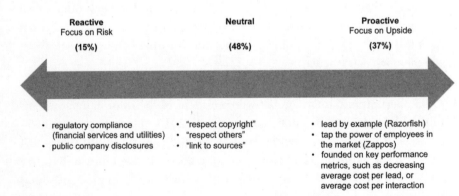

FIGURE 17.1 Focus of Publicly Available Social Media Policies.

Source: SocialMediaGovernance.com.

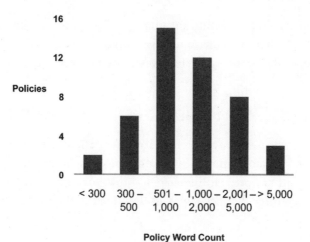

FIGURE 17.2 Length of Social Media Policies.

We found that very few organizations provide guidance for specific social utilities such as Facebook, LinkedIn, or Twitter. (See Figure 17.3.)

In particular, a few organizations provided guidance about Facebook and Twitter. Fewer advised about how to use wikis (such as Wikipedia), and only a couple discussed LinkedIn.

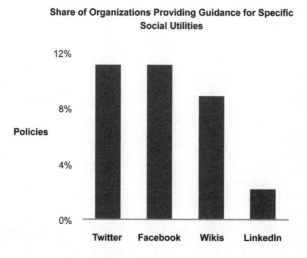

FIGURE 17.3 Social Utilities for Which Companies Provided Guidelines.

If a company finds a significant number of employees using a particular social utility, it should think about the unique features and impacts of that utility and consider writing guidelines on how employees should use each one.

What a Social Media Policy Should Be

After writing and studying the social media policies of companies across industries and business models, including business to business, business to consumers, and nonprofits, I determined that social media policies tend to evolve through three distinct stages, as described in the next subsections and shown in Figure 17.4.

Stage 1: Mitigation

Most organizations rush to create their first social media policy. They realize they need something quickly, and currently have nothing. So they look at what other companies have done and rapidly piece together a policy. As a result, their policy looks a lot like most social media policies. It says things like "respect copyright," "link to sources," "be authentic," and throws out lots of other catch-phrases that apply to every employee at every company in the world.

In addition, most organizations focus their initial policies just on protecting themselves from the risk. Examples of such policy content include

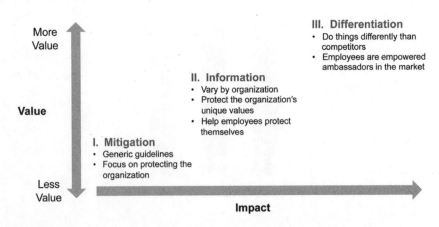

FIGURE 17.4 Three Stages of Social Media Policy Evolution.

prohibiting employees from accessing social media at work, prohibiting employee use of company trademarks, and ensuring that employees do not violate laws governing disclosures by public companies.

At this stage of evolution, most social media policies look very similar. To see if its policy is at this stage, a company should replace its name with another company's name from another industry and see if the policy still makes sense. If the policy still makes sense, the company is at Stage 1: Mitigation.

Because there is an abundance of readily available written checklists to guide organizations through the best practices of creating a policy that mitigates risk, we do not cover that information in this chapter.

Stage 2: Information

After an organization addresses the risk of social media, it must begin to use its social media policies in ways that are unique to its goals, culture, and business processes. It may seek to protect its unique values or help employees protect themselves in their use of social media. This is the stage where we start to see policies vary across organizations.

If a company provides training to personnel upon promotion to a management position, it should include its social media policy in the training. In addition, it should ensure that managers understand their legal boundaries with regard to their employees' social media activities. Without reliable evidence that an employee is damaging the employer's interests or violating company policies, tell managers to avoid password-protected sites or accounts used by employees. And, if a manager believes that she must seek access to a secured site or account, direct her to first consult HR or corporate counsel to ensure that her actions are appropriate. For an example of a company that failed to educate its managers, see the sidebar, "Snooping in Social Media Can Send Managers to Jail."

Make it easy for employees to find information that will help them use social media successfully. Link the policy document to other relevant documents, such as the privacy policy or policies on protecting company information, rather than re-creating that information in the social media policy.

If a company really wants to help employees to protect themselves in the hazardous world of social media, it should tell them what kinds of data the company will store and where employee ownership of their data begins and ends.

Snooping in Social Media Can Send Managers to Jail

By Chris Boudreau

In October 2009, a U.S. district court in New Jersey upheld a jury decision to hold Hillstone Restaurant Group liable for violations of the Stored Communications Act and New Jersey's parallel electronic surveillance statute after restaurant managers fired two employees over the content they created in a private MySpace group.*

The employees created a MySpace group to discuss their thoughts of the employer in a password-protected environment and invited other employees—but not managers—to join. When managers learned about the group, they asked an employee for access and read the group's pages. In those pages, the restaurant managers found negative remarks about the restaurant's customer service and quality guidelines, references to violence and illegal drug use, and a copy of the new wine exam that employees would need to take. After reading the content, the managers fired the two workers.**

The employee who gave the login information to the managers was not one of the group's creators, and she testified that she felt pressure to surrender the information. As a result, the court concluded that the managers did not have permission to enter the site.

When the suit was originally filed, the plaintiffs charged that the managers violated the Federal Wiretap Act, New Jersey Wiretap Act, Federal and State Stored Communications Act, along with Invasion of Privacy and Wrongful termination. Some of these statutes carry imprisonment in their potential punishments.

*Thanks to John H. Douglas of Foley & Lardner LLP for educating me about this case.
**Pietrylo v. Hillstone Restaurant (2008).
Source: Reprinted with permission from SocialMediaGovernance.com.

Stage 3: Differentiation

Finally, when an organization understands social media and how to use it to its advantage fairly well, it can craft more thoughtful guidance that empowers employees to differentiate the organization in the market. Such policies help employees do things differently from competitors and often turn employees into ambassadors to the market.

Role of Trust in Social Media Governance

Organizations desperately need social media policies because every employee can be a voice to the world for the organization, and social media is growing more deeply woven into our lives. Trying to control what employees say about their company in social media essentially would require controlling employees' thoughts and actions every hour of every day. It's just not possible. (And why would anyone want to do that, anyway?)

Instead, leaders must provide the right balance of empowerment and accountability. After all, trust and empowerment are inherently less expensive than control. Trust and empowerment do not require reporting, audits, or processes. In addition, trust and empowerment obliterate fear and diminish politics in the workplace.

As Stephen M. R. Covey states in his book *The Speed of Trust*, "Today's increasingly global marketplace puts a premium on true collaboration, teaming, relationships and partnering, and all these interdependencies require trust . . . partnerships based on trust outperform partnerships based on contracts. Compliance does not foster innovation, trust does."[6] In fact, Covey provides significant data to show that "high-trust organizations outperform low-trust organizations." We highly recommend his book to understand how to use trust to build a more competitive organization.

The right levels of trust and empowerment will vary based on an organization's regulatory environment and the nature of its customer relationships. However, every company must find the right balance of empowerment and accountability in social media for their organization.

In addition, executives must take the lead in defining boundaries. Bad things usually happen when leaders fail to get out in front of their people. Do not wait for an employee to do something in the absence of a social media policy and then frown on him or her. Stand up as a leader, take the initiative to understand social media, then determine appropriate boundaries for the organization and educate employees.

Finally, every organization should treat its social media policies as living documents, updating them as it learns about social media, as it increases its social media skills, as technologies and service providers evolve, and as the organization's priorities and goals change. After all, the beauty of the Web is that it allows us to change and republish these documents any time we like. They're just digital bits and bytes—not documents set in stone.

Every Policy Should Be Unique

Companies need to create social media policies with an understanding of the processes they intend to impact, the employees who will carry out those processes, the measures of success, their unique culture, and their context (regulations, business objectives, organizational history and other factors behind the policies). Figure 17.5 displays the interdependent components of a social media operating strategy. These components must be designed together, not independently.

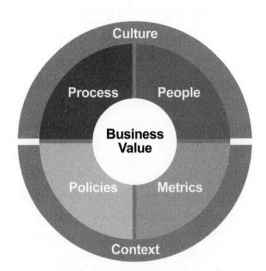

FIGURE 17.5 Interdependent Components of a Social Media Operating Strategy.

Every company should not strive to use social media just like Zappos or Dell does. The reason is that every company has a unique strategy, workforce, customers, processes, culture, technologies, and so on. In the words of online marketing guru Seth Godin, "The reason social media is so difficult for most organizations: It's a process, not an event. Dating is a process. So is losing weight . . . and building a brand. On the other hand, putting up a trade show booth is an event. So are going public and having surgery. Events are easier to manage, pay for and get excited about. Processes build results for the long haul."[7]

When a company excels in social media, its audience—its evangelists and fans—will be somewhat unique to the organization. A company that follows someone else's wake of social media success should expect its results to vary. The early adopters may give some examples of tactics to try, but their results will not be specific to any other company because each company's process has different inputs and should take different turns.

Companies should not hold out for someone in their industry to pioneer social media so that they can be the fast followers. They won't learn all that much. Instead, companies should start their exploration today.

18

Social Media, Collaboration, and Value Creation in Organizations

Robert J. Thomas

CHAPTER HIGHLIGHTS

Collaboration among employees has become increasingly critical to business success, especially as companies have become more diverse and geographically dispersed. Yet not all types of collaboration are created equal, and collaboration does not always add value.

An emerging set of applications based on social media can be useful in boosting collaboration by allowing employees to form and amend their own collaborative networks—and, consequently, raise the overall productivity and contribution of those networks.

Managers in business and government are curious about whether social media applications can be employed to enhance collaboration inside organizations. If the phenomenal growth of social media such as Facebook and Twitter are evidence of people's desire to connect, why shouldn't organizations use them to accelerate collaboration dramatically?

In this chapter, we explore the promise of social media for enhanced collaboration inside organizations. Drawing from a growing body of research and hands-on experience, we make three central points.

1. Collaboration does not always add value; therefore, investments in software that stimulates collaboration may not always pay off. Knowing the difference between collaboration that adds value and collaboration that destroys it can be quite helpful when deciding whether to invest in social media.
2. It is important to track the process as well as the outcomes of collaboration. Fortunately, advances in social networking applications have enhanced our ability to see collaboration and to measure its costs and benefits.
3. Managers need to prioritize their quest for collaboration because the preconditions for productive collaboration—like trust, respect, and the right technology—don't take root overnight.

Because collaboration is the object of interest here, we begin by clarifying what collaboration is and is not before exploring how social media can be used to enhance it.

Not All Collaboration Is the Same

The dictionary defines collaboration as "working together." Strictly speaking, then, any work that relies on the cooperation of two or more people would qualify as collaboration. However, managers need a definition that is practical and actionable.

After reviewing the diversity of work activities found in organizations, we identified two essential characteristics of collaboration. The first dimension has to do with purpose, or why collaboration is initiated. Sometimes collaboration is instigated by an intentional search—for example, someone is looking for the solution to a problem or a partner who can provide much-needed expertise. The initiator may not know all that she needs, but she knows that she must find people who have pieces to the puzzle. In other instances, collaboration results from discovering a shared interest in a topic; collaboration is therefore emergent, a by-product of a casual search. Search is not a random walk, but neither is it a focused investigation.

The second distinguishing characteristic of collaboration is its orientation—it can either be proactive or reactive. Sometimes collaboration is proactive: people assemble to pursue a common goal, usually one they consider to be constructive and aligned with a positive organizational objective. In other instances, collaboration may be reactive: It comes about in response to shortcomings in, or the failure of, a formal structure or process.

		Purpose	
		Emergent	Intentional
Orientation	**Proactive**	**Self-Organizing** • Formed out of casual search • Collaboration grows with the discovery of shared purpose or interest	**Progressive** • Formed out of casual search • Collaboration grows with the number and variety of exceptions and need for coordination
	Reactive	**Remedial** • Formed out of casual search • Collaboration grows with the discovery of shared purpose or interest	**Oppositional** • Formed out of casual search • Collaboration grows with the discovery of shared purpose or interest

FIGURE 18.1   Different Types of Collaboration.

Taken together, these two characteristics yield four distinctly different types of collaboration, as shown in Figure 18.1.

Self-organizing collaboration emerges from the discovery of shared purpose or interest on the part of previously unconnected individuals. Social media and networking web sites—including those that are part of a company's intranet—offer a place where people can post their interests and others can see them. Expert profiling systems like those used in Halliburton, 3M, and Verisign help employees quickly find authorities on a given topic or access compendia of lessons learned.[1] Similarly, commercial sites like Facebook and LinkedIn encourage people to explore the intersection between their interests and others'; some of these applications suggest links between pairs of people based on shared (but invisible) connections (for example, former employer, alumni association, geography, or declared interest).

Progressive collaboration often starts out as the product of chance encounters but grows into something much more durable as collaborators discover a shared need or passion and recruit others to it. Casual search quickly leads to richer conversation, a refined understanding, and, ultimately, a commitment to do something about the object of common interest. Relevant examples include communities of practice (CoPs) and centers of excellence (CoEs) in a wide variety of settings. In companies like ConocoPhillips, MWH (a global engineering firm), and Masterfoods (makers of M&M candies), CoPs are created with the explicit intent that they foster progress and knowledge-sharing among people who have invested in similar areas of expertise but who reside in distant organizational units.[2]

Remedial collaboration occurs as a constructive reaction to elements of the formal organization that do not work completely or well. Rather than throw up their hands in frustration or wait for someone else to repair a broken process, people find workarounds that enable them to complete their tasks. For example, employees at UPS improvised alternative approaches to make up for the fact that the software that determined shipping routes didn't take into account roadwork or construction projects.[3] Remedial collaboration fills the empty spaces left untouched by policies, answers the questions that procedures manuals don't, and makes it possible for people to secure resources, get approvals, and negotiate ambiguity in places where there is no documented process.

Oppositional collaboration does not seek to ameliorate or compensate for the shortcomings of a formal procedure; it seeks instead to leverage them to strike a more attractive effort bargain and/or to grow a counterculture and a distinctive identity based in opposition.[4] Creative energy that might be directed to fixing formal processes gets channeled into defensive routines, rate setting, and dissent. For example, people may use advanced communications technology to spread rumors faster or to transmit potentially embarrassing information to competitors, regulators or the media.

Having distinguished types of collaboration based on purpose and orientation—from chance encounter to intentional search, from desires to advance or to protect a set of interests—we now can refine our investigation of what it takes to establish and maintain these different types of collaboration.

Fostering Collaboration

Three of these four types of collaboration are attractive from a managerial perspective, and each poses unique requirements and challenges alongside the opportunities. Based on research conducted by a team from Accenture's Institute for High Performance and the Network Roundtable at the University of Virginia,[5] we have identified opportunities, requirements, challenges, and enablers for each type of collaboration. (See Table 18.1.)

Table 18.1 Opportunities, Requirements, and Challenges of Collaboration

Type of Collaboration	Opportunities	Requirements	Challenges	Enablers
Self-Organizing	• Unanticipated discoveries and breakthroughs • Increased employee engagement	• **Accessibility to a large percentage of employees** • Technology platform that supports peer-to-peer connectivity	• **Appearance of unproductive time spent online** • Difficulty of channeling activity to specific goals	• **Wikis and other easily accessible libraries and databases** • **Networking tools that quickly identify active conversations on topics of interest**
Progressive	• Leveraging/re-use of existing intellectual assets • Increased organizational agility • Increased employee engagement	• **Effective, continuously refreshed knowledge exchange** • System of rewards that promotes both voluntarism and trust	• **Reducing the time and energy it takes for people to find and qualify one another** • Expense associated with administering databases/portals and maintaining quality	• **Online expert profiles linked to corporate directories** • **Instant messaging and other team collaboration software**
Remedial	• Low-cost, informal solutions that complement the existing organization	• **Effective, widespread use of problem-solving methods** (e.g., Six Sigma) as a foundation for collaboration	• **Avoiding collaboration overload** • Reducing the time and energy it takes for people to find and qualify one another	• **Team collaboration software** • **Wikis and other easily accessible libraries and databases**

Self-organizing collaboration can enable a company to fluidly capitalize on new opportunities regardless of functional, hierarchical, geographic, or organizational lines. However, self-organizing collaboration challenges managers to accommodate themselves to the fact that success often involves high levels of uncertainty, nonlinearity, and serendipitous discovery. For example, a pharmaceuticals researcher casually scanning a corporate database found that someone in a different lab who shared an interest in the behavior of an obscure peptide already had proven the utility of that compound, albeit in a drug that had failed in clinical trials. Their chance encounter, enabled by user-friendly software that made search simple and straightforward, led to a collaboration that turned one person's failure into a significant organizational success. Without a platform for knowledge exchange and willingness on the part of management to encourage broad-based searches, such a discovery probably never would have happened.

Despite the occasional unearthing of gems hidden in the data, broad-based searches can appear to the untrained eye to be aimless time-wasting. In many organizations, and especially in those with managers unaccustomed to supporting broad-based searches, it is common to hear complaints about people idly surfing the Web or chatting on Facebook when, in fact, people may be scanning the environment garnering potentially valuable connections for the company.

Progressive collaboration can create reservoirs of functional expertise that enable a company to focus on products and customers without losing technical depth. A great example is the use of technical CoPs in companies like 3M and Ford Motor Company. However, a major challenge to progressive collaboration resides in finding ways to reduce the time and the energy required for people to find one another—that is, to root out who has expertise or experience in a particular domain—and then to "qualify" (gain comfort or trust) in the information or expertise the other person has to offer. For example, executives in a major North American consumer products company noted with concern that as the company had grown through acquisition, the percentage of its revenue coming from new products—in this case, packaged foods—was declining, despite a significant increment in investment in research and development. Analysis of data collected through employee surveys and interviews revealed that the integration of so many new companies and staffs overwhelmed the existing software and social relationships that previously had made it possible for people to find the in-house expertise they needed in a timely fashion. In employees' own words, growth in the company did not bring any reduction in the impulse or the desire to collaborate. They just couldn't find each other. Avoiding situations like this also requires a continuous refreshing (or scrubbing) of shared databases or knowledge exchanges to ensure that they remain current and don't lead people down blind alleys.

In another example of progressive collaboration, researchers and graduates of the West Point military academy pioneered peer-to-peer knowledge-sharing applications to enhance the connectivity of front-line leaders in different parts of the world. The key was to help forward-positioned troops to exchange the latest information (for example on improvised explosive devices [IEDs]) with people who already were credentialed as trustworthy sources. But to work effectively, the information had to be pushed to the edge of the organization instead of centralized in the Pentagon.[6]

Remedial collaboration is highly valued because it addresses bottlenecks, breakdowns, and failures in existing processes often in creative, improvisational ways. People pitch in to address shortcomings of a process without reverting to bureaucratic rules. However, in the absence of a clear set of priorities—which repairs or improvements really matter—and lacking a shared methodology for analyzing and repairing breakdowns (such as Six Sigma or total quality management), it is common for people to find themselves inundated with requests for collaboration. Technology that allows for instant communication and cross-platform connectivity (for example, presence-based applications that follow the subscriber from PC, to smart phone, to videoconference) can exacerbate problems they were meant to solve when all they do is multiply (and amplify) the number of calls for collaboration. For example, the new leader of an expanding consulting practice was stunned when she found her pleas for more collaboration between specialty groups were met with boos and catcalls at a unit retreat.[7] Subsequent investigation revealed to her that no one opposed the idea of collaboration but virtually everyone complained that they suffered from "initiative overload" and were expecting the new leader to reduce, not to expand, the number of strategic initiatives by applying a logical prioritization . . . and to do so without investing in even more communication technology (which already was perceived to be overly invasive).

In summary to this point: Managers who want to make the most out of collaboration need to understand what type of collaboration they want to foster and how. They need to be clear as to why they want collaboration because it is expensive, requires distinctive supports, and can easily consume the time and attention of some of the most valuable people. We hope these are useful admonitions—but that's all they will be without the ability to see collaboration (or detect its absence), measure it, and evaluate the benefits achieved from efforts to foster more of it. What can't be seen often does not get measured, and what does not get measured rarely gets managed. We describe next the utility of social network analysis for these tasks.

Seeing Collaboration and Its Consequences

Collaboration as we define it is a network phenomenon. It involves durable and often informal relationships of give-and-take, exchange, sharing and reciprocity among people. It is often not visible from the perspective of an organization chart or a formal table of responsibilities. The informal, voluntary side of collaboration is what gives these networks their distinctive flexibility—their capacity to sense and respond to breakdowns in formal processes.

Unfortunately, collaboration of any type is largely invisible without the right tools or lens with which to see it. In recent years, however, social network analysis (SNA) has emerged as a powerful new way for managers to see the patterns of interaction—information sharing, problem solving, and mentorship as well as collaboration—that make up the less visible, often informal side of an organization.[8] By asking simple survey questions online and identifying the people with whom they interact most frequently, SNA makes it possible to depict (in a network diagram such as Figure 18.2 or in a matrix) the networks that underlie or exist in parallel to the formal organization charts and process diagrams. Repeated surveys will, over time, reveal changes in networks or in patterns of collaboration—making it possible to assess whether interventions such as reorganization or targeted efforts to improve collaboration (for example, offsite events, new software/communications tools, or incentive programs) actually have their desired impact. Moreover, targeted questions can reveal different types of collaboration.

To illustrate the utility of SNA as a means to see as well as to seed collaboration, we offer a brief example from our research that features an example of progressive collaboration rendered visible through a network lens.

A very successful partner was tapped to lead a new business unit at one of the world's largest professional services organizations.[9] Because the organization she'd been given had recently been formed out of several disparate units,

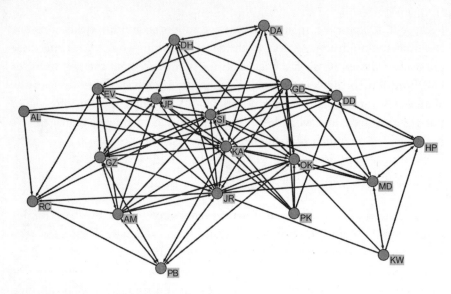

FIGURE 18.2 Typical Network Diagram.

she found herself leading people she did not know—many of whom had never worked together before. To make matters even more challenging, the group was tasked with achieving a significant increase in market share quickly so as to justify the reorganization.

To tackle her new challenge, she decided to approach collaboration systematically. Rather than rely on a few energetic collaborators or rush to install a much-hyped technological solution, she elected to start by asking a few basic questions: Which networks were in place that leveraged the expertise and project experiences within her business unit? How much did her employees know about the depth of skills residing in the group (and so whom to tap when certain opportunities appeared)? And which incentives were most likely to encourage value-added collaborations?

Knowing she could not answer any of those questions by looking at the unit's organizational chart or even by reading people's job descriptions, she carried out a social network analysis to find targeted ways to enhance collaboration—particularly progressive collaboration—among experts in the group. She focused on progressive collaboration because her organization relied on teams of experts to solve client problems and to do so in a way that leveraged not just the immediate team's knowledge but the knowledge of the unit as a whole.

To get a sense of these patterns of collaboration among her employees, she asked each employee to rate all other employees on this issue: "Please indicate the extent to which the following people are effective in providing you with information that helps you to learn, solve problems, and do your work." She was concerned that a lack of awareness of "who knows what" and trust in other colleagues' expertise was invisibly leading to missed sales opportunities and less-than-optimal delivery of services.

The SNA revealed barriers that were keeping the unit from combining expertise in key areas and differentiating itself from its competitors. A quantitative presentation of the network data (see Figure 18.3) helped her see the extent to which a pattern of recurring work assignments had created silos within and between key industry account groups and business units like hers. This table shows the percentage of information-seeking relationships that existed within and between each function out of 100 percent if every person were collaborating with every other person at that network juncture (either within or across units). For example, if everybody in High Tech had effective informational relationships with one another, the figure 100 percent would appear in the top left-hand cell (instead of the actual 35 percent).[10]

The table revealed several opportunities. Although she did not want to see high numbers in all the cells—everybody collaborating with everyone else would mean time probably was being wasted—she did want to see specific points of integration where fluid information flow was important to the success of the unit. Two things stood out. First, looking *down the diagonal*, she hoped to see 25 percent to 35 percent connectivity within each group to ensure that best practices and synergies were being realized in groups that

	High Tech	Banking	Government	Consumer Products	Natural Resources	Strategy	Other
High Tech (11)	35%	0%	0%	1%	3%	10%	0%
Banking (3)	0%	100%	11%	0%	6%	4%	0%
Government (3)	9%	22%	50%	7%	17%	10%	11%
Consumer Products (9)	3%	0%	0%	13%	2%	1%	0%
Natural Resources (6)	0%	6%	11%	4%	23%	5%	22%
Strategy (26)	7%	3%	6%	1%	4%	36%	36%
Other (3)	6%	11%	0%	0%	11%	36%	0%

FIGURE 18.3 Collaboration Matrix.

had similar expertise. Within Consumer Goods and Natural Resources, those figures were much lower. She knew that even though those functions were small, each had specialists who rarely worked together, yet collaboration could help to develop truly unique service offerings.

Second, she was keenly interested in building certain off-diagonal collaborations that could yield a competitive advantage with clients—especially where bringing together people from different functions produced a holistic solution to clients' problems. These key off-diagonal junctures represented the greatest opportunity to combine unique, tacit expertise in offerings to clients that competitors could not re-create. Collaborations often break down for simple reasons: Two leaders don't like each other, physical distance between people gets in the way, incentive schemes are incompatible, or there is a lack of technical infrastructure. The figures in this kind of grid help locate those breakdowns that will undermine strategy execution.

In this example, the SNA—and a network perspective more generally—made it possible see collective behavior as well as missed opportunities for collaboration. This gave a busy senior executive a basis for deciding how best to initiate and sustain collaboration.

Social Media as a Boost to Productive Collaboration

At the outset of this chapter we asked whether social media can enhance collaboration. We can now answer with a resounding yes—but a yes with reservations. That is, as we've shown, not all collaboration is productive, and different types of collaboration pose different requirements and benefit from different enablers. Self-organizing collaboration is fueled by tools like wikis that make expertise quickly visible and accessible and that illuminate the networks among people with common interests. Progressive collaboration benefits most from expert profiles and team collaboration software, particularly as collaboration moves from serendipitous discovery to durable CoPs. Remedial collaboration prospers when informal solutions and workarounds need to be cataloged and communicated to larger audiences or retrieved for later use by their creators.

To date, software tools that support these different forms of collaboration have tended to reside in different places and to work largely independently of one another. However, that is beginning to change—partially as a result of the evolution of social media such as Facebook and Twitter—where user behavior has revealed new uses for the application. That is, developers of new enterprise-based social media like Chatter, a product of Salesforce.com, have observed the behavior of Facebook users and discovered that simple messages often are preferred over lengthy e-mails, that short updates of individual or team activity can lead to impromptu meetings and surprising discoveries, and that participants are often quite satisfied to browse updates rather than engage in time-consuming exchanges through e-mail or even instant messaging. Although still in its infancy and therefore lacking evidence as to its effects on productivity, Chatter nonetheless combines a familiar Facebook-like interface with the capacity to track the doings of individuals, teams, documents, and even ideas through one's personal network. Participants can choose whom they wish to follow, set levels of accessibility so that they are not inundated with queries, and post notices on a personal blog. One of Chatters' greatest strengths is its integration with the suite of Salesforce.com's cloud-based applications. That means that any document, file, or database can be linked to a message or set aside in a team space for easy access.

Although it is not yet clear whether Chatter or a similar application will emerge as the Swiss Army knife of collaboration software, the idea of allowing employees to form and amend networks of collaboration holds enormous appeal. In that respect, it could serve as a boon to self-organizing collaboration. However, to prevent it from becoming yet another contributor to information overload, both managers and employees will need to prioritize where they need collaboration and where they don't.

Conclusion

In times like these—when increases in market volatility and complexity have delivered a one-two punch to many organizations—collaboration brings a richer and more diverse gene pool of interests, skills, and experiences to bear on a common topic. And perhaps most important, it encourages initiative from people who otherwise might wait for direction.

The building blocks of collaboration—the intense conversations and head scratching that are the preamble to defining a problem or discovering a solution and the trust needed to lubricate interaction—require time, attention, and a willingness to share. Without dedicated time and shared objectives, potential collaborators often find themselves stretched too thin. Excessive pressure to collaborate can kill the impulse to share. And, absent trust, collaboration can easily be starved by rigid organizational silos. Ironically, employees exhibit a lot of collaboration but much of it does not get recognized, and, in some cases, collaboration is actually aimed at accomplishing ends that are at odds with formal corporate objectives. Finally, if not configured properly, technologies intended to enhance collaboration can turn work into a labyrinth of meetings, phone calls, videoconferences, e-mail, instant messages, voicemail, blog posts, wiki entries, and tweets.

But it is important to recognize that not all collaboration adds value and not all value-adding collaboration is evident when it begins. Self-organizing collaboration helps people discover the common interests that often serve as the precursor to value-creating activity. Progressive collaboration produces value indirectly, largely by adding depth to the understanding of a process or an activity that directly creates value. Remedial collaboration helps achieve value when a system is incapable of monitoring and correcting itself. Oppositional collaboration usually destroys value or dissipates it.

Collaboration is most powerful when focused on the creation of intangible assets, such as ability to innovate, talent and human capital development, leadership development, reputation, and brand. Fortunately, tools such as social network analysis are making it possible to do something more than "water and wait" when it comes to cultivating collaboration. By utilizing more effective ways to depict collaborative networks, to see change in them as a result of targeted interventions, and to distinguish among the types of collaboration possible, managers are finding that they can encourage collaborations that are likely to yield fruit for the organization.

Appendix 1:
Solution Example: Putting
Sentiment in a CRM Package

There are many commercial search engines to choose from, including some that are working closely with major customer relationship management (CRM) vendors. Some technology providers, however, already have combined their search and sentiment technologies. In fact, there is an abundance of open source tools in this space.

One example of a CRM package that has sentiment analysis technology inside is RightNow's SmartSense. The product gives a company a real-time score of customer engagement using the visual image of a thermometer. (See Figure A1.1.)

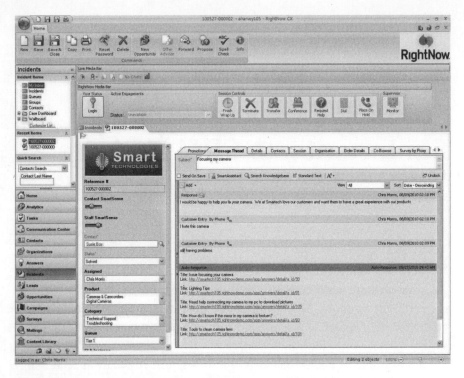

FIGURE A1.1 RightNow's SmartSense Gives a Company a Real-Time Score of Customer Engagement Using the Visual Image of a Thermometer (www.rightnow.com).

Appendix 2: Solution Example: Merging Structured and Unstructured Data

As mentioned earlier in the book, one of the major challenges in dealing with social media is the fact that much of the data generated by social media is unstructured. Thus, a tool that can manage and make sense of such data is vital to the effective use of social media.

To see the value and utility of such a tool, it's first helpful to understand the problem that structured query language (SQL) databases have with unstructured data. Take a simple example: the case notes of any memo field. A relational database (by definition) operates based on the relationships between data fields. Tables have keys, such as Customer ID and Customer Name. These keys have defined lengths (usually less than 255 characters) and are always single words. (This will be critical later, as we will discuss.)

Tables are linked together by the keys common to those tables. When someone issues a query to the database, it's by keys. A modern relational database is constantly querying its own keys to create an index of them. Using this index and query plans, the database can answer the query quickly. This is especially the case today, when indexes—if not the entire database—can be stored into a computer's memory, thanks to 64-bit addressing.

However, case notes are stored in memo fields, and those fields typically allow many words. Because SQL indexes have to be keyword based, one can't index a memo field in SQL. That means it's impossible to relate or connect the contents of one memo field to another memo field because there are no defined keys to make that relationship. That also means one cannot look within the SQL database to see if there is a pattern to the issue noted in the memo field.

Unless a company has a small number of database users and computer hardware with loads of unused capacity, likely its database administrator prevents users from doing text searches on memo fields. Many customer relationship management (CRM) technologies block these types of search as well. As of this writing, case history text search is prohibited in popular CRM packages such as Salesforce.com.

To be sure, there are ways to work around this limitation. One is adding a "list of values" field to the case record, called something like "Problem Code." This would include a list of issues one would expect to find for a product (e.g., "It won't turn on," "It won't turn off," etc.). An individual would ask call center agents to pick from that list to provide a shortcut to the problem. Then the company would be able to index all the case problem codes to generate a nice report, right?

Not quite. In the brave new world of social media, the list of problem codes could be the entire English language. Should a company create pick lists for all the negative and positive words? Pick lists for every product sold and all the possible problem codes? Clearly, the list expands infinitely quickly.

But search technologies come to the rescue here. Search technologies are designed to make sense of unstructured data and let us query that data. Some (such as Endeca and InQuira) have natural language query processing. Some (like Google) attach values to content by the number of times a link is clicked.

So at first blush, the work-around of merging the best of search and text-mining technology with the best of SQL databases seems like a good fix. However, keyword searching isn't enough to help a company navigate through the sea of unstructured social media data. Ideally, a company needs entity extraction, sentiment analysis, dynamic facets, and more. It should want as much machine learning as possible (i.e., over time the software gets better at recognizing the importance of certain words and patterns). A company can expect to be burdened with handling some manual tuning of the technology but not very much. And a company wants answers in real time without waiting for it.

Another common approach has flaws too: extracting, transforming, and loading data (so-called extract, transform, load [ETL] in database lingo) from the SQL database to an immediate location, such as a data warehouse or data mart. But this is likely to bog down quickly because of organizational politics. Database administrators don't like their transactional online databases to be loaded down with ETL requests, so they mandate that they be done once a day (and at night, at that). Additionally, ETL tools are not designed to take things in bits and pieces (as they happen in the world of social media), so this makes the ETL approach doubly hazardous.

Furthermore, specialists tightly control access to the data warehouse, often through data-reporting tools that only they know how to use. These specialists usually are overloaded with requests to generate reports, often on last year's data. Asking them to create a report based on an incident in the past 24 hours would be like a person asking a local ferry operator to take him to Europe. Additionally, data warehouse specialists are steeped in standard ETL approaches that call for "cleansing the data." With social media, a company wants raw data (not cleansed data), and wants it summarized. But it also wants to be able to drill down to the record of the very person it thinks precipitated an avalanche of rants (or raves).

There is a better approach to all this. It is indexing the data with a search tool that has work flow capabilities. As data enters a CRM database, it is sent to a search engine that takes a generational indexing approach. Ideally, the search engine also is combing through blogs, forums, and review data as they come in and thus is continuously updating its index. Endeca claims that the latest iteration of its product does this. The firm Attivio was founded on this principle. Its search technology has been clocked at 800 queries per second stand-alone and 300 queries per second while ingesting 30 gigabytes of unstructured content per hour. (Note: When shopping such technologies, a company always should ask for the query speed during ingest.) Both search engines perform entity extraction, sentiment analysis (which Attivio does at the entity level, not just the document level), and dynamic facets, which means they can provide a real-time picture of what is going on in both outboard and onboard social media channels.

These tools are proficient at doing things at the speed of call centers. A decision support system-based approach built on search technology is a great way to deal with the issue of combining structured and unstructured data in real time. (Figure A2.1 illustrates Attivio and Salesforce.com.)

In this demonstration, the Accenture Interactive group provided more than 10,000 reviews from Amazon, CNET, and BestBuy web sites. This data then was walked through the work flow steps we advocated earlier with

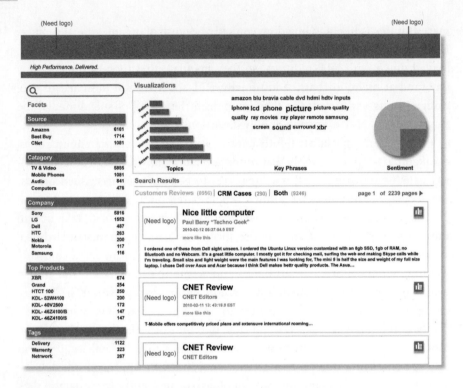

FIGURE A2.1 Combining Attivio and Salesforce.com to Provide Structured and Unstructured Data in Real Time.

Source: www.attivio.com/active-intelligence/aie-demo.html.

Attivio. The reviews were analyzed for sentiment and bucketed in facets by product and complaint type. Then they were merged with Case Memo data stored in Salesforce.com. The end result was a decision support system that merges offboard and onboard structured and unstructured data in real time. Any issue that is of interest can be compared immediately to see if it's a known issue, and if it is, an agent can respond quickly with the resolution or official company position. If it's a new issue, an agent creates a case, which enables regular CRM users—especially product management—to become aware of it right away. There's no waiting for ETL or daily batches.

Let's say a company wanted to go beyond what happened in the past 24 hours or even last week in the social media world. More than 40 tools are available today to understand more deeply customers' sentiments over a longer period of time. One is Clarabridge.

A company's choice of a text analysis tool should be based on whether the model used by a tool fits the model of the business. Take a tool called Attensity. It comes out of the military intelligence market and focuses on finding connections by mining intelligence data. This tool breaks down text into "triples"—Subject, Predicate, Object. Attensity then added a tool for entity extraction (ThingFinder from SAP's InXight group). It combined the two into a powerful tool set that analyzes text data to determine interesting relationships—that is, how social media text might relate to other text. But it does not focus on sentiment analysis. A company must tune Attensity to look for the kinds of triples it seeks; the software's strength is not finding anomalies or new triples. However, Attensity should be good at helping figure out if someone complaining on an outboard channel is a customer of a particular firm.

In contrast, Clarabridge grew up in the customer experience monitoring market. It is optimized for sensing sentiments and has entity extraction built in. So it does a fine job of analyzing buzz trends and impact. The firm also has a relationship with a vendor called Alterian Techrigy around social media feeds. Clarabridge has relationships with business intelligence software vendors MicroStrategy and BusinessObjects around reporting. At the time of this writing, Clarabridge had developed a fairly sophisticated approach for detecting anomalies in social media data and highlighting new issues with high frequency.

The approach one takes to solving this issue depends on the company's business model. Text-analytic vendors should be expected to improve their offerings continually. That means a company must refresh its knowledge of their products continually.

Notes

Introduction

1. www.web-strategist.com/blog/2010/01/19/a-collection-of-social-network-stats-for-2010/.
2. http://royal.pingdom.com/2010/05/07/how-much-we-will-be-tweeting-by-january-2011-chart/.
3. www.web-strategist.com/blog/2010/01/19/a-collection-of-social-network-stats-for-2010/.
4. Ibid.
5. http://econsultancy.com/blog/5324-20+-mind-blowing-social-media-statistics-revisited.
6. http://seniorhousingnews.com/2010/01/07/baby-boomers-represent-fastest-growing-segment-on-social-networking-sites/.
7. Accenture, "Consumer Electronics Products and Services Usage Report," 2009.
8. www.pamorama.net/2010/03/21/were-addicted-to-social-networks-48-of-us-check-them-in-bed/.
9. www.marketingcharts.com/television/socnets-web-video-radically-alter-online-behavior-8838/nielsen-landscape-time-spent-increase-video-social-media-february-2009jpg/.
10. www.readwriteweb.com/archives/social_networking_now_more_popular_on_mobile_than_desktop.php.

Chapter 1

1. www.washingtonpost.com/wp-dyn/content/article/2009/07/12/AR2009071200319.html.
2. Los Angeles Times Daily Travel and Deal Blog, http://travel.latimes.com/daily-deal-blog/index.php/smashed-guitar-youtu-4850/.
3. www.omo.com.au/features/dirt-is-good.aspx.

Chapter 2

1. "Dell Reports $3 Million in Twitter Revenue," *New York Times*, June 15, 2009, http://dealbook.blogs.nytimes.com/2009/06/15/dell-says-it-has-earned-3-million-from-twitter/.
2. Dell annual revenues taken from Dell Form 10-K, Annual Report for the Fiscal Year Ended January 31, 2010. http://i.dell.com/sites/content/corporate/financials/en/Documents/fy10-year-in-review/FY10_Form10K_Final.pdf.
3. Seth Godin Seth's Blog, "The Reason Social Media is So Difficult for Most Organizations," December 10, 2009. http://sethgodin.typepad.com/seths_blog/2009/12/the-reason-social-media-is-so-difficult-for-most-organizations.html.

Chapter 4

1. This is according to www.pingdom.com, which cites Google Ad Planner statistics. For more information, see http://royal.pingdom.com/2010/02/16/study-ages-of-social-network-users/.
2. Spencer Stuart Board Index Report, 2009. http://www.spencerstuart.com/research/bi/1390/].
3. www.ricg.com/marketing_articles/digital_marketing/one_quarter_of_baby_boomers_use_social_networks_says_aarp/.
4. According to digital marketing firm White Horse, www.whitehorse.com.
5. www.computerweekly.com/Articles/2010/06/10/241516/Interview-Top-CEOs-are-too-old-to-tweet-says-Forrester-Research.htm.
6. Ibid.
7. See the May 24, 2010, video of Best Buy CMO Barry Judge here: http://video.forbes.com/fvn/cmo/best-buy-cmo-barry-judge.
8. http://mashable.com/2010/01/07/vitamin-water-connect/.
9. www1.peanutlabs.com/.

Chapter 5

1. eMarketer, February 2009, according to Bazaarvoice web site page: www.bazaarvoice.com/resources/stats.
2. Econsultancy, July 2009, according to Bazaarvoice web site: www.bazaarvoice.com/resources/stats.
3. www.insurancenetworking.com/issues/13_7/insurance_technology_social_media_customer_service_USAA-24995-1.html.
4. From an interview with Bazaarvoice CEO Brett Hurt posted on March 14, 2010, on the web site of *Texas CEO Magazine*, http://texasceomagazine.com/?p=164.

Chapter 6

1. Sebastiani, F. 2002. Machine learning in automated text categorization. ACM Computing Surey 34, 1 (Mar. 2002), 1-47.
2. Ontogen. Jozerf Stefan Institute, Ljubljana, Slovenia. http://ontogen.ijs.si.

Chapter 7

1. www.slideshare.net/fred.zimny/boston-consulting-group-innovation-2010-a-return-to-prominence-and-the-emergence-of-a-new-world-order.
2. www.pressreleasepoint.com/battelle-rampd-magaz..ie-report-shows-emerging-economies-drive-global-research-and-development-growth.
3. Wells Fargo case study originally was published in Accenture's *Outlook* journal (September 2007), www.accenture.com/Global/Research_and_Insights/Outlook/By_Issue/Y2007/SustainProfitableGrowth.htm.
4. According to Larry Huston and Nabil Sakkab, "P&G's New Innovation Model," *Harvard Business Review* (March 2006), http://hbswk.hbs.edu/archive/5258.html.
5. Both quotes are from: www.ideastorm.com/ideaAbout?pt=About+IdeaStorm.
6. www.utalkmarketing.com/pages/Article.aspx?ArticleID=16954.
7. Scott Berinato and Jeff Clark, "Six Ways to Find Value in Twitter's Noise," *Harvard Business Review* (June 2010): 34.

Chapter 8

1. http://right-people.blogspot.com/2010/04/online-advertising-increase.html.
2. www.marketingcharts.com/television/new-auto-online-ad-spend-to-jump-114-11069.
3. http://managementchords.blogspot.com.
4. Accenture Research Report. "Onward and Up: How Marketers Are Refocusing the Front Office for Growth," 2010, www.accenture.com/Global/Consulting/Customer_Relationship_Mgmt/Marketing-Transformation/R-and-I/Onward-Growth.htm.
5. Ibid.
6. www.marketingcharts.com/direct/online-consumer-generated-reviews-have-big-impact-on-offline-purchases-2577/.
7. http://adage.com/article?article_id=129488.
8. http://mashable.com/2010/07/15/old-spice-stats/.
9. www.readwriteweb.com/archives/how_old_spice_won_the_internet.php.
10. www.ericsson.com/ericsson/corpinfo/publications/telecomreport/archive/2009/social-media/article1.shtml.
11. http://mashable.com/2010/04/19/dewmocracy-2-flavor-nations/.

12. Jennifer Aaker and Victoria Chang, "Obama and the Power of Social Media and Technology," *European Business Review*, May 18, 2010, www.europeanbusinessre view.com/?p=1627.

Chapter 9

1. Better Business Bureau, "US BBB 2009 Statistics Sorted by Complaint," www.bbb .org/us/storage/16/documents/stats percent20pdf/us_complaint.pdf.
2. "Auto Sales—Market Data Center," *Wall Street Journal*, July 1, 2010, http:// online.wsj.com/mdc/public/page/2_3022-autosales.html#autosales.
3. Joe Marchese, "JetBlue Gets Twitter", MediaPost Blogs Online Spin, June 22, 2010, www.mediapost.com/publications/?fa=Articles.showArticle&art_aid=130680.
4. E. York, "Game of Chicken Against Leader Pays Off for Chick-fil-A," *Advertising Age*, May 3, 2010, http://adage.com/article?article_id=143642.
5. R. Reisner, "Comcast's Twitter Man," *Bloomberg BusinessWeek*, January 13, 2009, www.businessweek.com/managing/content/jan2009/ca20090113_373506.htm.
6. "Intuit and User Contribution Systems," Contribution Revolution, usercontribution .intuit.com/Intuit-and-user-contribution-systems.
7. "Competition Description: Predict HIV Progression," http://kaggle.com/ hivprogression.
8. "The Zappos CEO and UPS Step In," *BusinessWeek*, February 19, 2009, www .businessweek.com/magazine/content/09_09/b4121030584631.htm?chan= magazine+channel_in+depth.

Chapter 10

1. Arbitron Inc. and Edison Research, "The Infinite Dial 2010: Digital Platforms and the Future of Radio," http://arbitron.mediaroom.com/index.php?s=43&item=682.
2. "Led by Facebook, Twitter, Global Time Spent on Social Media Sites up 82 percent Year over Year," http://blog.nielsen.com/nielsenwire/global/led-by-facebook-twitter-global-time-spent-on-social-media-sites-up-82-year-over-year/. (December 2009.)
3. Sass, The Social Graf, "20 percent of Social Network Users Have Shared Negative Brand Experiences," April 29, 2010, www.mediapost.com/publications/? fa=Articles.showArticle&art_aid=127224.
4. From an interview with Toby Richards, Microsoft general manager for communities and online support. (June 2010.)
5. Harvard Business School wrote a case study in 2010 on the "United Breaks Guitars" incident, which can be found here: http://hbr.org/product/united-breaks-guitars/an/ 510057-PDF-ENG?Ntt=united percent2520breaks percent2520guitars.

6. www.dianaswednesday.com/2009/07/united-breaks-guitars/.

7. Brett Snyder, BNET, "United Aggressively Responds to 'United Breaks Guitars Part 2,'" August 24, 2009, www.bnet.com/blog/airline-business/united-aggressively-responds-to-8220united-breaks-guitars-part-2-8243/1055.

8. http://mvp.support.microsoft.com/gp/aboutmvp.

9. Reena Jana, "How Intuit Makes a Social Network Pay," *BusinessWeek*, July 2, 2009, www.businessweek.com/magazine/content/09_28/b4139066365300.htm.

Chapter 11

1. You can read the full Federal Trade Commission Act at: www.ftc.gov/ogc/FTC_Act_IncorporatingUS_SAFE_WEB_Act.pdf.

2. www.ftc.gov/multimedia/video/business/endorsement-guides/endorse_mary-q1.shtm.

3. www.ftc.gov/opa/2009/10/endortest.shtm.

4. www.ftc.gov/opa/2009/10/endortest.shtm, as of May 21, 2010.

5. The FTC Guides state that "[a]n advertiser may satisfy this obligation by securing the endorser's views at reasonable intervals where reasonableness will be determined by such factors as new information on the performance or effectiveness of the product, a material alteration in the product, changes in the performance of competitors' products, and the advertiser's contract commitments."

6. http://allthingsd.com/about/walt-mossberg/ethics/.

Chapter 12

1. Paul Greenberg, *CRM at the Speed of Light: Capturing and Keeping Customers in Internet Real Time* (4th ed.), 2009, p. 32. Greenberg quoted from a 2006 blog by Seth Godin, who had talked to Disney executives about their version of CRM, http://books.google.com/books?id=YWOFpc2D_c8C&pg=PA32&lpg=PA32&dq=cmr+crm+greenberg&source=bl&ots=rJO69xMHLg&sig=42IEiDpxmf3WfmjdrVpz9yn1weg&hl=en&ei=jXg7TP2FMMH98Aat5MGRBw&sa=X&oi=book_result&ct=result&resnum=1&ved=0CBUQ6AEwAA#v=onepage&q&f=false.

2. Twitter stats according to a June 2010 article in *TechCrunch*: http://techcrunch.com/2010/06/08/twitter-190-million-users/.

3. Seth Grimes, "Defining Text Analytics," *Intelligent Enterprise*, February 8, 2007, http://intelligent-enterprise.informationweek.com/blog/archives/2007/02/defining_text_a.html.

4. www.scribd.com/doc/12828231/Lithium-Community-Health-Index.

Chapter 13

1. Hula Hoop reference: www.madehow.com/Volume-6/Hula-Hoop.html. Google reference here: www.mercurynews.com/breaking-news/ci_14940444?nclick_check=1.
2. "Marketers Get Wise, Design Mobile Apps with a Purpose" *AdAge*, September 14, 2009, http://adage.com/digital/article?article_id=138974.
3. J. Wortham, "Foursquare Raises $20 million in Venture Capital," *New York Times*, June 29, 2010, www.nytimes.com/2010/06/30/technology/30foursquare .html. S. Gustin, "Heavily Hyped Hipster Game Foursquare Shows It's Legit at SXSW," Daily Finance.com, March, 12, 2010, www.dailyfinance.com/story/company-news/heavily-hyped-hipster-game-foursquare-shows-its-legit-at-sxsw/19395678/.

Chapter 15

1. Don Tapscott, *Grown Up Digital: How the Net Generation Is Changing Your World* (New York: McGraw-Hill, 2009), p. 18.
2. Accenture, "Jumping the Boundaries of Corporate IT: Accenture Global Research on Millennials' Use of Technology," 2010.
3. Tapscott, *Grown Up Digital*, p. 46
4. Accenture, "Jumping the Boundaries of Corporate IT."
5. Accenture Aging Workforce Study.
6. "The Future of Work," Pew Research Center, *Time* magazine.
7. Susan Cantrell and David Smith, *Workforce of One: Revolutionizing Talent Management through Customization* (Boston: Harvard Business Press, 2010).
8. Regina Connell, Barbara Shuck, and Marion Thatch, "Social Networking for Competitive Advantage," Society for Marketing Professional Services, July 2009.
9. Accenture Innovation and Collaboration Survey, "Workforce of the Future," 2010.
10. Accenture, "Jumping the Boundaries of Corporate IT."
11. Mark Foster, "The Global Talent Crisis," *BusinessWeek,* September 2008, www.businessweek.com/managing/content/sep2008/ca20080919_403840 .htm.
12. Labor Data Show Surge in Hiring of Temp Workers. NY Times By LOUIS UCHITELLE Published: December 20, 2009 www.nytimes.com/2009/12/21/business/economy/21temps.html.
13. Connell, Shuck, and Thatch, "Social Networking for Competitive Advantage."
14. Cantrell and Smith, *Workforce of One.*
15. Statistics are from the Accenture Middle Manager Study.

Chapter 16

1. Andrew O'Connell, "Reading the Public Mind," *HBR* (October 2010).
2. David Armano, Sr. VP Edelman Digital, (blog for HBR) "Fire Your Marketing Manager and Hire a Community Manager," *HBR*, October 2010.
3. www.insidefacebook.com/2010/06/23/att-social-media-facebook/.
4. "Guide to Organization Design: Creating High Performing and Adaptable Enterprises," *Economist*, 2007.

Chapter 17

1. March 2010 survey of 257 security and information technology professionals by nCircle.
2. March 2010 Survey, Web security firm F-Secure.
3. American Century Investments, "Financial Professionals Social Media Adoption," March 29, 2010.
4. CNET, "Study: Social Media Puts Companies at Risk," June 8, 2010, http://news .cnet.com/8301-1023_3-20007071-93.html.
5. December 2009 study of publicly available social media policies on SocialMediaGovernance.
6. Stephen M. R. Covey, *The Speed of Trust*.
7. Seth Godin, http://sethgodin.typepad.com/seths_blog/2009/12/the-reason-social-media-is-so-difficult-for-most-organizations.html.

Chapter 18

1. Rob Cross, Jean Singer, Sally Colella, Robert J. Thomas, and Yaarit Silverstone (eds.), *The Organizational Networks Fieldbook* (San Francisco: Jossey-Bass, 2010): see chapters by Rob Cross and Guillermo Velasquez, "Driving Business Results through Networked Communities of Practice"; Barry Dayton, "Network Analysis for Engineering Small Practice Groups"; and Angelique Finan and Grady Bryant, "Building a Technical Community."
2. For a detailed depiction of how social media have helped spawn dozens of communities of practice in ConocoPhillips, see Peter Gray and Dan Ranta, "Networks of Excellence," in Cross et al., *Organizational Networks Fieldbook*. In MWH, see Christie Dowling, Betsy Smith Redfern, and Victor Gulas, "Forging Global Connections," in ibid. For Masterfoods, see Rob Cross and Robert J. Thomas, *Driving Results through Social Networks* (San Francisco: Jossey-Bass, 2008), pp. 113–115.
3. UPS case study.
4. See, for example, Michael Burawoy, *Manufacturing Consent* (Chicago: University of Chicago, 1979).

5. Cross and Thomas, *Driving Results through Social Networks*; and Cross et al., *The Organizational Networks Fieldbook*.

6. See David S. Alberts and Richard E. Hayes, *Power to the Edge: Command and Control in the Information Age* (Washington, DC: CCRP Foundation, 2003).

7. Rob Cross, Robert J. Thomas, Ana Dutra, and Carrie Newberry, "Using Network Analysis to Build a New Business," *Organizational Dynamics* (Spring 2008).

8. For a more detailed discussion of the origins and varieties of social network analysis, see: R. Cross and A. Parker, *The Hidden Power of Social Networks* (Boston: Harvard Business School Press, 2004); Cross and Thomas, *Driving Results through Social Networks*; M. Gladwell, *The Tipping Point: How Little Things Can Make a Big Difference* (Boston: Back Bay Books); R. Burt, *Structural Holes* (Cambridge, MA: Harvard University Press, 1992; M. Granovetter, "The Strength of Weak Ties," *American Journal of Sociology* 78 (1973): 1360–1380; T. Allen, *Managing the Flow of Technology* (Cambridge, MA: MIT Press, 1984); P. Monge and N. Contractor, "Emergence of Communication Networks," in F. Jablin and L. Putnam (eds.), *Handbook of Organizational Communication* (2nd ed.) (Thousand Oaks, CA: Sage, in press); E. Rogers, *Diffusion of Innovations* (4th ed.) (New York: Free Press, 1995.

9. See Cross, Thomas, Dutra, and Newberry, "Using Network Analysis to Build a New Business."

10. Of course, percentages in a table like this are affected by group size. It is much easier for a group of 10 to be fully connected than a group of 100.

Index